·2023·

何梁何利奖

HLHL PRIZE

何梁何利基金评选委员会　编

THE SELECTION BOARD OF HO LEUNG HO LEE FOUNDATION

中国科学技术出版社

·北　京·

图书在版编目（CIP）数据

2023 何梁何利奖 / 何梁何利基金评选委员会编．北京：中国科学技术出版社，2025. 3. -- ISBN 978-7-5236-1079-4

Ⅰ. K826. 1

中国国家版本馆 CIP 数据核字第 2024G17Y34 号

责任编辑	韩　颖
责任校对	张晓莉
责任印制	徐　飞

出　　版	中国科学技术出版社
发　　行	中国科学技术出版社有限公司
地　　址	北京市海淀区中关村南大街 16 号
邮　　编	100081
发行电话	010-62173865
传　　真	010-62173081
网　　址	http://www.cspbooks.com.cn

开　　本	787mm × 1092mm　1/16
字　　数	394 千字
印　　张	17.75
印　　数	1—3000 册
版　　次	2025 年 3 月第 1 版
印　　次	2025 年 3 月第 1 次印刷
印　　刷	北京荣泰印刷有限公司
书　　号	ISBN 978-7-5236-1079-4 / K · 457
定　　价	80.00 元

内 容 提 要

本书是何梁何利基金出版物——《何梁何利奖》的第三十集。书中简要介绍了2023年度何梁何利基金56位获奖人的生平经历和主要科技成就。为了便于海内外人士了解本奖背景，书中同时收入了反映何梁何利基金及其科技奖励情况的资料，作为附录刊出。

This is the thirty collection of the publications of Ho Leung Ho Lee Foundation—*Ho Leung Ho Lee Prize.* In this book, the biographical notes on the 56 awardees of the year 2023 and their main scientific and technological achievements are accounted briefly. This collection includes appendices concerning Ho Leung Ho Lee Foundation and its scientific and technological award in order to help the readers both in China and abroad to understand the background of this prize.

2023 年 12 月 19 日，何梁何利基金 2023 年度颁奖大会（第三十届）在北京钓鱼台国宾馆举行。中共中央政治局常委、国务院副总理丁薛祥出席大会并讲话。

On December 19, 2023, the 2023 Award Ceremony (30th) of HLHL Foundation is held at Diaoyutai State Guesthouse in Beijing. Ding Xuexiang, a member of the Political Bureau of the Communist Party of China (CPC) Central Committee and Vice Premier of the State Council, attends and delivers a speech.

2023 年 12 月 19 日，何梁何利基金 2023 年度颁奖大会（第三十届）在北京钓鱼台国宾馆举行。中共中央政治局常委、国务院副总理丁薛祥出席大会并讲话。全国人大常委会副委员长蔡达峰、全国政协副主席陈武出席大会。

On December 19, 2023, the 2023 Award Ceremony (30th) of HLHL Foundation is held at Diaoyutai State Guesthouse in Beijing. Ding Xuexiang, a member of the Political Bureau of the Communist Party of China (CPC) Central Committee and Vice Premier of the State Council, attends and delivers a speech at the 2023 Award Ceremony of HLHL Foundation. Cai Dafeng, Vice Chairman of the Standing Committee of the National People's Congress, and Chen Wu, Vice Chairman of the Chinese People's Political Consultative Conference, attend the Award Ceremony.

中共中央政治局常委、国务院副总理丁薛祥为何梁何利基金2023年度科学与技术成就奖获得者戚发轫颁奖。

Ding Xuexiang, a member of the Political Bureau of the Communist Party of China (CPC) Central Committee and Vice Premier of the State Council, present prizes to Qi Faren, the winner of 2023 HLHL Prize for Scientific and Technology Achievements.

何梁何利基金2023年度科学与技术成就奖获得者戚发轫院士在颁奖大会上发言。

Qi Faren, the winner of 2023 HLHL Prize for Scientific and Technology Achievements and academician of the Chinese Academy of Engineering, delivers a speech at the 2023 Award Ceremony of HLHL Foundation.

何梁何利基金（北京）代表处首席代表、何梁何利基金评选委员会秘书长段瑞春主持大会，并代表何梁何利基金信托委员会主席、评选委员会主任朱丽兰作评选委员会工作报告。

Duan Ruichun, the chief representative of the Beijing Representative Office of the Ho Leung Ho Lee Foundation (Hong Kong), and the Secretary-General of the Selection Board of HLHL Foundation, presides over the 2023 Award Ceremony of HLHL Foundation and delivers a report on the work of the Selection Board on behalf of Zhu Lilan, Chairwoman of the Board of Trustees and Director of the Selection Board of HLHL Foundation.

国家领导人、各界嘉宾为何梁何利基金 2023 年度获奖人颁奖并合影。

The state leaders and the honored guests present prizes to and have a group photo taken with the winners of 2023 HLHL Prize.

国家领导人、各界嘉宾为何梁何利基金 2023 年度获奖人颁奖并合影。

The state leaders and the honored guests present prizes to and have a group photo taken with the winners of 2023 HLHL Prize.

国家领导人、各界嘉宾为何梁何利基金 2023 年度获奖人颁奖并合影。

The state leaders and the honored guests present prizes to and have a group photo taken with the winners of 2023 HLHL Prize.

国家领导人、各界嘉宾为何梁何利基金 2023 年度获奖人颁奖并合影。

The state leaders and the honored guests present prizes to and have a group photo taken with the winners of 2023 HLHL Prize.

国家领导人、各界嘉宾为何梁何利基金 2023 年度获奖人颁奖并合影。

The state leaders and the honored guests present prizes to and have a group photo taken with the winners of 2023 HLHL Prize.

国家领导人、各界嘉宾为何梁何利基金 2023 年度获奖人颁奖并合影。

The state leaders and the honored guests present prizes to and have a group photo taken with the winners of 2023 HLHL Prize.

国家领导人、各界嘉宾为何梁何利基金 2023 年度获奖人颁奖并合影。

The state leaders and the honored guests present prizes to and have a group photo taken with the winners of 2023 HLHL Prize.

何梁何利基金 2023 年度颁奖大会会场。
The meeting hall of the 2023 Award Ceremony of HLHL Foundation.

何梁何利基金 2023 年度颁奖大会会场。
The meeting hall of the 2023 Award Ceremony of HLHL Foundation.

何梁何利基金科学与技术成就奖获得者传略

PROFILES OF THE AWARDEES OF PRIZE FOR SCIENTIFIC AND TECHNOLOGICAL ACHIEVEMENTS OF HO LEUNG HO LEE FOUNDATION

innovation, gather more social resources towards technological innovation, and provide strong support for scientific and technological undertakings.

The 2023 Ho Leung Ho Lee Foundation "Prize for Scientific and Technological Achievements" was awarded to Academician Qi Faren, the first chief designer of China's Shenzhou spaceships, and another 55 science and technology workers were awarded the "Prize for Scientific and Technological Progress" or the "Prize for Scientific and Technological Innovation".

Cai Dafeng and Chen Wu were present at the ceremony.

序

今年是何梁何利基金成立的三十周年。过去多年，社会以至整个世界都出现了巨大的转变，基金也多次经历了不同的挑战，但在历任信托委员会、投资委员会和评选委员会同人的努力应对下，基金都能迎难而上，同时不断优化运作和评选机制，公信力不断提升并得到社会的广泛认同，捐款人都非常欣慰。

三十年来，中国在科技和创新方面取得了极大的突破和成就，实力不断提升，在多个领域更跻身世界前沿，何梁何利基金能够透过奖励工作参与其中，感到非常光荣。

营造良好氛围、激发人才活力是科技创新发展的重要元素。中国国家主席习近平今年 6 月在国家科学技术奖励大会上，强调了科技现代化和创新在实现中国现代化和高质量发展中的重要性。同时指出:“新时代科技发展积累的经验必须坚持并在实践中不断丰富”“坚持走中国特色自主创新道路，坚持创新驱动发展，坚持深化改革激发创新活力，坚持教育、科技、人才良性循环，坚持培育创新文化，坚持科技开放合作造福人类。”

近年，中国在科技创新，包括智能生活、超级工程、航天科技以及医学探索等方面，都取得瞩目的成就，也展示了如何透过科技创新增进人类福祉。

过去三十年，基金始终坚守理念，努力配合国家的社会和经济发展方向，奖励杰出科学工作者，鼓励更多年轻人才积极研发高新科技，更好地推动中国的科技自主和创新发展。

展望未来，基金同人定会继续努力，积极配合国家的科研战略方针，把何梁何利基金的工作做得更好，为推动科技发展和奖励人才发挥最大作用，通过鼓励中国科技工作者的自主创新，让中国在竞争激烈的世界科技领域发挥更大影响力，继续为国家建设成为世界科技强国、实现高水平科技自立自强作出贡献。

何梁何利基金捐款人

何善衡慈善基金会有限公司　梁銶琚慈善基金会有限公司

何添基金有限公司　伟伦基金有限公司

2024 年 6 月于香港

Preface

This year marks the 30th anniversary of the establishment of the Ho Leung Ho Lee Foundation. Over the past years, there have been tremendous changes in society and the world at large, and the Foundation has faced various challenges on many occasions. However, thanks to the hard work of our colleagues in the successive Board of Trustees, Investment Committee and Selection Committee, the Foundation has been able to meet the challenges, while continuing to improve its operation and selection mechanism, further enhancing its credibility and gaining wide recognition in the community, which has been a source of great relief to contributors.

Over the past 30 years, China has made great breakthroughs and achievements in science, technology and innovation, and its strength has continued to grow, making it a world leader in a number of fields. It is an honor for the Foundation to participate in these achievements through its prize work.

Creating a favorable atmosphere and stimulating the vitality of talents are important factors in the development of scientific and technological innovation. At the National Science and Technology Award Conference held in June this year, Chinese President Xi Jinping stressed the importance of scientific and technological upgrading and innovation in achieving China's modernization and high-quality development. At the same time, he pointed out that "experience accumulated from the sci-tech development in the new era must be adhered to and continuously enriched in practice" and "We must insist on the path of independent innovation with Chinese characteristics, insist on novation-driven development and deepening reform to stimulate innovation vitality, the virtuous cycle of education, sci-tech development and talent, the cultivation of innovation culture, as well as sci-tech opening-up and cooperation for the benefit of mankind".

In recent years, China has made remarkable achievements in scientific and technological innovation, including smart living, super-engineering, aerospace technology and medical exploration, demonstrating how scientific and technological innovation can contribute to the well-being of mankind.

Over the past three decades, the Foundation has always adhered to its philosophy of supporting the country's social and economic development, rewarding outstanding scientists, encouraging more young talents to actively research and develop new technologies, and better promoting China's technological autonomy and innovative development.

Looking into the future, our colleagues will continue to work hard to actively co-operate with the State's strategic direction on scientific research, to make the work of the Ho Leung Ho Lee Foundation even better, to maximize the role of the Foundation in promoting scientific and technological development and rewarding talents by encouraging Chinese scientists to innovate on their own, to enable China to exert greater influence in the highly competitive world scientific and technological arena. We will continue to build our country into a world power in science and technology and realize a high level of self-reliance in science and technology.

Donors of Ho Leung Ho Lee Foundation

S. H. Ho Foundation Limited　Leung Kau Kui Foundation Limited

Ho Tim Foundation Limited　Wei Lun Foundation Limited

June 2024, Hong Kong

何梁何利基金评选委员会
2023年度工作报告

信托委员会主席、评选委员会主任　朱丽兰

（2023年12月19日）

尊敬的丁薛祥副总理，
尊敬的蔡达峰副委员长，
尊敬的陈武副主席，
同志们，朋友们：

初冬北京，瑞雪傲梅。北京钓鱼台国宾馆一片喜庆风光。今天，我们在此隆重举行何梁何利基金2023年度颁奖大会，向56位科技工作者授予何梁何利基金科学与技术奖的崇高荣誉。中共中央政治局常委、国务院副总理丁薛祥同志亲临颁奖大会，传达党中央、国务院对获奖科学家的热烈祝贺和对广大科技工作者的亲切问候。全国人大常委会副委员长蔡达峰同志、全国政协副主席陈武同志、科技部部长阴和俊同志和各部门领导以及香港捐款人代表光临大会，给予我们莫大激励和鼓舞。在此，我谨代表基金同仁，对党和国家领导同志的亲切关怀表示衷心感谢，对内地和香港各界嘉宾出席本次大会表示热烈的欢迎。

下面，我代表评选委员会作工作报告。

一、关于2023年度信托委员会决定

今年6月9日，何梁何利基金信托委员会全体会议在香港中银大厦举行。会议审议并接受基金投资委员会投资情况报告；审议并通过基金评选委员会2022年度工作报告和2023年度工作设想，决

定继续聘任罗兵咸永道会计师事务所为基金稽核师，并通过了评选委员会委员更替等其他事项。

这里，我想做两点说明。

一是近年来，世界经济形势复杂，投资环境持续波动，金融市场起伏动荡，基金资本运营面临较大挑战。投资委员会把握变局、沉着应对，基金财务状况尚属稳定。截至 2023 年 3 月 31 日，基金市值为 6.68 亿港元。与基金创立之初总值 3.9 亿港元相比，保持着较高增长。考虑到未来全球投资环境尚存诸多变数，根据综合经济评估，2023 年度用于发放奖金的预算总额以过去五年的平均数为基数，确定为 1200 万港元，与上年持平。

二是在评选委员、专业评委和各界志愿者的共同努力下，评选委员会圆满完成三大奖项的评审工作。基金北京代表处依法履行职责，健全评选机制，自主开发完成的“何梁何利基金科技奖评选管理和网络安全系统”已经投入使用，大大提升了评选工作的信息化水平。为了弘扬科学家精神、促进创新发展，评选委员会和省市、部门联合举办高峰论坛、西丽湖论坛和学术报告会等活动，取得圆满成功，产生热烈反响。

二、关于 2023 年度评选委员会工作

今年年初，评选委员会向境内外提名人共发出提名通知 2400 多份，在规定期限内收到提名推荐书 927 份，其中有效被提名人 917 人。7 月 5—7 日，2023 年度专业评审会在北京外国专家大厦举行。130 多位专家组成的各专业评审组遵循公平、公正、公开的评选方针，按照 10 ∶ 1 的入选率，评选产生“科学与技术进步奖”候选人 67 名、“科学与技术创新奖”候选人 36 名；此外，经过考察听证，提名“科学与技术成就奖”候选人 1 名，一并提交评选委员会全体终评。8 月 26 日，何梁何利基金评选委员会全体会议在北京友谊宾馆举行。经科学评议、优中选优，以无记名投票表决方式，终评产生何梁何利基金三大奖项共 56 位获奖人。

今年，何梁何利最高奖项——“科学与技术成就奖”落户中国

空间技术研究院。我国著名战略科学家、杰出空间技术专家获得此项殊荣。他是我国东方红一号卫星技术负责人，是神舟五号飞船首任总设计师，为我国首次载人航天作出了卓越贡献。他五十年如一日献身祖国空间技术事业，精心培养新一代领军人才，为神舟飞船与空间站交互对接奠定了坚实基础。他是“两弹一星”精神的践行者，是新时代“爱国、创新、求实、奉献、协同、育人”崇高科学家精神的榜样。

今年，32 名荣获“科学与技术进步奖”和 23 名荣获“科学与技术创新奖”的科技工作者，是在科技战线上始终坚持“四个面向”，在科学技术深度和广度进军赛道上不断探索的优秀代表。人人都有一张亮丽的成绩单，其中，有科学家在基础科学及其交叉学科领域取得原始性成果，引领了学科发展；有研究员在关键核心技术、前沿技术实现重大突破，改写了世界领先纪录；有技术专家在高新技术产业攻坚克难、打破封锁，实现了技术链、产业链、营销链全新畅通；有科学家在新疆、西藏、青海、广西等边远省份和民族自治地区，以特色科技创新振兴地方经济发展，为“一带一路”倡议作出了积极贡献。今年首次有“大国工匠”进入获奖人行列，他是一位特级技师，把工匠精神根植于心、付之于行，反复试验、摸索，创造独特的焊接工法，为保障国之重器的高精度、高可靠性作出宝贵贡献。

各位领导、各位嘉宾，在中央人民政府和香港特区政府的亲切关怀下，在科技界、教育界和社会各界的大力支持下，何梁何利基金走过了 29 载春秋，共奖励祖国杰出科技人才 1582 位，为我国科教兴国战略、人才强国战略和创新驱动发展战略作出了应有贡献。令人遗憾的是，当年创立基金的四位爱国金融实业家何善衡、梁銶琚、何添、利国伟先生都已在九旬高龄驾鹤仙逝。我们深深地怀念他们。2005 年，何梁何利基金修订《信托契约》，完成捐款人法人化。基金捐款人变更为何善衡慈善基金会有限公司、梁銶琚慈善基金会有限公司、何添基金有限公司、伟伦基金有限公司。而今，当年捐款人的后辈秉承先辈宏愿，传承爱国、爱港、爱科学、爱人才的精神，推进新时期何梁何利基金行稳致远。这里，我们谨对年轻一代捐款人代表致以崇高敬意。

同志们、朋友们，伟大时代需要伟大精神，伟大精神需要榜样引领。奖励杰出科技人才是国家和全社会的神圣使命，是一项功在当代、泽被永远的崇高事业。让我们紧密团结在以习近平同志为核心的党中央周围，以习近平新时代中国特色社会主义思想为指导，努力把何梁何利基金办成国际一流科技大奖，鼓舞和激励广大科学技术工作者努力攀登科学技术高峰，为加快实现高水平科技自立自强、以中国式现代化全面推进强国建设和民族复兴伟业作出更大贡献！

谢谢各位！

2023 Work Report of the Selection Board of Ho Leung Ho Lee Foundation

Zhu Lilan, Chairperson of the Trust Board and Director of the Selection Board

(December 19, 2023)

Vice Premier Ding Xuexiang,

Vice Chairman Cai Dafeng,

Vice Chairman Chen Wu,

Comrades and Friends:

Blessed with snow and plum blossoms of early winter, the Diaoyutai State Guesthouse in Beijing is in a festive mood. At the 2023 Ho Leung Ho Lee Foundation Award Ceremony solemnly held here today, 56 science and technology workers will be awarded the high honor of Ho Leung Ho Lee Foundation Science and Technology Award. Comrade Ding Xuexiang, Member of the Standing Committee of the Political Bureau of the CPC Central Committee and Vice Premier of the State Council, attended the award ceremony to convey the warm congratulations of the Party Central Committee and the State Council to the award-winning scientists and the warm greetings to the vast number of science and technology workers. The presence of Comrade Cai Dafeng, Vice Chairman of the Standing Committee of the National People's Congress, Comrade Chen Wu, Vice Chairman of the National Committee of the Chinese People's Political Consultative Conference, Comrade Yin Hejun, Minister of Science and Technology, leaders of various departments, as well as representatives of donors from Hong Kong gave us utmost motivation and encouragement. On behalf of my colleagues at the foundation, I would like to express my heartfelt thanks to the leaders of the Party and the State for their kind attention, and extend a warm welcome to the guests from all walks of life from the mainland and Hong Kong.

Next, on behalf of the Board of Selection, I will present a work report.

I. On the Decisions Made by the Board of Trustees in 2023

On June 9 of this year, the plenary meeting of the Board of Trustees of Ho Leung Ho Lee Foundation was held at Bank of China Tower in Hong Kong. At the meeting, the Investment Report of the Investment Board of the Foundation was reviewed and accepted, the Work Report of 2022 and Work Plan for 2023 of the Selection Board of the Foundation was reviewed and approved, it was decided to continue to appoint PricewaterhouseCoopers as the auditor of the Foundation, and other matters such as the replacement of members of the Selection Board were also approved.

Here, I would like to make two explanations.

First, in recent years, the world economic situation has been complex, the investment environment and the financial market have been volatile, and capital operations of the Foundation have faced significant challenges. The Investment Board has calmly dealt with the changes, and the financial situation of the Foundation remained stable. As of March 31, 2023, the market capitalization of the Foundation recorded HKD 668 million, maintaining a relatively high growth rate compared to the initial total value of HKD 390 million at the commencement of the Foundation. Considering the variables in the future global investment environment and based on a comprehensive economic assessment, the total budget for bonus distribution in 2023 is determined to be HKD 12 million based on the average of the past five years, which is the same as the previous year.

Second, with the joint efforts of members of the Selection Board, professional judges, and volunteers from all walks of life, the Selection Board has successfully completed the evaluation of the three major awards. The Beijing Representative Office of the Foundation has fulfilled its responsibilities in accordance with the law and improved the selection mechanism, and the "Selection Management and Network Security System for Ho Leung Ho Lee Foundation Science and Technology Awards" independently developed by it has been put into use, greatly improving the informationization level of selection. In order to encourage dedication to science and foster innovative development, the Selection Board co-hosted activities such as the summit forum, the X-Lake Forum, and the symposium with relevant provincial and municipal governments and departments, all of which were complete success and received warm response.

II. On the Work of the Selection Board in 2023

Early this year, the Selection Board sent call for nominations to more than 2400 nominators at home and abroad, and received 927 recommendation letters within the prescribed period, including 917 valid nominees. The 2023 Professional Evaluation Meeting was held on July 5–7 at Foreign Experts Building Beijing. The professional evaluation panels composed of more than 130 experts followed the principles of fairness, impartiality, and openness in their selection processes. With a selection rate of 10 : 1, the panels selected 67 candidates for the "Prize for Scientific and Technological Progress" and 36 candidates for the "Prize for Scientific and Technological Innovation". In addition, after investigation and hearing, one candidate for the "Prize for Scientific and Technological Achievements" was nominated and submitted to the final evaluation by the entire Selection Board. On August 26, the plenary meeting of the Selection Board of Ho Leung Ho Lee Foundation was held at Beijing Friendship Hotel. After scientific evaluation and picking the best of the best, and by secret ballot, a total of 56 winners were finally selected for the three major awards of Ho Leung Ho Lee Foundation.

This year, the highest award of Ho Leung Ho Lee Foundation, the "Prize for Scientific and Technological Achievements", went to the China Academy of Space Technology. As China's renowned strategic scientist and an outstanding space technology expert, the winner was the tech lead of China's Dong Fang Hong I satellite and the first chief designer of the Shenzhou V spacecraft, making outstanding contributions to China's first manned spaceflight. He has devoted himself to China's cause of space technology for fifty years, carefully cultivating new generations of leading talents and laying a solid foundation for the interactive docking between Shenzhou spaceship and the space station. He is a practitioner of the spirit of the national defense scientists, and a model of dedication to science characterized by "patriotism, innovation, pragmatism, dedication, collaboration, and education" in the new era.

The 32 winners of the "Prize for Scientific and Technological Progress" and the 23 winners of the "Prize for Scientific and Technological Innovation" this year are outstanding representatives of science and technology workers who have always focused on the "Four Orientations" (major challenges in the world's scientific and technological frontier, the main economic battlefield, major national needs and people's life and health) on the scientific and technological front and continuously explored the depth and breadth of scientific and technological advancement. All of them have made outstanding achievements. Among them, there are scientists who have made original achievements in basic science and its interdisciplinary fields that lead the development of the respective discipline; there are researchers who have achieved significant breakthroughs in key core and cutting-edge technologies, rewriting world-leading records; there are technical experts who have tackled difficulties in high-tech industries and broke through blockades, achieving completely new and smooth flow of technology, industry and marketing chains; and there are scientists who have revitalized local economic development with distinctive scientific and technological innovation in remote provinces and ethnic autonomous regions such as Xinjiang, Xizang, Qinghai and Guangxi, making positive contributions to the "Belt and Road" strategy. This year, a "national-level master artisan" has entered the list of award winners for the first time. He is a top-level technician who has rooted the spirit of craftsmanship in his heart and put it into practice. Through repeated experiment and exploration, he has created a unique welding method, making valuable contributions to ensuring the high precision and reliability of vital instruments of national strength.

Leaders and guests, under the kind attention of the Central People's Government and the Government of the Hong Kong Special Administrative Region, and with the strong support of the scientific, technological, educational, and social sectors, Ho Leung Ho Lee Foundation has awarded a total of 1582 outstanding scientific and technological talents in our country in 29 years, making due contributions to the strategy for invigorating China through science and education, the workforce development strategy, and the innovation-driven development strategy. Unfortunately, the four patriotic financial industrialists who founded the Foundation, Mr. Ho Sin Hang, Mr. Leung Kau-Kui, Mr. Ho Tim and Mr. Lee Quo-Wei, have all passed away in their nineties. We deeply miss them. In 2005, Ho Leung Ho Lee Foundation completed the corporatization of donors upon revision to its trust instrument, and donors of the Foundation changed to S. H. Ho Foundation Limited, Leung Kau Kui Foundation Limited, Ho Tim Foundation Limited and Wei Lun Foundation Limited. Today, upholding the grand aspirations of the founding donors, their younger generation are carrying forward the spirit of loving the motherland, loving Hong Kong, loving science, and loving talents, ensuring the steady development of Ho Leung Ho Lee Foundation in the new era. Here, we would like to pay high tribute to the representatives of the younger generation of donors.

Comrades and friends, a great era needs a great spirit, and a great spirit requires exemplary guidance. Rewarding outstanding scientific and technological talents is a sacred mission of the country and the whole society, and a noble cause that is accomplished in contemporary times and will benefit our future generations. Let us unite closely around the CPC Central Committee with Comrade Xi Jinping at its core, and seek guidance from Xi Jinping Thought on Socialism with Chinese Characteristics for a New Era. Let us strive to make Ho Leung Ho Lee Foundation Awards international first-class science and technology awards, and encourage and inspire the vast number of science and technology workers to strive to climb the peaks of science and technology, and make greater contributions to move faster to achieve greater self-reliance and strength in science and technology, and build a great country and advance the rejuvenation of the Chinese nation on all fronts through a Chinese path to modernization!

Thank you.

目　录

何梁何利基金科学与技术创新奖获得者传略

CONTENTS

丁薛祥出席何梁何利基金2023年度颁奖大会

（2023年12月19日）

12月19日，中共中央政治局常委、国务院副总理丁薛祥在北京出席何梁何利基金2023年度颁奖大会并讲话。

丁薛祥指出，党的十八大以来，以习近平同志为核心的党中央高度重视科技创新工作，推动我国科技事业实现了历史性、整体性、格局性重大变化。新时代新征程上，以中国式现代化全面推进中华民族伟大复兴，必须加快实现高水平科技自立自强。

丁薛祥强调，人才是科技创新的第一资源。实现高水平科技自立自强，归根结底要靠高水平创新人才。要深化科技体制改革，完善人才发展体制机制，营造良好创新生态，充分激发各类人才创新活力。希望获奖科学家把奖励和荣誉化为动力和担当，多出关键性、原创性、引领性重大科技成果。希望广大科技工作者大力弘扬科学家精神，服务国家重大需求。希望何梁何利基金秉承“爱国、爱港、爱科学、爱人才”初心，为推动国家科技进步贡献更大力量。希望社会各界关注创新、参与创新、支持创新，将更多社会资源集聚到科技创新上，为科技事业提供强有力的支撑。

2023年度何梁何利基金“科学与技术成就奖”授予我国神舟飞船首任总设计师戚发轫院士，另有55位科技工作者荣获“科学与技术进步奖”和“科学与技术创新奖”。

全国人大常委会副委员长蔡达峰、全国政协副主席陈武出席大会。

Ding Xuexiang Attended the 2023 Award Ceremony of Ho Leung Ho Lee Foundation

(December 19, 2023)

On December 19, Ding Xuexiang, the Member of the Standing Committee of the Political Bureau of the CPC Central Committee and Vice Premier of the State Council, attended and addressed the 2023 Award Ceremony of Ho Leung Ho Lee Foundation in Beijing.

Ding Xuexiang pointed out that since the 18th National Congress of the CPC, the Party Central Committee with Comrade Xi as the core has attached great importance to the work on scientific and technological innovation, and has facilitated major changes of historical, holistic, and structural significance in China's scientific and technological undertakings. To advance the rejuvenation of the Chinese nation on all fronts through a Chinese path to modernization on the new journey that lies before us in the new era, we must speed up efforts to achieve greater self-reliance and strength in science and technology.

Ding Xuexiang emphasized that talents are the primary resource for technological innovation. Greater self-reliance and strength in science and technology ultimately depends on high-caliber innovators. Efforts need to be made to deepen structural scientific and technological reform, improve institutional systems for talent development, create an environment favorable for innovation, and fully inspire greater creativity of talent of all types. He hopes that award-winning scientists will turn their rewards and honors into motivation and responsibility, and produce more significant scientific and technological achievements that are crucial, original, and pioneering; science and technology workers will vigorously encourage dedication to science and serve the major needs of the country; the Ho Leung Ho Lee Foundation will uphold the original intention of "loving the motherland, loving Hong Kong, loving science, and loving talents", and contribute more to promoting national scientific and technological progress; all sectors of society will pay attention to, participate in, and support

戚发轫

戚发轫，1933年4月出生于辽宁省复县（今大连市瓦房店市）。1957年毕业于北京航空学院飞机系，同年到中国运载火箭技术研究院工作。1967年调入中国空间技术研究院，从事卫星和飞船研制，先后担任副院长、院长；1983年担任中国航天科技集团公司第五研究院院长；1992年担任神舟飞船总设计师。曾任北京航空航天大学宇航学院院长，国际空间研究委员会中国委员会副主席，中国航天科技集团有限公司科技委顾问。现任中国空间技术研究院技术顾问、北京航空航天大学宇航学院名誉院长。中国工程院院士，国际宇航科学院院士。

戚发轫是我国著名的空间技术专家，是我国载人航天器的开拓者和奠基人，先后担任过多个卫星型号和飞船的总设计师，在载人航天器、卫星、宇航元器件等工程技术领域以及我国空间事业战略发展中作出了系统的、创造性的重大贡献。曾荣获国家科技进步奖特等奖2次，一等奖、二等奖、三等奖各一次；中国工程科技奖、何梁何利科技奖、国际宇航联合会“名人堂”奖等奖项，以及全国五一劳动奖章、2020年“最美教师”称号等荣誉。

一、我国神舟飞船首次载人飞行的开创者

他是神舟飞船首任总设计师，带领团队实现我国载人航天器技术从无到有的重大突破。

提出符合中国国情的高可靠、高安全的载人飞船发展路线，明确我国神舟飞船研制指导思想，确定我国神舟飞船总体方案，突破了神舟飞船关键技术，解决了一大批工程难题，为我国自主突破载人天地往返飞行作出突出贡献。带领团队圆满完成神舟一号至四号无人飞行任务、神舟五号“一人一天”、神舟六号“多人多天”载人飞行任务。2003年10月，神舟五号成功发射，首次实现了中国人的千年飞天梦。

在我国航天工程基础薄弱、载人航天无技术积累、试验验证条件匮乏、人才储备不足的条件下，带领团队突破载人环境、应急救生、返回再入、回收着陆等载人航天关键技术。工程中制定重大问题解决方案，攻克防热结构、降落伞系统、着陆缓冲系统和有害气体控制等技术难题；亲自制定空投试验方案和零高度逃逸救生飞行试验方案，在地面验证回收着陆技术、降落伞系统及故障条件下航天员救生方案，为航天员正常及故障条件下的安全性保驾护航。

神舟五号载人飞行任务的圆满成功验证了神舟飞船的技术体系，包括承载与密封、姿态与轨道控制、载人环境控制、能源管理、信息管理、返回再入、回收着陆、应急救生等8类20项关键技术，奠定了我国载人航天器的技术基础。

二、我国载人航天器的开拓者和奠基人

他创建了我国载人航天器技术体系、管理体系和质量体系，全面应用于后续空间实验室、货运飞船、空间站等任务。

他注重系统工程方法论的实践，建立技术状态管控、风险、进度、质量、人才队伍管理和基础建设的载人航天器工程管理体系，其中重点关注试验覆盖性分析和质量问题“双五条”，确保了载人航天器研制质量受控、地面试验覆盖飞行工况，是系统工程方法在载人航天器全周期研制中的创新实践。

他提出“依据国情、立足当下、兼顾长远”的指导思想，主张独立自主完成神舟飞船地面试验，全力推动北京五院航天城建设，建成了当时亚洲最大空间环境模拟器（KM6）、世界最大高低频振动试验室和电磁兼容试验室，确保神舟飞船任务的成功，在

后续100多个大中型航天器研制任务中发挥了重要作用，支撑了我国空间事业的长远发展。

他构建了我国载人航天可靠性安全性设计和验证体系，有力保证了迄今为止我国全部27个载人航天器任务100%成功，航天员26人次顺利进入太空并已安全返回。他构建了载人航天器高可靠、高安全质量管理体系，形成了“零缺陷、零疑点、零故障”的质量文化，锻造了“求真务实、追求卓越”的工作作风，保证了18名中国航天员顺利进入太空。

他开创了具有中国特色的载人航天器发展路线，形成了影响深远的神舟文化，为载人航天器的连续成功奠定了坚实的技术和管理基础。

三、我国卫星领域的先行者

他历任东方红一号主要技术负责人，东方红二号副总师、总师，东方红二号甲、三号总师兼总指挥，为我国通信卫星从无到有、从弱到强、高水平持续发展、达到国际先进水平作出重要贡献。

作为我国第一颗人造地球卫星——东方红一号的主要技术负责人，他主持完成正样星研制和发射技术工作，使我国掌握了研制人造卫星的能力。针对卫星各项飞行任务，制定并实施完整的地面模拟试验方案；建立东方红一号卫星研制全过程的工作规范，在发射场及时解决电磁干扰等技术故障和难题，确保卫星首次发射成功。

他制定东方红二号“一步走”方案，直接研制地球静止轨道卫星，实现我国通信卫星零的突破，使我国空间技术从试验阶段进入应用阶段。他通过技术改进、系统优化等手段，实现东方红二号甲通信容量提高10倍，实现我国通信卫星从试验型到应用型的转型升级。

他首创公用平台和模块化设计思想，决策东方红三号卫星采用三轴姿态稳定方案，成为我国当时最先进的卫星公用平台，并广泛应用于通信、导航、深空探测等领域共36颗卫星和探测器。

四、我国宇航元器件可靠性体系的创建者

他识别出元器件可靠性是制约卫星长寿命的关键，开创性地提出元器件“五统一”原则，创建了中国首个宇航元器件质量保证机构，将元器件可靠性提升两个数量级，有力保证了3颗东方红二号甲卫星在轨长期服役。

2003年以后，他融合载人航天工程元器件管理经验，进一步丰富“五统一”原则，构建型号全寿命周期元器件管理模式，提出我国宇航元器件可靠性体系，系统性保障不同型号元器件需求，全面推广应用至今，推动了载人航天、通信、导航、深空探测、遥感等多领域航天器元器件可靠性工程的发展和自主可控，带动了工程研制和建设水平的整体跃升。其中，北斗导航卫星元器件全部国产化，载人空间站元器件全部自主可控。

他为我国航天器可靠性提升和长寿命运行作出卓越贡献，有力支撑了我国航天器高水平自立自强。

五、我国空间事业战略发展的推动者

他致力于空间事业战略发展，主持航天强国空间应用、载人航天等重大战略课题研究，并呈报《关于加快航天强国建设的路径及建议》《关于开展我国载人登月前期综合论证的建议》等院士建议，得到中央领导批复和认可，推动了国家航天战略规划制定和重大工程立项，并促进了中央航天领导小组的成立。

Profile of Qi Faren

Qi Faren was born in Fuxian County of Liaoning Province in April 1933. After graduating from the Aircraft Department of Beijing Institute of Aeronautics in 1957, he was assigned to work at China Academy of Launch Vehicle Technology. In 1967, he was transferred to the China Academy of Space Technology to engage in the development of satellites and spacecrafts, and successively served as the Vice President and President of the academy. In 1983, he served as the President of the 5th Research Institute of China Aerospace Science and Technology Corporation. In 1992, he was appointed chief designer of the Shenzhou spacecraft. He has served as chief designer of multiple satellites and spacecrafts, dean of the School of Astronautics at Beihang University, vice chairman of the China Committee of the International Space Research Committee, and the science and technology consultant of China Aerospace Science and Technology Corporation. He is currently the technology consultant of the Chinese Academy of Space Technology, honorary dean of the School of Astronautics of Beihang University, academician of the China Academy of Engineering, and academician of the International Academy of Astronautics.

Qi Faren, a Chinese space technology luminary and the forerunner of China's manned spacecraft program, has made seminal contributions in the engineering and technological arenas of manned spacecraft, satellites, and aerospace components, and has charted the strategic course of China's space industry. So far, he had achieved National Science and Technology Progress Special Prize for twice, First Prize for once, Second Prize for once and Third Prize for once, as well as the China Engineering Science and Technology Award and the Ho Leung Ho Lee Award for Technology and Science. He also won the Qiushi Outstanding Science and Technology Achievement Collective Award. He is a recipient of the National May Day Labor Medal and the "Hall of Fame" award from the International Astronautical Federation in 2019 and the title of "Most Beautiful Teacher" of China in 2020.

何梁何利基金科学与技术进步奖获得者传略

PROFILES OF THE AWARDEES OF PRIZE FOR SCIENTIFIC AND TECHNOLOGICAL PROGRESS OF HO LEUNG HO LEE FOUNDATION

物理学奖获得者

万 宝 年

万宝年，1962 年 6 月出生于江苏省海安市。1992 年获德国维尔茨堡大学物理系理学博士学位，随后开展博士后研究工作。1993 年回国至今，在中国科学院等离子体物理研究所工作，先后任研究所托卡马克物理研究室主任、副所长、所长，2014—2019 年任中国科学院合肥物质科学研究院副院长。现任中国科学院等离子体物理研究所首席科学家，兼任中国科学技术大学等离子体物理与聚变工程系主任。ITER 国际托卡马克物理活动中方联系人，国家磁约束核聚变专家委员会成员。2021 年当选中国科学院院士。

万宝年长期从事磁约束聚变等离子体物理研究，先后主持了我国两代超导托卡马克聚变实验装置的物理实验，在托卡马克高约束稳态运行模式探索中取得一系列创新性成果。曾获国家科技进步奖创新团队奖、国家科技进步奖一等奖等。

一、解决了射频波稳态加热 / 电流驱动的关键问题，使实现高约束长脉冲运行成为可能

解决了射频波耦合、加热和电流驱动等基本问题，探索了射频波驱动旋转、多波协同作用等前沿物理问题：发现低杂波驱动边界旋转并为芯部提供动量源，以及离子回旋波模转换产生流剪切，揭示了离子伯恩斯坦波朗道阻尼加热及其与低杂波产生局域电流的协同机制，成为控制等离子体输运和稳定性的重要手段；揭示了参量衰变等多种非线性过程是限制电流驱动效率的关键物理因素，通过抑制参量衰变、电子协同加热、改善可近性等手段，解决了低杂波在高密度下电流驱动效率急剧下降的关键难题。基于上述手段，实现了高效非感应电流驱动和多种加热 / 电流驱动方式下的高约束模式；形成了基于射频波加热和电流驱动的高约束稳态运行途径。

二、发现了形成高约束的关键机理，并发展出缓解边界局域模又不牺牲约束性能的新方法，实现了稳态等离子体高约束性能的稳定维持

在国际上较早地获得了带状剪切流存在并与背景湍流耦合的实验证据；在临界阈值功率下，揭示了带状剪切流在抑制湍流形成高约束过程中的关键作用并给出了直观物理图像；发现了磁轴位移致稳效应中密度梯度的作用机制等，使等离子体约束性能得以大幅提升和更易稳定维持。

发现三维磁扰动非线性作用机理并首次实现低旋转条件下的边界局域模（ELM）控制；开创性地利用射频波驱动边缘电流带以改变磁拓扑，实现 ELM 控制；阐明了微观不稳定性对 ELM 的缓解机理，并发展为一种主动调控的新途径；发现自发高频小幅度 ELM 的形成机理等；在 ELM 缓解的同时高约束性能稳定维持，消除了 ELM 对高约束稳态运行的威胁。

三、在国际上率先成功示范了基于射频波驱动的高约束、长脉冲稳态运行模式，为未来聚变堆稳态运行模式提供了可行性验证

瞄准稳态运行模式发展需求，带领实验团队相继完成了与 ITER 贴近的辅助加热系统布局、偏滤器结构的升级改造。克服超导装置可近性差的技术瓶颈，研发了多项适用于稳态运行的先进诊断和控制系统，解决了射频波加热与电流驱动下分布参数测量等关键技术难题，构建了配套的数据库和集成模拟平台，为稳态运行模式的发展和验证提供了重要基础。

通过对物理和技术的集成，在集成模型预测的基础上优化加热 / 驱动配置和控制，改善芯部约束和边界稳定性控制的兼容性，在国际上率先成功示范了基于射频波驱动的高约束、长脉冲稳态运行模式。在低动量注入纯射频波加热、钨偏滤器等类似国际热核聚变实验堆 ITER 未来运行条件下，获得约束性能优于 ITER 基本运行模式的、小 / 无边界局域模的、超过 100 秒的高约束等离子体，物理上实现完全的稳定和稳态，使 EAST 成为率先实现百秒级的稳态高约束模运行的托卡马克聚变实验装置，在国际上最早具备了开展稳态物理验证实验的能力。

Awardee of Physics Prize, Wan Baonian

Wan Baonian was born in Haian City of Jiangsu Province in June 1962. He has dedicated his career to researching magnetic confinement fusion plasma physics, yielding a range of innovative breakthroughs in the realm of steady-state, high-confinement (H-mode) tokamak operation scenarios. He and his team have not only established the theoretical underpinnings, but also devised experimental techniques on radio frequency (RF) wave-plasma interactions. They resolved key scientific challenges including RF power coupling, RF heating accessibility, non-inductive current drive in high-density H-mode plasmas, enabling a long-pulse plasma operation. He achieved a series of important breakthrough at the access and sustainment of H-mode plasmas, particularly in addressing the origin of zonal flows and explaining how shear flows lead to turbulence suppression. Moreover, he has developed several novel methods for controlling instabilities so-called "Edge Localized Modes" (ELMs) without deteriorating plasma performance. The threads from the transient heat load associated with ELM are eliminated. By bridging the advantages gained in physics and technology, RF-driven fully non-inductive high-performance H-mode operation over 100 s has been successfully demonstrated, for the first time, in the Experimental Advanced Superconducting Tokamak (EAST) tokamak of China. This achievement has positioned EAST as the first tokamak device worldwide capable of ITER-relevant experiments at a time scale of hundred seconds. This accomplishment also provides crucial feasibility verification for the efficient steady-state operation of future fusion reactors. Wan Baonian and his team offers a successful scheme in high-confinement, steady-state tokamak operation through RF-wave heating and fully non-inductive current drive. His research work has a profound impact on the international fusion community. As a key scientist in the field, he also received the National Science and Technology Progress Innovation Team Award and the prestigious National Science and Technology Progress First Prize, among other accolades. Additionally, Wan Baonian played a pivotal role in the physical concept design of the China Fusion Engineering Test Reactor. His unwavering commitment extended to actively promoting EAST openness, sharing, and collaboration. This dedication has significantly contributed to the advancement of magnetic confinement fusion physics in China, establishing him as a pioneering scientist in the field.

化学奖获得者

韩布兴

韩布兴，1957年7月出生于河北省遵化市。1982年毕业于河北科技大学化学工程系，1985年获中国科学院长春应用化学研究所硕士学位，1988年获中国科学院化学研究所博士学位，1989—1991年在加拿大萨斯喀彻温大学做博士后研究。1991年至今在中国科学院化学研究所工作。中国科学院院士，发展中国家科学院院士，英国皇家化学会会士，英国诺丁汉大学荣誉教授，国际纯粹与应用化学联合会绿色化学委员会主席，中国化学会常务理事。

韩布兴主要从事物理化学与绿色化学的交叉研究，在绿色溶剂体系物理化学、CO_2、生物质、废弃塑料、有机垃圾转化利用研究方面取得了系统性成果，推动了物理化学、绿色化学与技术的发展。

一、发展了一系列实验方法与技术，研制多套仪器装置

开展超临界流体、离子液体、水等绿色溶剂及其混合体系的化学热力学性质及应用研究是发展绿色化学与技术的重要基础。开展相关研究需要特殊装置，商用仪器不能或难以满足创新研究需要。针对相关研究难题，韩布兴带领团队发展了一系列新的研究方法，研制了超临界流体/离子液体体系相平衡仪、超临界流体量热计、超临界流体化学反应装置、各类高压原位光谱测定装置等宏观和微观性质研究仪器和装置，为开展化学热力学与绿色化学交叉的原创研究提供了重要条件。

二、在绿色溶剂复杂体系性质研究方面取得系统性原创成果

绿色溶剂复杂体系性质研究是其在各领域应用的基础。韩布兴带领团队构建了数百个具有结构和组成特征的绿色溶剂复杂体系，利用上述研制的仪器装置，或与其他手段相结合，对其化学热力学性质、分子间相互作用和微观结构进行了系统研究，揭示了宏

观性质与微观性质的内在联系；首次发现离子液体可以大量吸收 SO_2，开辟了利用离子液体吸收 SO_2 研究新方向；率先发现离子液体可形成微乳液这一重要现象，创制了一系列新型绿色微乳液体系，开辟了离子液体微乳液研究的新方向；提出用超临界 CO_2 调控表面活性剂体系热力学性质和微观结构的学术思想，发现超临界 CO_2 可诱导胶束与液晶之间可逆相转变等重要现象。以上系统性和创新性成果不仅推动了相关理论发展，而且为开发变革性绿色技术奠定了重要科学基础。

三、发展了多种 CO_2、生物质、废弃塑料、有机垃圾高效绿色转化的新方法、新路线

在 CO_2 转化利用方面，带领团队在创制、构建新型高效绿色溶剂－催化剂催化体系基础上，采用热催化、电催化、光催化方法，原创性提出了多种 CO_2 高效绿色转化制备醇、烷烃、烯烃、羧酸、合成气、含氮化合物等重要化学品和燃料的新方法和新途径。例如，实现超临界 CO_2 加氢制备甲酸的高效反应，利用离子液体特性解决了该反应热力学受限这一挑战性难题；率先实现甲醇、CO_2 加氢羧化合成乙酸，这是在 H_2 气氛下 CO_2 直接参与 C–C 偶联并生成羧酸的首例报道；创新催化剂，不经过 CO 中间物种，实现了 CO_2 和 H_2 在催化剂表面直接高选择性生成 C_5～C_{26} 液体烃，发现了 CO_2 化学反应的一个新机制；针对 CO_2 电催化转化过程中催化剂容易失活问题，提出原位脉冲再生催化剂的新方法，使催化剂保持长期稳定。

在生物质、废弃肥料转化利用方面，韩布兴带领团队创制了多种基于绿色溶剂的新型高效催化体系，发展了生物质及其衍生物、废弃塑料高效绿色转化制备表面活性剂、酚、醇、芳烃、羧酸、环己酮、苯醌、含氮化合物等重要化学品和燃油的一系列新方法和新路线，揭示了催化机制。例如，开创性地提出了木质素及其衍生芳香醚自供氢制备芳烃的反应路线，芳烃产率达到 100%，为木质素高效转化制芳香化学品提供了新思路；率先实现木质素直接转化制苯酚，打通了由造纸行业废弃木质素制环己酮这一重要化学品的新路线。首次提出选择性利用木质素上的甲氧基制备纯化学品的思路，通过选择性断裂 C–O 键制备了乙酸、乙醇、甲酰胺等。

与多家企业合作，开发推广可再生碳资源、废弃碳资源转化利用技术。例如，与河北隆盛生物质能源开发有限公司合作开发生物炭及生物质基清洁燃料制备技术；与北京福海兰天（北京）环保科技有限公司成立了中科－福海资源循环利用技术与产业化联合研究中心，合作开发废弃塑料制油技术；与广东海纳百川环保科技有限公司合作开发推广餐厨垃圾制有机肥料技术，目前 25000 吨 / 年水溶肥技术已实现产业化，在数十种农作物中应用并取得良好效果。

Awardee of Chemistry Prize, Han Buxing

Han Buxing was born in Zunhua City of Hebei Province in July 1957. He received B.S. degree in Chemical Engineering at Hebei University of Science and Technology in 1982, M.S. degree in Inorganic Chemistry at Changchun Institute of Applied Chemistry, CAS in 1985, Ph.D. degree in Physical Chemistry at Institute of Chemistry, CAS in 1988, and did postdoctoral research in Chemical Engineering at the University of Saskatchewan, Canada from 1989 to 1991. He worked in Institute of Chemistry, CAS since 1991. He is an Academician of Chinese Academy of Sciences, a Fellow of The World Academy of Sciences for the Advancement of Science in Developing Countries, and a Fellow of Royal Society of Chemistry. He is also the Chairman of Interdivisional Committee on Green Chemistry for Sustainable Development, International Union of Pure and Applied Chemistry.

His research interests include physicochemical properties of green solvent systems and application of green solvents in green chemistry, especially on transformation of CO_2, biomass, and organic wastes into valuable chemicals and fuels. The main achievement of Han Buxing includes design and build various types of apparatuses, study physiochemical properties of solvent systems, and catalytic transformation of CO_2, biomass, waste plastics and kitchen wastes.

天文学奖获得者

景 益 鹏

景益鹏，1964 年 1 月出生于浙江省绍兴市。1984 年获杭州大学物理系理学学士，同年进入中国科学技术大学攻读天体物理学博士学位。1989 年因去意大利访学而中断国内研究生学习，于 1991 年和 1992 年在意大利高等研究生院分别获硕士和博士学位。1993 起先后在美国亚利桑那大学、德国马普天体物理研究所、日本东京大学从事博士后和研究员工作。2000 年回国后先后在上海天文台、上海交通大学工作。2015 当选中国科学院院士。曾任中国天文学会理事长。

景益鹏主要从事宇宙结构和星系形成的研究，在宇宙结构的数值模拟、宇宙结构基本单元暗物质晕（简称暗晕）的物理性质以及宇宙大尺度结构的观测分析等研究中取得了一系列开创性成果。

一、开展国际领先的数值模拟研究，系统研究暗晕的空间分布和内部结构

发展了一套针对高密度区域的多层网格、自适应 P3M 方法，独立建立了模拟宇宙结构形成的N体计算程序，计算了一系列在国际上同类模拟研究中精度高、样本全的宇宙学模拟。利用这些模拟对暗晕的空间分布和内部结构开展系列性研究，获得以下重要结论。

1. 暗晕空间成团和暗晕空间取向

发现小质量暗晕的成团性比经典 Press-Schechter（PS）理论的预言要强得多，同时提出了暗晕成团的精确公式。该成果已被广泛用于预言星系和暗物质的成团性质，引发了对经典 PS 理论的修改；严格修正了数值计算精度对暗晕取向相关性测量的影响，并得到了暗晕取向相关的精确结果，被同行称为“景模型”。

2. 暗晕的内部密度径向分布：暗晕密度轮廓

发现了暗晕的密度轮廓随暗晕的动力学状态而变化的规律，提出了描述密度轮廓密

集因子的对数正则分布公式；该成果被用来解释 Tully-Fisher 关系的观测弥散和强引力透镜时间延迟的统计等重要观测现象。获得了暗晕密度轮廓的高精度模型数据，为其后的数值模拟和理论研究提供了权威性的参考样本，成为高精度研究暗晕结构方面最有影响的三个工作之一。

3. 暗晕形状的理论：三轴椭球模型

发现暗物质晕的形状与其质量、形成时间、宇宙学模型之间存在一个关键而又简单的标度关系，在此基础上首次提出描述暗晕内部物质分布的三轴椭球密度模型，已被广泛用于观测宇宙学的多个研究领域，如预言引力透镜、星系团的 SZ 效应、星系团的 X 射线分布、暗物质分布等。

4. 暗晕内部结构的演化理论：密度轮廓与质量增长之间的关系

发现暗物质晕的质量增长历史包含了诸多特性截然不同的两个阶段，即早期并合主导、密集因子不变的质量快速增长阶段和晚期吸积主导、密集因子快速变化的质量缓慢增长阶段；发现了暗物质晕演化的统一规律，构建了预言暗物质晕质量增长历史、暗物质晕密度轮廓及其演化历史的精确模型，该模型异常简单，但精确普适，在各种情况下的精度都远好于当时在国际上被大量运用的模型；相关成果被编入国际最著名的天文学教科书《星系动力学》的第二版，用以讲解暗物质晕的结构与其形成历史之间的联系。

5. 重子冷却效应对宇宙物质分布的影响

采用宇宙结构形成的流体力学 N 体模拟，首次自洽研究重子宏观物理过程对宇宙暗物质结构形成和对暗物质晕内物质分布的影响，定量计算了这些物理过程对预言弱引力透镜功率谱的影响，指出了对未来弱引力透镜实验结果的影响。研究结果被欧洲空间局 / 欧洲南部天文台未来十五年的发展报告和美国大型综合巡天望远镜项目 LSST 的科学绿皮书所引用，作为在未来大型引力透镜观测研究中必须考虑重子冷却效应的证据。

二、提出广泛用于国际大型星系红移巡天的暗晕占有数模型方法

为建立星系与暗晕间的观测联系，提出了构造星系大尺度分布和运动规律的模型——星系团低权重偏袒模型，并将该方法应用于 Las Campanas 星系红移巡天，首次测量了暗晕内星系数目与暗晕质量间的关系（即星系占有数），并限制宇宙学模型参量。斯隆、2dF 等后来的国际巡天组都用该模型方法分析星系分布与宇宙学模型的联系，测量暗晕内星系占有数。

从星系红移巡天数据，系统研究了星系物理性质与周围环境之间的关系，发现星系的相对速度弥散随星系的光度非单调的变化关系，首次测量了星系的成团强度随星系恒星质量的变化关系，成为检验理论模型和与其他观测结果比对的重要观测结果。

Awardee of Astronomy Prize, Jing Yipeng

Jing Yipeng was born in Shaoxing City of Zhejiang Province in January 1964. He got his PhD from the International School for Advanced Studies, Trieste, Italy in 1992. Afterwards, he did his postdoc research at the University of Arizona, Max-Planck Institute for Astrophysics, and the University of Tokyo before he returned to China in 2000, when he became a professor of Shanghai Astronomical Observatory. In 2012, he moved to Shanghai Jiao Tong University.

His research area is centered on the formation and evolution of galaxies and of the large-scale structures in the Universe. He uses supercomputers to simulate the growth of cosmic structures with his own N-body code, and has generated a set of most advanced cosmological simulations. Based on the simulations, he made a number of important discoveries on the dark matter halos that are basic building blocks of the cosmic structures. For examples, he obtained an accurate formula for the clustering of dark matter halos. He found an accurate model that describes the shape and internal structures of dark matter halos. With his collaborators, he established a universal relation that links the structure of a dark matter halos to its growth history. Many of his findings have become essential ingredients to current theories of structure formation in the Universe. He also uses the galaxy surveys to measure the cosmic structures in the real Universe in order to understand how the universe evolves and to test the theories. He proposed a framework that can connect the galaxies in galaxy surveys to the dark matter halos in the theories, which is so successful that it has become a standard approach to use galaxy surveys to study both cosmology and galaxy formation.

气象学奖获得者

李　俊

李俊，1965年6月出生于江苏省宜兴市。1987年毕业于北京大学数学系，1996年获中国科学院大气物理研究所理学博士学位。历任中国科学院大气物理研究所副研究员，威斯康星大学（麦迪逊）Distinguished Scientist、Permanent Principal Investigator，现任中国气象局国家卫星气象中心首席科学家。国际欧亚科学院院士。

李俊长期从事气象卫星遥感反演理论和方法、数据同化、观测系统规划设计的数值模拟和评估等研究，对大气科学的两大核心问题（遥感探测和数值天气预报）均作出杰出贡献。建立了中国新一代天气卫星定量产品开发标准和体系，指导和带领团队从无到有开发了20多种定量产品科学算法和软件，并全部获得业务化应用，极大提升了定量应用效果，尤其在台风、暴雨等灾害天气监测和预报中发挥了重要作用，取得了显著的社会和经济效益。曾荣获赵九章优秀中青年科学工作奖、美国国家海洋大气局戴维·约翰逊奖、美国威斯康星大学杰出研究校长奖等多个奖项和荣誉。

一、系统性建立了大气垂直廓线反演理论和计算方法

快速、准确地由卫星探测提取气象要素一直是卫星气象界面临的重大挑战。李俊针对大气垂直廓线反演的不适定问题，从理论上证明了约束反演的正则参数存在唯一解，提出了交互求解大气垂直廓线和正则参数的高效计算方法，实现了正则参数的确定从经验到客观的跨越。发现并改正了国际主流算法中反演水汽的原则性错误，解决了海量数据最优反演中难以兼顾时效和精度的国际性难题。建立了有效分离快变和慢变地球物理参数的反演理论，解决了地表和大气多参数反演中的不稳定性难题。李俊提出的反演方法自2000年成为国际通用算法，被中、美、欧等国家和地区的卫星业务中心用于生成大气廓线业务产品，也被美国宇航局和欧洲气象卫星组织用于处理卫星观测历史数据，产生长时间序列科学数据集。以此为基础，李俊领导中、美科学家于1999年研制完成第二

代国际先进大气垂直探测处理软件包（IAPP），大大提高了对暴雨和台风等灾害性天气的监测和预警能力。自 2012 年起，威斯康星大学组织开发国际卫星处理软件包（CSPP）并收入 IAPP，被包括中国在内的 100 多个国家和地区的 2900 多个卫星用户（单位或组织）广泛应用。

通过卫星观测的反演和分析，李俊首先在国际上揭示了地表发射率的日变化特征，对数值天气和气候模式中长波辐射的准确计算有重要意义；揭示了水汽反演对改进台风预报的重要作用。

二、建立了同化云区红外探测数据的理论和方法

从理论上阐述了直接同化云区探测数据中存在的高度非线性、Jacobian 矩阵的不连续性、卫星观测和大气模式的不一致性等一系列难题，提出"最优清云"处理方法，可有效清除探测仪视场内云的影响，得到"等效晴空"探测数据，解决了高光谱红外大气探测云区数据的同化问题，极大提升了数值天气预报模式同化卫星大气探测数据的能力和效率，从而显著改进了台风和暴雨等灾害天气的预报效果。

三、建立了大气探测系统规划设计的数值模拟和评估方法

建立了红外波段全天候快速精确辐射传输模式，提出了平衡仪器噪声、光谱范围、光谱分辨率和空间分辨率的科学方法，建立了关联仪器指标和科学指标的物理模型，并被用于制定气象卫星规划。建立了集轨道模拟、导航模拟、观测模拟、影响试验和评估于一体的综合系统，可以模拟和评估多种轨道上大气探测系统，用于优化轨道确定和星座配置及仪器指标的组合，该评估方法成为新一代国际地球同步气象卫星大气探测系统需求规划的主要手段。此外，首次认证了采用多星座小卫星大气探测可以达到传统卫星大气探测对灾害数值天气预报的同样效果。

四、建立高质量关键科学数据集

带领团队攻克多卫星历史观测数据非均一性难题，在国际上首次建立了基于卫星历史资料的陆地气溶胶光学厚度 30 年（1980—2010 年）长时间序列科学数据集，填补了陆地气溶胶历史数据的缺失。对全球多个静止气象卫星高空水汽资料作均一化处理，得到了关键气候因子之一且常规观测难以获取的全球均一化的高空水汽数据集。气溶胶和水汽这两个关键科学数据集为气候模式检验和评估、气候变化研究提供了重要观测依据。

Awardee of Meteorology Prize, Li Jun

Li Jun was born in Yixing City of Jiangsu Province in June 1965 . He graduated from the

Department of Mathematics at Peking University in 1987 and obtained his Ph.D. from the Institute of Atmospheric Physics (IAP) of the Chinese Academy of Sciences (CAS) in 1996. He has successively served as an Associate Scientist at the IAP/CAS, a Distinguished Scientist, and Permanent Principal Investigator at the University of Wisconsin–Madison. He is currently the Principal Scientist at the National Satellite Meteorological Center of the China Meteorological Administration.

Dr. Li has long been engaged in research on meteorological satellite remote sensing data inversion, data assimilation, observing system simulation, and evaluation. He played leadership roles in the development of quantitative products from the new generation of weather satellite series. These products have been widely used in high–impact weather nowcasting and numerical weather prediction.

Dr. Li has received multiple national and international awards and honors, including the Zhao Jiuzhang Outstanding Young Scientist Award, the David Johnson Award from the National Oceanic and Atmospheric Administration, and the Chancellor's Award for Excellence in Research from the University of Wisconsin–Madison.

Dr. Li has established meteorological satellite based quantitative inverse theory and methodologies for quickly and accurately extracting quantitative information of geophysical parameters from meteorological satellite observations and solved the instability problem of simultaneously retrieving multiple atmospheric and surface parameters. The theory and related algorithms have been widely used by international satellite operational centers for real–time satellite data processing and atmospheric production generation. To expand the satellite data assimilation from clear skies to cloudy skies, Dr. Li has developed an "optimal cloud–clearing" methodology to allow effectively assimilating the satellite–based infrared sounder data in cloudy skies into numerical weather prediction models, which substantially improves the forecasting of severe storms and tropical cyclones. In addition, he has guided and led his team to develop a comprehensive OSSE (observing system simulation experiment) system integrating orbit simulation, navigation simulation, observation simulation, impact experiment and evaluation, the research outcomes from OSSE have been used in planning the advanced atmospheric sounding systems for the new generation of international geostationary weather satellites.

地球科学奖获得者

陈 发 虎

陈发虎，1962年12月出生于陕西省丹凤县。1990年获兰州大学自然地理学博士学位。1995—1997年在英国利物浦大学地理系从事博士后研究。1995年起进入兰州大学工作，2007—2018年任兰州大学副校长，2018年起任中国科学院青藏高原研究所所长。2019年起任中国地理学会第十二届理事会理事长。中国科学院院士，发展中国家科学院院士。曾获全国先进工作者、全国杰出专业技术人才、第二届全国创新争先奖等荣誉。

陈发虎长期从事气候与环境变化以及史前人－环境相互作用研究，在我国晚第四纪东亚夏季风和黄土粉尘、亚洲中部干旱区气候变化的“西风模态”、史前人类向青藏高原扩散和定居等方面取得了一系列原创性成果，成果曾获国家自然科学奖二等奖、世界十大科学突破、中国科学十大进展等。

一、推动我国晚第四纪东亚夏季风和黄土粉尘研究

系统开展黄土高原西部和青藏高原东北边缘地区的黄土地层、沉积年代和气候记录研究，建立了适用于区域对比的黄土－古土壤序列；开展晚第四纪冰期/间冰期状态的气候快速变化研究，较早提出我国末次冰期冬、夏季风均存在快速变化观点。定量重建了我国华北可靠的全新世降水变化历史，发现历史时期人类活动诱发了强沙尘暴现象。部分成果获2007年度国家自然科学奖二等奖。

二、开创亚洲中部干旱区气候变化的“西风模态”研究

系统开展我国西部和中亚干旱区湖泊演化和湖泊记录研究，发现西风环流主导的亚洲中部干旱区的湿度（降水）变化模式与亚洲季风区存在显著差异，提出了全新世气候变化的“西风模态”新观点，并从高－中－低纬和海－陆－气耦合框架下的多尺度和多动力因子研究层面提出驱动机制框架。成果获2018年度国家自然科学奖二等奖。

三、提出青藏高原史前人类活动与高海拔适应的新观点

发现夏河丹尼索瓦古老型人类在中更新世已生活在青藏高原东北部，经历多个冰期-间冰期旋回并适应了青藏高原高寒缺氧环境，开创了古蛋白解析东亚古人类演化的新方法；提出跨大陆交流引起的农业技术革新推动了史前人群在晚全新世大规模定居青藏高原的新观点，推动了国际上对青藏高原史前人类活动及其高海拔适应的研究。部分成果被 *Archaeology* 杂志评为 2019 年度世界十大考古发现、被 *Science* 杂志评为世界十大科学突破、被 *Science News* 评为世界十大科学新闻，以及 2019 年度中国高校十大科技进展、中国十大科技进展新闻、中国科学十大进展。

Awardee of Earth Sciences Prize, Chen Fahu

Chen Fahu was born in Danfeng County of Shaanxi Province in December 1962. He is CAS Academician elected in 2015, Member of the World Academy of Sciences (TWAS) elected in 2016, a research professor and director of Institute of Tibetan Plateau Research, Chinese Academy of Sciences (CAS). He is the president since 2019 and fellow of Geographical Society of China, and associate Chairman of Environment Evolution Commission of IGU since 2012. He worked in Lanzhou University during 1995–2018. He was chairman of Rapid Climatic Changes in the Central-Asia's Dryland under INQUA RACHAD Working Group during 1999–2007, and now is vice presidents of China Society on Tibetan Plateau, and China Quaternary Research Associate.

His scientific work involves Quaternary environmental changes (especial during Holocene), climate changes, environmental archeology, loess record, desert evolution and paleolimnology with special focus on paleoenvironmental reconstruction, past human-environment interactions in Arid Central Asia and the Tibetan Plateau. His main scientific contributions include three aspects: i) Promoted research on East Asian summer monsoon and loess-dust in China during the late Quaternary, ii) Pioneering the study of the "westerlies-dominated climatic regime" of climate change in the arid central Asia drylands, iii) Proposed a new perspective on human occupation history and high-altitude adaptation on the Tibet Plateau.

生命科学奖获得者

骆清铭

骆清铭，1966 年 1 月出生于湖北省蕲春县。1986 年获西北电讯工程学院技术物理系工学学士学位，1989 年、1993 年先后获得华中理工大学光电子工程系理学硕士、工学博士学位。1993—2018 年在华中科技大学（现华中理工大学）工作，其间 1995 年 6 月—1997 年 2 月在美国宾夕法尼亚大学医学院生物化学与生物物理系任博士后副研究员。2018 年 9 月至今担任海南大学校长。中国科学院院士，中国医学科学院学部委员，国际医学与生物工程学院、美国医学与生物工程院、国际光学工程学会、英国工程技术学会、美国光学学会和中国光学学会会士。

骆清铭长期从事生物医学光子学与生物影像学新技术新方法及应用研究，围绕解决生物信息“看得见、看得清、看得全”的难题，在生物结构、功能及多分子事件信息获取方面作出了系统性、创新性贡献，实现了在全脑范围和介观分辨水平的神经连接测绘原理与关键技术的突破，研制的全脑显微光学成像仪器成为中美脑计划研究中广泛应用的装备，为脑科学研究作出了贡献。曾获国家技术发明奖二等奖、国家自然科学奖二等奖、黄家驷生物医学工程奖一等奖。

在单神经元分辨水平绘制整个大脑的神经连接图谱是认知脑功能与疾病的重要基础，是“脑计划”优先发展方向。磁共振成像和电镜成像都不能同时实现单细胞分辨和厘米级大范围全脑成像。美国艾伦脑研究所曾耗巨资测绘小鼠全脑图谱，仅得到百微米轴向分辨率的间隔图像，远未达到单神经元分辨水平。缺乏既“看得清（三维高空间分辨）”又“看得全（大视场）”的成像新原理是制约该领域发展的瓶颈。

针对光学成像难以同时满足微米级轴向分辨率及大范围全脑成像的难题，骆清铭率先建立光折射率差异组织切片成像理论，发明了一种反射式切片成像技术，突破传统的“先切片再成像”模式，解决人工收集样本薄片无法准确、快速自动成像的问题，奠定了生物组织高分辨连续成像的基础；创制出具有亚微米体素分辨率的全脑显微光学切片断层成像（MOST）装置，该装置在国际上首次绘制出单细胞分辨水平的小鼠全脑三维神经元图谱，与传统 130 张间断的鼠脑图谱相比，MOST 获取了 15380 张连续薄层图像，轴向分辨率提高了 2 个数量级，成果入选“2011 年度中国科学十大进展”。

针对解析特定基因、蛋白相关神经环路需要荧光标记，而传统样本制备方法会造成荧光淬灭的难题，骆清铭率领团队阐明了树脂包埋时荧光蛋白的荧光淬灭与恢复机理，发明了荧光 MOST 及相关样品制备方法，实现了在全脑范围内对荧光蛋白特异性标记神经元的追踪。

针对在全脑范围内追踪神经元长程投射的同时需要解剖精准定位投射靶区的难题，揭示了荧光染料在树脂包埋脑组织中的渗透规律，发明两种荧光信号同步获取的双色荧光 MOST 技术，建立了单细胞分辨水平空间定位神经环路投射靶区的成像新方法。

针对介观脑影像 PB 级大数据，创建了三维图像大数据的编码、存储格式及快速归档处理构架，解决了普通工作站无法处理 PB 级图像大数据的难题。

通过上述原理与技术改进的创新，获得了包括全脑标记和样本制备、全自动三维高分辨光学成像和图像大数据处理的介观脑图谱绘制全链条自主知识产权，并研制了稳定可靠的一系列 MOST 仪器装备。系列装备已在脑科学重要问题研究中得到应用示范。中外已有 60 余个实验室应用这些技术开展神经环路与脑疾病研究，如美国科学家利用荧光 MOST 产生的数据建立哺乳动物初级运动皮层的多模式细胞普查和图谱，中国科学家利用该技术建立了国际最大的小鼠全脑介观神经联接图谱数据库。

围绕生物功能的光学表征和光学检测的机理研究，他系统性地解决了生物功能信息“看得见、看得清”有关问题。

发现活细胞中绿色荧光蛋白探针存在双光子高阶光漂白效应，揭示了双光子成像中光漂白影响成像准确性的规律——光漂白速率与激发光强呈 4 次方关系。该理论已成为解析蛋白质分子相互作用、分子运动、离子浓度等生物功能的重要依据。

合作揭示了飞秒激光经角色散后时空色散的传播规律和耦合关系，精确预测了高斯脉冲激光在快速显微成像中的行为。这是飞秒激光无惯性扫描技术实现高时间分辨成像的理论依据。

发现了激光散斑时间与空间衬比统计特性对动态血流检测的等效性，且对静态背景组织干扰的敏感程度具有差异性。综合这些规律，提出了激光散斑时间衬比高分辨脑血流成像方法，使血流成像空间分辨率较传统提高 5 倍、信噪比提高 2 倍。发明了系列基于荧光蛋白的功能型探针和能同时检测单个活细胞内三对蛋白质间相互作用的方法。多个实验室采用上述成果开展生物医学研究，研制的激光散斑血流成像系统和荧光蛋白分子探针已用于哈佛大学、解放军 301 医院等单位。

Awardee of Life Sciences Prize, Luo Qingming

Luo Qingming was born in Qichun County of Hubei Province in January 1966. After graduating with a B.Eng. degree in Technical Physics from Xidian University in 1986, he received an M.Sc. degree in Optics and a Ph.D. degree in Physical Electronics from Huazhong University of Science and Technology (HUST) in 1989 and 1993, respectively.

Dr. Luo's research interests focus on multi-scale optical bioimaging and cross-level information integration. In 1995–1997, he went to work with the founder of biomedical photonics, the world-renowned Professor Britton Chance of the University of Pennsylvania. After returning to HUST, he immediately built one of the most comprehensive research centers in China in biomedical photonics. He has been devoted to new techniques and novel applications in life sciences, including optical molecular imaging, laser speckle imaging (LSI) in combination with optical intrinsic signal imaging (ISI), small animal imaging of fluorescence diffusion optical tomography (fDOT) coregistered with micro-CT, functional near-infrared (NIR) imaging, and micro-optical sectioning tomography (MOST).

His team created "the most detailed three-dimensional map of all the connections between the neurons in a complete mouse brain" and "demonstrated the first long-range tracing of individual axons in the mouse brain" with their homemade Brain-wide Positioning Systems (BPS). He is the winner of the Second Prize of the State Technological Invention Award, the Second Prize of the State Natural Sciences Award, and the First Prize of the Huang Jiasi Biomedical Engineering Award.

Recognizing Dr. Luo's contributions to the field of optical bioimaging and optical neuroscience, he was inducted as the Academician of the Chinese Academy of Sciences in 2019 and the Chinese Academy of Medical Sciences in 2020. Furthermore, he is also elected to be a Fellow of The International Academy of Medical and Biological Engineering (IAMBE), The American Institute for Medical and Biological Engineering (AIMBE), Optica (formerly OSA), The Institution of Engineering and Technology (IET), The International Society for Optics and Photonics (SPIE) and Chinese Optical Society (COS).

生命科学奖获得者

林 圣 彩

林圣彩，1963 年 10 月出生于福建省尤溪县。1984 年获厦门大学生物系学士学位，1991 年获美国得克萨斯大学西南医学中心生物化学专业博士学位。1991—1995 年在美国 Howard Hughes 医学研究所从事博士后研究。1995—2001 年、2001—2006 年、2006—2017 年分别在新加坡国立大学分子与细胞生物学研究所、香港科技大学生化系、厦门大学生命科学学院工作。现任中国生物化学与分子生物学会副理事长，中国抗癌协会肿瘤代谢专业委员会主任委员。中国科学院院士。

林圣彩长期致力于代谢稳态调控的分子机理和生物学功能研究，并取得系统性研究成果，为了解糖脂代谢相关疾病的成因及其药物研发提供了新理论和新策略。

一、揭示细胞感知葡萄糖并调节代谢稳态关键激酶 AMPK 的原理

AMPK（AMP 依赖的蛋白激酶，抑制合成代谢）和 mTOR（雷帕霉素靶蛋白激酶，促进合成）在调控分解代谢和合成代谢平衡、细胞生长和机体寿命中起到中枢作用，并因此成为研发治疗代谢类疾病的药物靶点。以前的理论认为 AMPK 是感知细胞能量水平的蛋白质激酶，林圣彩团队通过对 AMPK 的激活和葡萄糖感应机制与功能的系统研究，作出了一系列发现。

发现细胞内 AMPK 被上游激酶 LKB1 的激活需要 AXIN 这一架构蛋白质作为桥梁；当葡萄糖水平下降时，AXIN 和 LKB1 的复合体转运到溶酶体膜上激活 AMPK，同时竞争性地抑制了 mTOR 复合体 1（mTORC1）的活性，创立了 AMPK 激活的“溶酶体通路”；发现二甲双胍激活 AMPK 也是通过这一溶酶体途径进行的，为揭示其降低肿瘤发生率和延长寿命的机制提供了理论依据。

发现葡萄糖酵解途径中的醛缩酶即是葡萄糖代谢物果糖 -1,6- 二磷酸的感受器，通过溶酶体途径以不依赖 AMP 水平升高的方式激活 AMPK，被评价揭示了细胞响应葡萄糖水

平下降诱导 AMPK 激活及其同步调控合成代谢与分解代谢之间转换的“路线图”，是该领域的“范式转换”。研究成果“葡萄糖的感知及其生物学意义”入选 2017 年度中国生命科学十大进展。

发现不同程度的营养和能量水平的缺乏对 AMPK 调控的时空异质性及其生理意义。当醛缩酶感知低葡萄糖水平时，它通过抑制位于内质网的 TRPV，将低葡萄糖信号转换成低钙信号而激活 AMPK；发现醛缩酶也可感知高葡萄糖水平，让 mTORC1 保持活力，揭示了葡萄糖的重要信息性——同时管控 AMPK 和 mTORC1。

二、发现生长因子调节糖脂代谢稳态的通路与机理

揭示了细胞在该应激状态下启动自噬的多接点的信号通路，即 GSK3-TIP60-ULK1 途径，发现该途径是生长因子缺乏情况下启动细胞自噬的关键；生长因子缺乏时，ULK1 能调控葡萄糖代谢途径中的多个酶，进而控制糖代谢的流量和流向分配，以维持能量与氧化还原稳态，从而揭示了生长因子缺失下的葡萄糖分解代谢重编程机制；在生长因子调控脂质合成方面，发现最常见突变原癌基因之一的产物 Src 直接磷酸化并调控脂肪合成酶 lipin-1，重塑癌细胞脂代谢，使肿瘤细胞具有增殖和转移的优势，提供了一种肥胖促进肿瘤生长的内在机制。其研究成果“揭示营养匮乏引发细胞自噬的分子机制”入选 2012 年度中国科学十大进展。

三、二甲双胍靶点的发现及其延缓衰老的机制阐明

发现一种称为 PEN2 的蛋白质是二甲双胍的靶蛋白，并揭示了该靶点通过“借道”该团队发现的葡萄糖感知通路起到降糖、治疗脂肪肝、延长寿命等的生理作用，进一步证明了葡萄糖感知溶酶体通路的生理意义；筛选到一个能模拟辟谷效应（卡路里限制）的化学药物（俗称“辟谷精”），具有降糖、治疗脂肪肝、延长寿命的效果；发现了“辟谷精”和二甲双胍一样均借道先前他们发现的葡萄糖（卡路里限制）感知通路，从而偶联到 AMPK 长寿相关通路，达到治疗糖尿病和脂肪肝等重大代谢性疾病以及延缓衰老等作用。这些新的原理性具有十分重要的应用转化价值，提出了为干预困扰现代社会的代谢综合征问题，药物靶点必须以 AMKP 激活的时空调控为依据来加以选择，解释了国际制药巨头投入重金研发 AMPK 激动剂失败的原因。基于 AMPK 溶酶体通路调控时空调控理论，提出了系列代谢性疾病的新药创新靶点，相关专利已申请并转让给有关公司进行药物开发，该靶点药物 aldometanib 正在推向临床，目前已取得阶段性重要突破。其研究成果“二甲双胍靶点的发现及其延缓衰老的机制阐明”入选 2022 年度中国生命科学十大进展。

四、发现脂肪吸收储存、利用的新调控机制

分离了与 AXIN 相互结合的蛋白质并命名为 AIDA，发现其是应激条件下脂质代谢

调节的关键分子：①通过介导多种甘油三酯合成的关键酶的降解，减缓甘油三酯重合成，以减缓脂肪吸收来控制体重、抑制肥胖发生，提出 AIDA 是一种“浪费基因”的新概念——有别于长期广泛持有的“节俭基因”理论；②发现在寒冷环境下，AIDA 受交感神经信号调节，并直接结合棕色脂肪关键产热蛋白质 UCP1 将其活化，促进脂质代谢生成热量以维持体温，揭示了交感神经调控体温的直接机制，也揭示了脂肪合成酶 lipin-1 的翻译后修饰影响甘油三酯和磷脂合成。这些成果从脂质吸收、合成和利用多角度对个体脂稳态调节机制的认知作出贡献。

Awardee of Life Sciences Prize, Lin Shengcai

Lin Shengcai was born in Youxi County of Fujian Province in October 1963. He obtained his bachelor's degree from Xiamen University in 1984, and obtained his doctorate of biochemistry in 1991 from University of Texas Southwestern Medical Center. He then became a postdoctoral fellow at the Howard Hughes Medical Institute, University of California at San Diego and stayed until 1995. Dr. Lin then moved to Asia, working at the Institute of Molecular and Cell Biology, Singapore during 1995–2001, then working at the Department of Biochemistry, Hong Kong University of Science and Technology during 2001–2006. During this period, from 2001 to 2006, he was also an adjunct professor—Cheung Kong Professorship—at the School of Life Sciences, Xiamen University, and acted as dean of the school from 2003. Finally, in 2006, Dr. Lin moved back to Xiamen University, his alma mater, and continued his deanery until 2017. He was elected into the Academy of Sciences of China. He is currently serving as a vice president of the Chinese Society of Biochemistry and Molecular Biology, and Chair of the Division society of Cancer Metabolism of the Chinese Society of Medicine.

Dr. Lin's long-term research interest has been with metabolic homeostasis and the underlying mechanisms. The recent, main achievements include the identification and characterization of the glucose sensing pathway that links glucose availability to AMPK and mTORC1. They revealed that aldolase associated with the lysosomal proton pump acts as a sensor for fructose-1, 6-bisphosphate, which reflects the availability of glucose. The quintessence of the finding is that glucose and its metabolites can act as messengers, in analogy to hormones, to directly control the switch between mTORC1 and AMPK. They also identified the long-missing target of metformin, showing that PEN2, lysosomally localized, binds to metformin, relaying to the (inactivation of) v-ATPase proton pump, thereby activating AMPK and inhibiting mTORC1. Beyond that, the finding that metformin intersects the glucose sensing pathway testifies that metformin is a pro-longevity mimetic. Based on the glucose sensing pathway, Dr. Lin's team have identified a chemical compound, termed Aldometabnib, that can mimic glucose starvation and extends both lifespan and healthspan.

农学奖获得者

何 光 存

何光存，1956 年 4 月出生于湖北省麻城市。1982 年获华中农业大学硕士学位，1989 年获日本爱媛大学博士学位，1994 年在英国诺丁汉大学从事博士后研究，1995 年进入武汉大学生命科学学院工作。何光存先后在华中农业大学、湖北省农业科学院、国际水稻研究所、日本香川大学、日本爱媛大学、英国诺丁汉大学、美国新泽西州立大学 Waksman 研究所和武汉大学从事水稻遗传育种相关研究，在水稻抗褐飞虱种质发掘、基因克隆、机理研究和育种应用等方面作出了系统性创新成果，突破水稻抗褐飞虱关键科学问题与育种技术瓶颈，推动我国抗褐飞虱育种实现多项突破并进入世界领先行列，在解决作物抗虫学科前沿性与基础性科学问题和褐飞虱防控国家重大需求方面作出了重要贡献。

一、国际首次克隆水稻抗褐飞虱基因，奠定水稻抗飞虱育种关键基础

国际上早在 20 世纪 60 年代就开始水稻抗褐飞虱研究，但基因克隆一直没有成功，是一个世界性难题和激烈竞争的目标。何光存率先在我国开展水稻抗褐飞虱研究，建立了大规模褐飞虱养殖与抗虫鉴定技术，从野生稻和传统农家品种资源发掘天然抗褐飞虱基因。应用远缘杂交和幼胚拯救技术克服种间杂交障碍，通过回交、染色体原位杂交与 RFLP 标记选择，构建异源单体附加系和渗入系群体，实现了野生稻有利基因的发掘、转移与利用。在野生稻杂交后代中发现和定位了两个抗褐飞虱基因位点，并带领课题组从种质资源中定位和命名了多个抗褐飞虱基因（*Bph6*、*Bph7*、*Bph9*、*Bph12*、*Bph14*、*Bph15*、*Bph30*、*Bph37*、*Bph43*）和抗白背飞虱基因（*Wbph7*、*Wbph8*），其中包括成功分离了世界上第一个水稻抗褐飞虱基因 *Bph14*；是国际上定位抗飞虱基因位点最多的实验室。

这些基因在水稻育种中有特别重要的应用价值，改变了我国抗飞虱基因匮乏的局面。研究成果系统揭示了抗褐飞虱遗传基础，得到了广泛认可和高度评价。

二、国际首次鉴定被植物免疫受体识别的昆虫唾液蛋白，革新了植物抗虫认知

何光存利用抗褐飞虱基因及材料，在国际上最先揭示了水稻抗褐飞虱基因编码细胞膜受体或胞内受体，首次鉴定了被植物受体识别的昆虫唾液蛋白 BISP，揭示了细胞自噬精细调控植物抗虫性与生长发育平衡的机制。揭示了 BPH6-EXO70-SAMSL 和 BPH14-WRKY46-RLCK281 等抗虫信号通路及 SA 和 CK 等植物激素在抗褐飞虱中的作用；发现了褐飞虱取食行为与水稻叶鞘表面特征及内部结构的关系；揭示了抗性水稻通过强化细胞壁或堵塞筛管使褐飞虱不能取食而饿死的抗虫机制，相关原创性成果是作物抗虫分子机理的奠基性工作，为培育高产抗虫品种提供了理论依据。

三、突破抗虫育种技术瓶颈，推动我国抗飞虱育种实现零的突破

抗褐飞虱基因蕴藏于野生稻和古老农家品种中。何光存克服种间杂交障碍，成功创制了首个带野生稻抗褐飞虱基因并被广泛应用的核心种质；揭示抗褐飞虱基因互补产生更强抗虫性，创制了双基因聚合的抗虫恢复系。开发了抗褐飞虱基因功能标记，应用于育种材料的抗褐飞虱基因检测，显著提升了我国抗飞虱育种能力。应用何光存发掘的抗褐飞虱基因与种质，我国育种单位培育了首个抗褐飞虱不育系、恢复系和超级稻。*Bph14*、*Bph15*、*Bph6*、*Bph9*、*Bph30* 是目前水稻育种中应用最广的抗飞虱基因，育成了 40 多个新品种并大面积推广应用，为稻飞虱绿色防控和粮食生产安全提供了支撑。

Awardee of Agronomy Prize, He Guangcun

He Guangcun was born in Macheng City of Hubei Province in April 1956. He obtained his master's degree from Huazhong Agricultural University in 1982. In 1989, he earned his Ph.D. from Ehime University in Japan, and in 1994, he received a Marie Curie Fellowship to conduct postdoctoral research at the University of Nottingham in the United Kingdom. In 1995, he became a professor and doctoral advisor at Wuhan University's College of Life Sciences.

He has conducted research on rice genetics and breeding at institutions such as Huazhong Agricultural University, Hubei Academy of Agricultural Sciences, International Rice Research Institute, Kagawa University (Japan), Ehime University (Japan), University of Nottingham (UK), Waksman Institute of Microbiology at Rutgers University (USA), and Wuhan University.

He Guangcun's research has focused on the genetic improvement of rice, particularly in the context of resistance to brown planthopper (BPH), one of the most destructive pests in rice cultivation. Over more than 30 years of dedicated research, he has made significant contributions to the BPH-resistant germplasm discovery, BPH resistance gene cloning, molecular mechanism study, and breeding applications of BPH resistance genes. He Guangcun's research has a profound impact on rice genetics, breeding for pest resistance, making him a leading figure in the field of pest resistance in crop in China and globally.

1. Cloning of rice BPH resistance genes

He Guangcun was the first to successfully clone rice genes conferring resistance to BPH, laying the crucial foundation for breeding BPH-resistant rice. He established large-scale BPH breeding and resistance identification techniques and explored natural BPH resistance genes from wild rice and land race germplasm. He has mapped and named multiple BPH resistance genes (*Bph6*, *Bph7*, *Bph9*, *Bph12*, *Bph14*, *Bph15*, *Bph30*, *Bph37*, *Bph43*) and whitebacked planthopper resistance genes (*Wbph7*, *Wbph8*), making his lab one of the world's leading groups in terms of the number of isolated BPH resistance genes. Cloning BPH resistance genes was a longstanding challenge worldwide, and He Guangcun's achievement had a significant impact on the field.

2. Understanding molecular mechanism of rice resistance to brown planthopper

He Guangcun's research provided valuable insights into the molecular mechanisms underlying plant resistance to insects, particularly BPH. He was among the first to reveal that rice genes conferring resistance to BPH encode cell membrane or intracellular receptors, and he identified the first BPH salivary protein, BPH14-Interacting Salivary Protein (BISP), recognized by plant receptor. These discovered autophagy fine-tunes the balance between plant resistance and growth. His work also uncovered signaling pathways involved in BPH resistance, including BPH6-EXO70-SAMSL and BPH14-WRKY46-RLCK281, and the roles of plant hormones like SA and CK in BPH resistance.

3. Advancements in BPH-resistant rice breeding

He Guangcun played a crucial role in breaking through technical barriers for breeding BPH-resistant rice. He successfully created the core germplasm carrying BPH resistance genes from wild rice, which has been widely applied in breeding programs. He demonstrated that combining multiple BPH resistance genes can enhance resistance and developed functional markers for detecting BPH resistance genes in breeding materials, significantly improving China's ability to breed BPH-resistant rice. Breeders have utilized the BPH resistance genes discovered by He Guangcun's group and developed the first BPH-resistant sterile lines, restorer lines, and super rice varieties. Genes like *Bph14*, *Bph15*, *Bph6*, *Bph9*, and *Bph30* have been widely used in rice breeding, contributing to sustainable rice production and food security in China.

农学奖获得者

吴义强

吴义强，1967年7月出生于河南省固始县。1987年考入中南林学院（现中南林业科技大学）木材机械加工专业，毕业后留校任教。2005年获日本国立爱媛大学生物资源利用学博士学位。2022年10月起任中南林业科技大学校长。兼任中南林业科技大学木材科学与技术国家重点学科带头人，第六、第七、第八届国务院学位委员会林业工程学科评议组成员，教育部高等学校林业工程类专业教育指导委员会副主任委员，中国林学会副理事长、中国竹产业协会副会长等。中国工程院院士，国际木材科学院院士。

一、创新人造板绿色环保节能制造技术，攻克人造板产业甲醛污染重、能耗高的重大技术瓶颈，有力推动产业结构调整升级和绿色低碳发展

创新胶黏剂多元杂化共聚理论及交联技术，发明有机－无机杂化无醛环保胶黏剂，从源头上解决人造板产业甲醛污染世界难题。创新多级联控节能制造技术与智控系统，突破了多工序协同节能“卡脖子”技术瓶颈，生产能耗降低40%以上，技术在多家大中型人造板企业推广应用，每年节能近千亿度电，每年新增产值超8000亿元。成果获2018年度国家科技进步奖二等奖。

二、创新人造板阻燃抑烟协同防火及长效防潮防水技术，突破人造板易燃发烟、吸潮变形重大技术难题，有力保障人居环境安全

构建人造板阻燃抑烟功能叠加耦合理论，创新固－液－气立体屏障防火技术，攻克阻燃抑烟难以协同国际难题，人造板阻燃性能国内外领先（达A2级），在1300℃火场长时间不燃烧、不发烟。创新醇胺网络交联防潮、无机桥联防水等技术，人造板在高湿环境中不变形、不破坏。产品及制品广泛用于人民大会堂、国家图书馆等标志性工程。成果获2010年度国家科技进步奖二等奖。

三、创制秸秆人造板高效制造技术与装备，破解秸秆代木人造板难以胶合成型关键技术瓶颈，实现秸秆资源规模材料化利用

创新物理刻蚀与化学赋能联合界面调控技术，攻克秸秆表面富集蜡质层胶合困难国际难题。发明叠压自加热成形技术，创制秸秆破碎/多级分选一体化、分级连续铺装与预压一体化等核心装备，建成全球首条秸秆无机人造板自动化生产线和全球最大产能无醛秸秆人造板产业集团。近 5 年利用秸秆超 3 亿吨，减少木材砍伐近 2 亿立方米。成果获 2017 年度教育部科技进步奖一等奖、2020 年度湖南省科技创新团队奖。

吴义强先后主持国家重点研发计划/科技支撑项目课题、中国工程院战略咨询项目、国家自然科学基金重大/重点/面上项目 20 余项，荣获国家科技进步奖二等奖 2 项、国家教学成果奖二等奖 1 项、全国创新争先奖 1 项，以及教育部科技进步奖一等奖、梁希科技进步奖一等奖等省部级奖励 10 余项。

Awardee of Agronomy Prize, Wu Yiqiang

Wu Yiqiang was born in Gushi County of Henan Province in July 1967. In 1987, he was admitted to the Wood Machinery Processing major of Central South Forestry College (now Central South University of Forestry and Technology, CSUFT) and stayed on campus to teach after graduation. Graduated from National Ehime University in Japan in 2005 with a PhD in Biological Resource Utilization. Since October 2022, he has served as the President of CSUFT. He concurrently serves as the leading expert in the National Key Discipline of Wood Science and Technology at the CSUFT. He has also been a member of the Evaluation Committee for Forestry Engineering Discipline of the 6th, 7th, and 8th State Council Academic Degrees Committee, Deputy Director of the Teaching and Supervisory Committee for Forestry Engineering Majors in Higher Education Institutions under the Ministry of Education. Additionally, he holds positions such as Vice Chairman of the Chinese Forestry Society, and Vice President of the Chinese Bamboo Industry Association. He is also an academician of the International Academy of Wood Sciences, and an academician of the Chinese Academy of Engineering (CAE) Member.

Prof. Wu and his groups innovated green, environmentally-friendly, and energy-efficient manufacturing technologies for wood-based panels, overcoming major technological bottlenecks such as heavy formaldehyde pollution and high energy consumption in the industry. His efforts have greatly contributed to the adjustment and upgrading of the industrial structure as well as the promotion of environmentally-friendly and low-carbon development. He won the second prize of the 2018 National Science and Technology Progress Award based on the above achievements.

Prof. Wu and his groups innovated flame-retardant synergistic fire protection and long-lasting moisture-proof and water-proof technology for wood-based panels, breaking through the major technical problems of flammable and smoke generation, moisture absorption and deformation of wood-based panels, effectively ensuring the safety of the living environment. He won the second prize of the 2010 National Science and Technology Progress Award based on the above achievements.

Prof. Wu and his groups created the efficient manufacturing technology and equipment for straw-based panels, cracking the key technical bottleneck of difficult gluing molding of straw wood-based panels which can substitute the wood-based panels, realizing the large-scale material utilization of straw resources, innovating the interface control technology of physical etching and chemical empowerment, and overcoming the international problem of gluing difficulties caused by the enrichment of wax layer on the surface of straw. He won the first prize of Ministry of Education Science and Technology Progress Award in 2017 and the Science and Technology Innovation Team Award of Hunan Province in 2020.

He has presided more than 20 projects of National Key Research and Development Plan, National Science and Technology Support Project, the Strategic Consultation Project of Chinese Academy of Engineering, and National Natural Science Foundation Projects. He has won 2 awards of second prizes of the National Science and Technology Progress Award, 1 of second prize of the National Teaching Achievement Award, 1 of National Innovation Competition Award, and more than 10 provincial and ministerial awards of the first prize of Ministry of Education Science and Technology Progress, and the first prize of Liang Xi Science and Technology Progress.

农学奖获得者

周 继 勇

周继勇，1963 年 10 月出生于重庆市开县。1989 年获中国人民解放军兽医大学农学硕士学位。1999 年获浙江大学生物医学工程专业理学博士学位。1989 年 7 月—1996 年 2 月在四川畜牧兽医学院（现西南大学）工作，1996 年 2 月—2000 年 12 月在浙江农业大学（现浙江大学）动物科学学院工作，2020 年 3 月起任浙江大学动物医学中心主任。国务院学位委员会第七届学科评议组成员、全国兽医专业学位研究生教育指导委员会委员、教育部高等学校动物医学类专业教学指导委员会委员、第二届全国动物防疫专家委员会委员。中国畜牧兽医学会生物技术学分会副理事长。先后获得国家自然科学奖二等奖、国家技术发明奖二等奖、国家科技进步奖二等奖、全国创新争先奖。

周继勇从事兽医病毒学与生物制品研究，在畜禽免疫系统损伤性病毒的基础理论研究和防控技术产品研发等方面作出了一系列创新性工作。

一、发现人兽共患的新病毒

通过长期病原监测与病毒分离鉴定，掌握了 PCV2 型、PCV3 型在我国的流行传播动态，首次发现新的猪圆环病毒 4 型，发现并命名了具有人兽共患特征的阿龙山病毒；首次发现高原鼠兔的禽流感病毒自然感染，并分离到 H5N1、H7N2、H9N2 亚型的禽流感病毒，揭示了它们调控天然免疫的差异机制。上述工作丰富了病毒生态学知识，为国家动物疫病防控技术开发提供了病毒基础资源，为禽流感的生物防治措施提供了新的科学证据。

二、创立免疫系统损伤性病毒感染的天然免疫自噬调控与衣壳变构理论模型

1. 建立了宿主感染过程中传染性法氏囊病病毒抑制天然免疫应答的自噬调节模型

首次发现并阐明了磷酸肌醇激酶依赖性蛋白激酶 1（PDPK1）的 SUMO 修饰及其调控细胞自噬的机制；揭示并阐明了 IBDV 的衣壳蛋白 VP2 在感染过程中通过不同信号转导

途径启动细胞自噬、VP3 蛋白借助 PDPK1 关闭细胞自噬并抑制天然免疫应答的系列机制，从而发现 VP2 是病毒激活自噬的蛋白标识、VP3 是病毒关闭自噬并抑制天然免疫应答的蛋白标识。这一系列研究结果形成了 IBDV 通过细胞自噬拮抗宿主天然免疫应答的理论模型，为传染性法氏囊病新型疫苗设计、抗病毒药物创制提供了全新的理论指导。

2. 揭示了宿主感染过程中猪圆环病毒 2 型衣壳变构的病毒基因组释放机制

发现病毒衣壳蛋白基因在提升 PCV2 复制能力中的关键作用，发现并鉴定了 PCV2 的新编码蛋白 ORF4 及其诱导细胞凋亡的机制，发现并阐明了 PCV2 粒子通过改变衣壳蛋白构象结合受体的入侵细胞机制、结合细胞微管相关蛋白的胞浆移行机制，以及结合细胞输入蛋白 5 进入细胞核的机制。在此基础上，发现猪圆环病毒 2 在细胞核内不解聚衣壳释放病毒核酸的机制。这些研究结果形成了猪圆环病毒在感染宿主过程中通过改变衣壳构象释放病毒核酸的理论模型，为猪圆环病毒 2 复制能力提升、抗病毒药物创制的策略制定提供了重要的理论依据。

三、创建免疫系统损伤性病毒 PCV/IBDV 感染的以检测诊断试剂、高效疫苗制品为核心的免疫预防技术体系

1. 创制了标准化的猪圆环病毒抗体检测试剂盒等生物制品

率先建立了基于 2D-MS 蛋白质组和病毒－宿主互作的感染标识挖掘技术，首次鉴定出 PCV2、IBDV 感染的标识蛋白。建立了具有发明专利授权的、表达基因工程蛋白的原核、真核制备系统。创建了系列基因工程病毒抗原、宿主蛋白的单克隆抗体细胞库以及 IBDV 强弱毒鉴别手段。发明了拥有自主知识产权的、鉴别猪圆环病毒基因型的抗原检测卡。基于 PCV2 衣壳蛋白基因工程抗原，建立了抗体检测试剂的标准化生产工艺，创制了获得国家 II 类新兽药注册证书的抗体检测试剂盒制品。该制品是我国第一个准予上市销售的猪圆环病毒病防控用商品，实现了“安全、精准、特异、低成本”目标，为疫苗免疫效果评价、流行病学调查提供了标准化的检测试剂。

2. 创制了高效的疫苗制品

建立了基于传染性法氏囊病病毒免疫原 VP2、猪圆环病毒的亚单位和病毒样颗粒疫苗技术。构建了具有中国发明专利授权的、比野生型病毒高 10～100 倍的高繁殖力猪圆环病毒 2 型毒株，解决了病毒体外培养繁殖力低的技术难题。利用该毒种，率先建立了我国首个悬浮细胞生产病毒抗原的工厂化标准工艺，制定了疫苗的工艺与免疫效力标准，创制出产生免疫保护力最快的猪圆环病毒 2 灭活疫苗（ZJ/C 株），并获得国家新兽药注册证书，为猪圆环病毒病的免疫预防提供高效的疫苗产品。

四、推进技术产品转化为生产力，为中国兽用疫苗产业发展作出贡献

积极推动技术产品向现实生产力转化，将本人创制的专利技术、获批国家新兽药注册证书的疫苗、检测试剂盒制品在 13 家兽用生物制品企业进行全面量产，获得农业部颁

发的 13 个制品的国家批准生产文号。2010 年至今，指导企业先后建成 6 条疫苗生产线和 6 条 ELISA 抗体检测试剂盒生产线，包括第一条 GMP 条件下的猪圆环病毒 2 抗体 ELISA 检测试剂盒生产线，促进了我国兽用生物制品行业的发展。量产上市的疫苗、诊断试剂制品打破了国外产品的市场垄断，在全国 28 个省市得到广泛应用，有效控制了猪圆环病毒病的流行。

Awardee of Agronomy Prize, Zhou Jiyong

Zhou Jiyong was born in Kaixian County of Chongqing City in October 1963. He received a master's degree of Veterinary Pathology from Veterinary University of the People's Liberation Army of China in July 1989, and a PhD degree in Biomedical Engineering from Zhejiang University in December 1999. He worked in Sichuan College of Animal Husbandry and Veterinary Medicine from July 1989 to February 1996, and Zhejiang Agricultural University from February 1996 to December 2000. He was a professor of Veterinary Virology at Zhejiang University since August 1998 and the director of Zhejiang University Veterinary Science Center since March 2020. He was a member of the 7th Discipline Evaluation Group of Academic Degrees Committee of the State Council, a member of the National Veterinary Graduate Education Steering Committee, a member of Veterinary Medicine Teaching Steering Committee of Higher Education Institutions of the Ministry of Education, a member of the National Animal Epidemic Prevention Expert Committee, and a vice president of Biotechnology Branch of Chinese Society of Animal Husbandry and Veterinary Medicine. He has won the second prize of the National Natural Science Award, the National Technological Invention Award and the National Science and Technology Progress Award.

Jiyong Zhou focused on viral diseases and biological products, and has made a series of innovative research work in the basic research of animal immune system-damaging viruses and the development of immune control products. He found the mechanism that different subtypes of avian influenza virus differentially regulated host innate immunity and the previously unidentified alongshan virus (a tick-borne zoonotic virus), porcine circovirus type 4 and pika-origin avian flu virus, etc. He established an autophagy regulatory model in which infectious bursal disease virus suppresses the innate immune response during host infection, and revealed the viral genome release mechanism of porcine circovirus type 2 capsid allosterism during host infection. He created the immune system damaging PCV/IBDV infection with detection and diagnostic reagents, effective vaccine products as the core of the immune prevention technology system, and contributed to the development of China's animal vaccine industry.

医学药学奖获得者

葛 均 波

葛均波，1962年11月出生于山东省五莲县。1993年获德国美因兹大学医学博士学位。1995—1999年任德国埃森大学医学院血管内超声室主任。1999年回国至今，先后担任复旦大学附属中山医院心导管室主任、心内科主任，上海市心血管病研究所所长，同济大学副校长，复旦大学生物医学研究院院长，中国科学技术大学附属第一医院院长，国家放射与治疗临床医学研究中心主任。兼任中国医学科学院学部委员、中国心血管健康联盟主席、中华医学会心血管病学分会主任委员、中国医师协会心血管内科医师分会会长、亚太介入心脏病学会主席、美国心脏病学会国际顾问、世界心脏联盟常务理事等职务。中国科学院院士。

葛均波长期致力于冠心病等重大心血管疾病关键诊疗技术革新和转化研究，在冠状动脉腔内影像诊断、复杂介入诊疗技术创新、新型器械研发等领域作出了一系列成果。2023年被授予全国创新争先奖章。

一、推动血管内超声技术临床应用

传统冠脉造影容易漏诊。葛均波运用血管内超声技术在国际上首先发现了冠脉心肌桥的影像学特征——“半月现象”，被国际学界称为“葛氏现象”，使心肌桥检出率由冠脉造影的0.51%～2.5%提高到95%以上，成为业界公认的金标准；同时还发现了心肌桥的多普勒血流频谱特征——“指尖现象”，揭示硝酸甘油加重心肌桥对冠脉的挤压作用并加重心肌缺血，从而修订了硝酸酯类药物治疗心肌桥导致心肌缺血的传统观点。研究成果被写入国际经典心血管病教科书《Braunwald心脏病学》和全国《内科学》统编教材，获2006年国家科技进步奖二等奖。

二、引领我国冠脉慢性完全闭塞病变介入治疗

冠脉慢性完全闭塞病变（CTO）是冠脉介入治疗领域有待攻克的“最后堡垒”，传统正向介入技术成功率仅为60%左右。2005年，作为我国大陆首位受邀手术演示学者，葛均波在美国TCT会议（国际最权威心脏介入会议）上创造性地应用“逆向导丝技术”，成功开通一例高难度冠脉CTO病变，开启了CTO病变“逆向开通”时代，使手术成功率提高到90%以上。目前该技术已成为CTO治疗的三大常规术式之一。

2015年，葛均波再创其姊妹技术“主动迎客技术”，显著提高了逆向导丝体外化效率和成功率。据2019年中国CTO介入俱乐部数据库统计，112例CTO病变采用该技术均顺利完成逆向导丝体外化，手术成功率100%，*Science Bulletin* 评价“该技术对简化复杂CTO介入操作贡献卓越”，目前已获业内广泛应用。

三、实现我国冠脉支架自主研发重大突破

针对传统冠脉支架涂层材料因不可降解而增加支架内血栓风险的设计缺陷，2005年主持研制我国首个可降解涂层冠脉支架，2006年被评为国家“863”计划新材料领域两项优秀研究成果之一，使晚期致死性支架内血栓发生风险由原来的1.2%～1.9%降至0.34%，显著降低了医疗费用和出血风险。自上市以来，该支架国内市场占有率达20%～25%，在全国超过900家医疗机构获得临床应用，同时出口俄罗斯、印度、新加坡等多国，每年节约医疗费用超过10亿元人民币，相关成果获2011年国家技术发明奖二等奖。

在此基础上，2013年再次成功研制出我国首个具有完全自主知识产权的生物可吸收冠脉支架Xinsorb，2020年批准上市，标志我国冠脉介入治疗的“第四次革命”；支架植入3～5年后完全降解，血管恢复自然状态，血管治疗失败率（5.3%）显著低于国外同类产品（13.4%）。在可降解支架领域国内市场占有率超过50%。

四、开启我国心脏瓣膜病微创介入治疗新时代

突破传统外科手术禁区，围绕心脏瓣膜全系统，探索高危患者微创介入治疗新方法。先后完成我国首例经皮主动脉瓣植入术、我国首例经皮肺动脉瓣植入术、亚洲首例经皮二尖瓣夹合术、亚洲首例经皮异位三尖瓣植入术。针对国外器械手术入路受限、操作复杂等问题，2018年首创经心尖二尖瓣夹合术式及其微创器械ValveClamp，显著缩短了手术时间（平均27分钟，国际同类157分钟），实现我国二尖瓣微创治疗技术和产品创新的重要突破。2019年获国际心血管创新大会年度唯一终身成就奖。2023年，ValveClamp器械成功上市，成为国内首个二尖瓣反流介入治疗器械。

五、深耕心脏损伤修复新理论新策略的全景式科学探索

针对缺血性心脏病“危险因素－心肌损伤－心肌修复”全事件链开展系列研究，确

立了大气污染和气候变化是心肌梗死全新的危险因素，同时揭示了 PCSK9 等在促进血小板活化和心肌梗死发生中的新机制；阐明了细胞焦亡参与心肌缺血再灌注损伤的关键机理，为心肌保护提供了新思路；提出并验证了线粒体代谢和巨噬细胞调控（Legumain、IL-35 等）促进心肌损伤修复的新策略。

Awardee of Medical Sciences and Materia Medica Prize, Ge Junbo

Ge Junbo was born in Wulian County of Shandong Province in November 1962. He is an academician of the Chinese Academy of Sciences. He graduated as a M.D. from the University of Mainz in Germany in 1993. From 1995 to 1999, he served as the director of the Vascular Ultrasound Laboratory at the University of Essen Medical School in Germany. In 1999, he returned to China and has been working at Zhongshan Hospital, Fudan University. Since then, he has held various positions, including Director of the Cardiac Cath Lab, Director of the Department of Cardiology, Director of the Shanghai Institute of Cardiovascular Diseases, Vice President of Tongji University, Dean of the Biomedical Research Institute of Fudan University, Dean of the First Affiliated Hospital of the University of Science and Technology of China, Director of the National Center for Radiological and Therapeutic Clinical Medicine Research, Member of the Chinese Academy of Medical Sciences, President of the Chinese Cardiovascular Association, President of the Chinese Society of Cardiology, President of Chinese College of Cardiovascular Physicians, President of the Asia-Pacific Society of Interventional Cardiology, International Consultant of the American College of Cardiology , and Board Member of the World Heart Federation.

Prof. Ge has been dedicated to the technological innovation and transformation study of the major CVD, such as coronary heart disease. He is awarded National Innovation Competition Medal. He has made fruitful achievements in terms of intra coronary imaging diagnosis and complex interventional diagnosis technology, and the research and development of new devices.

医学药学奖获得者

裴 国 献

裴国献，1954年10月出生于河南省临颍县。裴国献多年来从事严重肢体创伤的救治与研究工作，是我国显微骨科领域具有重要国际影响力的主要领军人之一和数字骨科学的开拓者、奠基人。兼任国务院学位委员会学科评议组成员、中华医学会显微外科学分会第七届主任委员、国际手和复合组织异体移植学会首任秘书长等职务。他创建了我国严重肢体创伤救治理论与新技术体系，解决了极重度肢体创伤保肢的重大技术难题；在国际上最先开展长段骨缺损组织工程再生骨修复研究；在亚洲率先成功开展异体肢体移植，代表了当今世界同类手术的最高水平，是世界肢体缺失重建领域的一个里程碑，入选2000年中国医药科技十大新闻。相关成果曾荣获国家科技进步奖一等奖、二等奖各1项，教育部自然科学奖一等奖1项，军队及省部级一等奖3项和军队重大科技成果奖2项。

一、创立极重度肢体创伤救治理念与新技术体系，在亚洲率先成功开展异体肢体移植，实现了对传统肢体创伤救治技术的革命

1. 提出“借用健侧供血”新理念，创立避免截肢、保全肢体的“健供式桥式移植”新术式

针对小腿及足部复合型创伤常面临截肢的临床重大难题，提出“借用健侧供血”新理念，首次揭示其血管形态学和血流动力学循环通路重塑规律，创立“健供式桥式移植”新术式，突破了肢体创伤传统修复理念和技术，创立了一项保全肢体、避免截肢的全新技术，救治患者246例，成功率100%。

2. 提出“序贯再植”新理念，创立手指多平面离断再植关键技术，创造了10指离断再植手术多项全球纪录

基于手指多平面离断再植极其复杂、致残率极高这一难题，提出“序贯再植”新理念，创立全部离断平面“统一吻接”“一次通血”的再植核心技术，解决了此类极复杂手

指再植的多项重大技术难题，成为我国显微外科标志性成果。裴国献领衔团队成功开展3例10指离断再植手术，创下10指离断再植例数最多、术时最短、功能最佳的全球纪录。

3. 创立四肢同时离断综合救治新理念新技术，全球唯一一例救治成功，为极重度多肢体创伤救治提供了前所未有的重大关键技术

四个肢体同时离断是极其严重的致死性创伤，全球未有挽救生命与肢体再植同获成功的先例。裴国献领衔团队最先成功救治并完全恢复功能，原创性提出多肢体离断综合救治理念和再植关键技术，解决了多项重大技术难题。成果获国家科技进步奖一等奖1项、二等奖1项，军队及省部级科技进步奖一等奖3项。

4. 创立异体肢体移植特异性免疫耐受理论和关键技术，在亚洲率先成功开展异体肢体移植，手术疗效国际最佳

异体肢体移植成功是国际外科移植技术的重大突破。继法国、美国之后，裴国献在亚洲率先成功开展3例异体肢体移植，因其独特的供体PBMC输注诱导特异性免疫耐受理论和技术，并与法国、美国2例依Carroll标准统一评分显示效果最佳，被评价为国际领先并被誉为Guangzhou Experience，为国际采用。入选2000年度“中国医药科技十大新闻”。

二、提出血管、神经与组织工程骨同步构建的耦合理论，建立长段骨缺损组织工程再生骨修复新技术体系，颠覆了长段骨缺损传统修复理念与技术

1. 提出血管、神经与组织工程骨同步构建的耦合理论，揭示了神经与血管因素具有同等促成骨效应与协同促成骨机制

基于组织工程骨大体积构建中心性坏死的技术瓶颈，从组织器官营养和代谢的二维角度，提出血管神经与组织器官同步构建的耦合理论。首次发现神经肽CYP40促成骨的独特作用与机制，提出感觉神经－破骨细胞－骨缺损修复的三元调控理论；发现血管/神经通过CGRP–OPG/RANK/RANKL通路协同促成骨的作用机制。制定我国首部组织工程骨通用技术标准。

2. 建立组织工程再生骨构建技术体系并在全球率先成功转化，实现骨缺损修复由移植变再生的重要理论与技术突破

针对长段骨缺损修复全球性难题，首创组织工程再生骨构建和修复新理念及技术体系，突破了大体积组织工程骨构建的技术瓶颈；推出国内首个临床转化路径和标准，成功修复全球首例长达12厘米的胫骨缺损，在43所三甲医院推广应用346例。项目关键技术实现产业化，制定了我国本领域的唯一一项产品标准。成果获国家科技进步奖一等奖1项、教育部自然科学奖一等奖1项。

三、提出数字骨科学理念，创建我国数字骨科学科，引领我国数字智能骨科技术的应用与发展

在国际上首次提出仿真梯度孔隙设计假体构建新理念，揭示假体材料的强度韧性力

学提升机制，根据人体松质骨梯度孔隙结构特点，提出多孔钛合金梯度孔隙设计理念，显著提高了其力学性能；揭示假体内部骨生物整合机制，3D 打印多孔钛合金材料，其抗压强度从多孔钽材料的 112 兆帕提升至 197 兆帕，孔隙内部骨长入效率从多孔钽的 16.8% 提升至 42.6%。

率先开展 3D 打印钛合金个性化植入物临床应用研究，2014 年完成全球首例 3D 打印钛合金假体修复锁骨、肩胛骨缺损和亚洲首例半骨盆缺损，救治患者 317 例，假体并发症发生率由 33% 降低至 3.1%，实现了长段骨缺损机械与生物学的仿生重建。组织制定 3D 打印模型、导板、矫形器和定制式医疗器械医工交互全过程监控等 5 项专家共识及标准。

在国际上首次提出数字骨科学理念，牵头成立中华医学会数字骨科学组和 SICOT 中国部数字骨科学会；领衔团队成功开展全球首例 5G 环境 MR 骨科机器人手术。建立我国首家具有引领性的粤港澳智能医疗创新研究院，我国 70% 数字智能骨科专业人才由裴国献团队培养。

Awardee of Medical Sciences and Materia Medica Prize, Pei Guoxian

Pei Guoxian was born in Linying County of Henan Province in October 1954. He is one of the leaders in the field of microsurgical orthopedics in China with great international influence and the pioneer and founder of digital orthopedics. He created the theory and new technology system for the treatment of severe limb injuries in China and solved the major technical problems of limb preservation in extreme limb injuries. He was the first to explore regenerative bone repair by tissue engineering of long segmental bone defects in the world, and he was the first to perform allograft transplantation in Asia, which is the highest level of this type of surgery in the world today. It is a milestone in the field of missing limb reconstruction in the world and was selected as one of the top ten news in China's medical science and technology in 2000.

He was the first complete person to win the first prize (2020) and the second prize (2002) of the National Science and Technology Progress Award, the first prize of the Natural Science Award of the Ministry of Education, three first prize awards of the Province (Army) and two major awards of the Army for scientific and technological achievements.

Pei Guoxian is a member of the Disciplinary Review Group of the Academic Degrees Committee of the State Council, seventh chairman of the Branch of Microsurgery of the Chinese Medical Association, and first secretary-general of the International Hand and Composite Tissue Allotransplantation Society, etc.

医学药学奖获得者

王 辉 山

王辉山，1965 年 6 月出生于辽宁省沈阳市。北部战区总医院副院长兼心血管外科主任，全军及辽宁省重点实验室主任。兼任中国医师协会心律失常组组长，中国研究型医院学会心房颤动专业委员会主任委员，中华医学会胸心血管外科学分会常务委员，全军胸心血管外科学专业委员会副主任委员，美国胸外科学会会员。

王辉山长期致力于复杂先心病外科、瓣膜及心律失常外科、心血管创伤、危重冠心病外科的临床救治和相关基础研究，在复杂先心病、心房颤动、心血管创伤等心脏外科治疗领域取得了多项具有重要影响的创新性学术成果。曾荣获国家科技进步奖二等奖 2 项、军队及省部级一等奖 4 项。

成功建立方坦手术慢性动物模型，进一步提出“低压肺血管重塑理论”，据此创用 Y 型心外管道方坦新术式引领功能性单心室外科治疗领域进入新阶段；应用上述研究成果，使方坦手术死亡率由 22.7% 下降至 7.5%、顽固性胸腔积液并发症由 38% 下降至 7%，且低氧血症、运动耐力等明显改善，疗效居国际领先水平。系列成果已成为美国胸外科协会研究生培训教材，写入耶鲁大学及英国帝国学院主编的两部心外科专著，并被《心脏外科学》等多部国内权威专著引用。相关成果获国家科技进步奖二等奖及辽宁省科技进步奖一等奖。

首次提出心脏自主神经稳态失衡为核心的房颤发生新机制：阐明创伤激活的炎症、氧化应激、纤维化反应过程，通过诱发自主神经酪胆酶比值分泌失衡进而导致房颤发生的神经机制，进一步证实心外膜脂肪垫内去自主神经化有助于恢复稳态、抑制新发房颤的发生，为外科预防提供理论依据与靶点。基于上述理论突破，国际首创自主神经化学靶向消融新术式。利用高浓度氯化钙的可逆神经毒性，针对新发房颤高危患者，在开胸手术过程中对心外膜脂肪垫实施定点注射，纠正自主神经稳态失衡，将心脏术后新发房颤发生率由 36% 降至 15%，解决了心脏术后新发房颤精准预防的国际性难题。

首次提出房颤精准治疗新理念：依据房颤持续时间及左房大小、纤维化程度，将持续性房颤分为早、中、晚三期，不同时期针对性采用不同消融技术手段，打破了房颤外科治疗禁区。自主设计研发房颤外科射频与冷冻消融系统，获医疗器械注册证 4 项，填补国内空白，实现成果转化。作为第一完成人，获辽宁省科技进步奖一等奖。主编《心脏外科学》专著，作为主任委员牵头成立中国研究型医院学会房颤专委会，成果收入《2015 年房颤外科治疗专家共识》，多次在国内外学术会议进行手术示教，推动我国房颤外科治疗进步与推广。

主持攻克磁耦合驱动等系列工程技术难题，研制出首个具有自主知识产权的野外便携式生命支持系统，成果荣获国家科技进步奖二等奖、军队医疗成果奖一等奖及辽宁省科技进步奖一等奖。

Awardee of Medical Sciences and Materia Medica Prize, Wang Huishan

Wang Huishan was born in Shenyang City of Liaoning Province in June 1965. He is the Vice President and Director of cardiovascular surgery of General Hospital of Northern Theater Command, Director of Key Laboratory of Chinese People's Liberation Army and Liaoning Province. He is also designated the head of Chinese Medical Doctor Association of Arrhythmia Group, chairman of Committee of Atrial Fibrillation Professional of Chinese Research Hospital Association, senior member of Thoracic and Cardiovascular Surgery Committee of Chinese Medical Association, vice chairman of Association of Thoracic and Cardiovascular Surgery of Chinese People's Liberation Army, and the member of AATS. He has long been dedicated to the basic and clinical studies on congenital heart surgery, valve and atrial fibrillation surgery, cardiovascular trauma and critical coronary surgery. As the first completer, he has won the second prize of National Scientific and Technological Progress Awards in 2019 and 2012, the first prize of Medical Achievement Award Chinese People's Liberation Army and Liaoning Provincial Scientific and Technological Progress Award 4 items.

医学药学奖获得者

徐 瑞 华

徐瑞华，1967年2月出生于江西省丰城市。博士毕业于中山医科大学。2002—2005年赴美国得州大学MD Anderson癌症中心开展临床进修及合作研究。先后担任中山大学附属肿瘤医院内科副主任、副院长，现任院长、华南恶性肿瘤防治全国重点实验室主任。兼任中国医学科学院学部委员、中国临床肿瘤学会理事长、中国抗癌协会副理事长等。

徐瑞华是我国消化系统肿瘤诊治的学术带头人，针对此类重大疾病早诊率低、疗效差难题，开展临床和科研工作30余年，取得系列国际性创新性成果。曾荣获国家科技进步奖二等奖2项、中华医学科技奖等省部级一等奖6项，以及第三届全国创新争先奖、谈家桢临床医学奖、吴阶平医学创新奖等奖项和荣誉。

一、实现结直肠癌诊治系统创新，达到国际先进水平

1. 创建新型肿瘤早诊、疗效预测手段，显著提升诊疗水平

创新循环肿瘤DNA（ctDNA）甲基化检测技术，建立肠癌早诊特异性ctDNA甲基化分子标签，敏感性达90%；建立ctDNA精准疗效预测体系，发现ctDNA可以大幅提高肠癌复发预测准确率，避免过度化疗或治疗不足；确立肠癌ctDNA动态检测指导治疗的价值；研发ctDNA甲基化诊断试剂盒和检测试剂盒，其中一项已获国家NMPA医疗器械注册批准。系列研究成果获2019年国家科技进步奖二等奖。

2. 创新结直肠癌治疗策略，多个方案成为国际标准

首创局部晚期直肠癌（MSI-H类型）的新辅助免疫治疗方案，完全缓解率达75%，使患者免于放化疗和手术，避免了毒性、手术创伤和人工肛，颠覆了现有治疗模式；首创高效低毒的晚期肠癌化疗维持治疗及亚洲方案。

在国际上率先建立卡培他滨维持治疗方案，延长晚期患者生存期；创新UGT1A1基因指导下的伊立替康联合卡培他滨治疗新方案，提高患者生存期，降低药物毒性。上述

两个老药新用创新方案成为新的国际标准，被写入美国 NCCN 指南、欧亚指南等。

建立靶向治疗新策略。创新靶向药物瑞戈非尼亚洲患者三线治疗标准，改写 NCCN 指南；引领我国靶向新药呋喹替尼三线治疗研究。

创建以无临床病灶为目标的多学科治疗模式，结合上述创新方案，建成晚期肠癌治疗新体系，晚期患者生存期大幅延长，部分晚期患者实现根治。研究成果获 2016 年国家科技进步奖二等奖。

二、创新上消化道肿瘤免疫治疗体系，达国际领先水平

1. 开展分子标志物指导下免疫治疗研究，创新免疫精准治疗

首次发现胃癌肿瘤突变负荷可鉴定 PD-1 抗体治疗有效的人群；国际首次报道 POLE 基因突变肿瘤患者对 PD-1 抗体有效，为该类患者找到治疗新方法；精准筛选出免疫治疗敏感类型，提高了疗效。

2. 创建免疫联合化疗新策略，将免疫治疗不敏感的“冷”肿瘤转为敏感的“热”肿瘤

前期研究发现，紫杉醇相较 5-FU 具有更强免疫激活效应，肿瘤杀伤型 T 细胞比例增加。国际首创 PD-1 抗体联合紫杉醇（代替欧美常用的 5-FU）食管癌中国免疫联合治疗方案，取得全球最高有效率 72%，明显高于欧美方案的 45%；通过另一项研究再次证实该方案有效性，将晚期食管癌一线治疗的中位生存期延长至全球最高，成为国内食管癌应用最广泛方案。进一步研究证实方案对 PD-L1 低表达患者有显著疗效，打破该类患者对免疫联合化疗无效的欧美传统观点；通过基因测序，首创可精准预测免疫化疗疗效的 EGIC 分型，指导精准免疫治疗策略。作为全球首席科学家，牵头全球新靶点 CLDN18.2 抗体药物（免疫机制）治疗晚期胃癌并取得巨大成功。

牵头负责多个国产创新药临床研究并推动创新药物上市，同时开展系列肿瘤代谢、微环境及免疫治疗机制研究，取得多项成果；鉴定出免疫治疗增效肠道活性菌 RX-af 01，成果已获得专利及转化并进行新药临床报批。系列研究获 2023 年全国创新争先奖。

Awardee of Medical Sciences and Materia Medica Prize, Xu Ruihua

Xu Ruihua was born in Fengcheng City of Jiangxi Province in February 1967. He obtained his doctorate from Sun Yat-sen University Cancer Center. He undertook clinical training and collaborative research at the University of Texas MD Anderson Cancer Center from 2002 to 2005. Currently, he serves as the president of Sun Yat-sen University Cancer Center and director of the State Key Laboratory of Oncology in South China. As the lead researcher, he has received two Second Prizes of National Science and Technology Progress Awards.

Xu Ruihua is the committee member of the Chinese Academy of Medical Sciences, president of the Chinese Society of Clinical Oncology, vice president of the China Anti-Cancer Association, etc.

He developed ctDNA methylation as a novel detection technology for circulating tumor DNA (ctDNA), and a new diagnostic model for colorectal cancer (CRC).

He found that ctDNA greatly enhances the accuracy of CRC recurrence prediction and validated the clinical value of dynamic ctDNA detection for on-treatment monitoring.

Pioneered neoadjuvant immunotherapy for locally advanced rectal cancer (MSI-H), achieving a 75% complete remission rate. Established the maintenance regimen of CRC using capecitabine. Developed the modified irinotecan plus capecitabine regimen guided by the UGT1A1 gene Led third-line standard treatment trials with regorafenib or fruquintinib.

He reported the identification of effective anti-PD-1 treatment candidates by tumor mutation burden (TMB) in gastric cancer. Discovered the benefit of anti-PD-1 treatment for cancer patients with POLE mutations.

He established the first combined anti-PD-1 and paclitaxel regimen for esophageal cancer, achieving the best response rate and overall survival globally, confirmed its effectiveness in patients with low PD-L1 expression, and discovered the EGIC classification for guiding precision immunotherapy.

医学药学奖获得者

杨晓明

杨晓明，1962年2月出生于甘肃省甘南藏族自治州。1985年获兰州医学院理学学士学位，1995年获卫生部兰州生物制品研究所免疫学硕士学位。1985—2002年在卫生部兰州生物制品研究所工作，其间1986—1987年、1996年、1997—2002年分别赴日本国立感染症研究所、美国食品药品管理局、美国国立卫生研究院访学。2002年回国后，先后在武汉生物制品研究所、中国生物技术股份有限公司工作。2022年12月起任中国生物技术股份有限公司首席科学家，2023年4月起任新突发传染病新型疫苗研发全国重点实验室主任。先后担任科技部“863”计划疫苗项目首席科学家，国务院联防联控机制科技攻关专家组成员，国家药典委员会执行委员，中国医学科学院学部委员，中华预防医学会生物制品分会主任委员，中国医药生物技术协会副理事长等。

杨晓明长期从事医药健康领域新型疫苗研发工作，聚焦传染病疫苗应用基础研究、工程技术体系创建和重大产品创制，为重大传染病防控和国家生物安全保障作出系统性贡献。

一、揭示新冠病毒抗体被动免疫保护规律

国际首次发现新冠患者恢复期血浆和特异性免疫球蛋白抑制新冠病毒体外感染细胞、降低患者体内病毒载量，显著提高临床疗效，揭示人体免疫系统防御和清除新冠病毒的作用机制，安全性良好。

二、创建新型病毒灭活疫苗工程技术体系

1. 创建疫苗生产用细胞大规模培养和病毒性疫苗大规模量产技术

针对微载体生物反应器等被国外“卡脖子”的困境，突破细胞高密度培养、病毒大规模量产和连续逐级放大三大卡点，创建基于篮式反应器的病毒性疫苗工程技术，使

我国病毒性灭活疫苗年产能从百万级跨越至亿剂级。在此基础上研发成功国家一类新药 sIPV 疫苗，年产能 2 亿剂并获 WHO 认证，保障我国脊灰疫苗序贯免疫新策略顺利实施，为全球最终根除脊灰作出中国贡献。

2. 创建超大规模病毒灭活疫苗工程技术体系，首创全球首个新冠疫苗并供应全球，加速中国疫苗国际化发展

首次应用二代测序技术和宏基因组分析新冠病毒候选疫苗株基因组，使疫苗株选育时间从 7 个月缩短到 16 天，从源头上确保疫苗研发成功；创建智慧工厂系统控制的大规模细胞和病毒的培养、收获、灭活和纯化连续生产工艺流程，形成标准；建立新型病毒灭活疫苗工程技术体系，98 天内完成疫苗开发，单批产能达到 4800 万剂，病毒灭活疫苗年产能全球历史性突破 50 亿剂；国内Ⅰ、Ⅱ期以及国际大规模、多中心Ⅲ期临床研究结果显示疫苗安全有效，保护效力达 79%，重症和死亡保护效力达 95%，血清学阳转率 100%，成为支撑疫苗批准上市、WHO 认证和西方国家认可的关键依据。2020 年 12 月 9 日和31 日，分获阿联酋和中国批准上市，是全球最早批准的新冠疫苗。截至2023 年5 月，全球供应超 35 亿剂，在 121 个国家、地区和国际组织应用。

3. 创新研究人用疫苗新型细胞基质

发现调控 MDCK 细胞生长方式关键基因，设计国际首创低成瘤、不致瘤 MDCK 细胞系，以此为基础研发中国首个 MDCK 细胞流感疫苗，并首先完成Ⅰ期临床研究，推动人用疫苗细胞基质从经验筛选跨越到科学设计阶段。

三、创建联合疫苗工程技术体系

1. 创新百日咳杆菌大规模培养和抗原制备技术，研发成功中国首个无细胞百日咳疫苗，确保免疫规划大品种更新换代

发明百日咳杆菌发酵培养基配方，研究培养体系对百日咳杆菌生长和产毒量的影响，实现了百日咳杆菌从静态培养向动态培养的转变，提高单位体积百日咳杆菌生物量和百日咳毒素产量，突破 500 升到 5000 升规模化生产工程技术瓶颈，年产能首达 7000 万剂；发现赖氨酸与百日咳毒素抗原性的量效关系，发明脱毒新技术和建立脱毒新工艺，解决百日咳毒素脱毒后毒性易逆转和抗原活性难保持的难题，比全细胞百日咳疫苗副反应降低 10～20 倍，研发成功我国首个无细胞百日咳疫苗，保障国家免疫规划大品种更新换代。

2. 突破多联多价疫苗研发技术瓶颈，提升多联多价疫苗技术系统创新能力

以自主研发的无细胞百日咳疫苗为基础，研发成功我国首个 DTaP 疫苗，联合自主研发 sIPV 疫苗。通过研究缓冲体系、佐剂磷酸盐 / 铝比例、抗原吸附顺序及吸附条件，解决抗原组分相容性、免疫干扰、鉴别和检测等技术难题，研发出 DTaP–sIPV 等高价次联合疫苗；建立轮状病毒专属细胞均质释放工艺，发明病毒保护剂配方，研制全球最高价次（六价）轮状病毒减毒活疫苗，已申报生产注册。使我国多联多价疫苗技术达到国际

先进水平。

四、设计、制定和建成中国首个人用疫苗高等级生物安全综合体等国家重大科技基础设施，形成标准体系

针对我国缺乏人用疫苗高等级生物安全生产设施、严重影响高致病性病原体疫苗产业化的问题，融合全球通用生物安全等级标准和药品生产质量管理规范，主持设计和制定中国人用疫苗高等级生物安全生产车间建设标准、运行规范和操作规程，建成国家级重大科技基础设施——全球最大规模人用疫苗高等级生物安全车间，被誉为“国之重器”。

Awardee of Medical Sciences and Materia Medica Prize, Yang Xiaoming

Yang Xiaoming was born in Gannan Tibetan Autonomous Prefecture of Gansu Province in February 1962. Chief Scientist and Chief Engineer of Sinopharm Group, Director of National Key Laboratory for Research and Development of Novel Vaccines for Emerging Infectious Diseases, Director of National Combined Vaccines Engineering Research Center.

For 38 years, Yang has been dedicated in the development of novel vaccines in the field of medicine and health. He focused on the application fundamental research of vaccines for infectious diseases, the establishment of engineering technology system and development of major products. Yang has established an international leading engineering technology system for novel inactivated viral vaccine and a national advanced engineering technology system for combined vaccines, developed five major products for infectious disease prevention and control, such as the first inactivated COVID-19 vaccine in the world, the national first-class new drug inactivated poliomyelitis vaccine (IPV) and bivalent live attenuated vaccine, and the first acellular pertussis-diphtheria-tetanus combined vaccine (DTaP) in China. He designed of the first MDCK Cell lines in the world with low tumorigenicity and no oncogenicity. The first influenza vaccine developed based on this cell line in China has completed the Phase I study. He has established the rotavirus cell homogenization process, invented the formula of virus protectants, and developed live attenuated hexavalent rotavirus vaccine with the broadest serotype coverage in the world, which has applied the marketing authorization. Yang presided over the design and construction of the national major scientific and technological infrastructure-the high-level biosafety research-and-production complex for human vaccines, promoted the high-quality and systemic development of vaccines in China, and enhanced the ability of prevention and control of infectious diseases and biosafety in China.

医学药学奖获得者

赵 家 军

赵家军，1961 年 5 月出生于山东省邹城市。1994 年获上海第二医科大学（现上海交通大学）医学博士学位。2000 年赴新加坡国立大学医院访学。现任中华医学会内分泌学分会主任委员、国家卫健委临床重点学科学术带头人。

赵家军围绕慢病最为常见的危险因素——脂代谢紊乱，系统开展“成因 – 危害 – 干预”转化医学研究并取得一系列创新成果。曾荣获国家科技进步奖二等奖 2 项、全国创新争先奖、吴阶平医学药学奖等奖项，以及全国优秀科技工作者、首届国家名医 – 国之名医（卓越建树）等荣誉称号。

一、明确垂体激素水平异常是脂代谢紊乱的新成因，提出“非经典垂体靶腺轴”新学说，革新临床诊疗方案，创建早期干预新策略

1. 提出“非经典垂体靶腺轴”新学说，开创垂体激素功能研究新领域，为临床干预提供证据

研究发现 TSH 升高是高胆固醇血症的独立危险因素，首次证实 TSH 促进胆固醇合成、抑制胆固醇转化，导致高胆固醇血症；增加肝脏脂质蓄积，导致脂肪肝；TSH 激活炎症通路、诱发氧化应激，导致动脉粥样硬化。

发现并证实女性绝经后垂体促性腺激素卵泡刺激素（FSH）水平升高是血脂异常的重要病因，靶向阻断 FSH，改善高胆固醇血症。揭示多种垂体激素作用于传统靶腺外的其他组织器官（肝脏、心脏等）发挥生物学效应，提出“非经典垂体靶腺轴”新学说，开拓了垂体生物学功能研究的新领域。

2. 建立甲减早期分层干预标准化方案，实现防治关口前移

依据 TSH 水平分层制定甲减早期精准干预方案，TSH 水平每降低 1 mIU/L，血清总胆固醇下降 15.9 mg/dl；纠正甲减，使脂肪肝患病率降低 8.9%。证实甲减早期干预的必要

性，牵头制定中国《成人甲状腺功能减退症诊治指南》并推广应用。

二、揭示脂代谢紊乱危害多脏器的新机制，创建“干预脂毒性防治内分泌代谢病”新模式，推动防治关口前移

1. 明确脂毒性是甲减发生的新病因，破解甲减高发难题，为早期精准防控提供科学依据

牵头全国多中心流行病学研究，发现高甘油三酯血症是甲减发生的独立危险因素，可使甲减患病风险增加 1.35 倍。证实游离脂肪酸抑制甲状腺对碘的摄取及活化，减少甲状腺激素合成，导致甲减。纠正血脂异常，使 50% 甲减患者恢复正常。

2. 揭示脂毒性导致糖尿病的新机制，为早期精准干预提供科学依据

以糖尿病防控的黄金窗口期为切入点，开展逆转糖尿病前期相关研究。发现高甘油三酯血症增加糖尿病发生风险 1.56 倍；率先明确游离脂肪酸抑制胰岛素合成的关键分子 PPARα/PDX1，其导致胰岛 β 细胞功能障碍、诱发胰岛素抵抗，是导致糖尿病的关键核心机制，为精准干预提供依据。

3. 创建以干预脂毒性为核心遏制糖尿病高发的新方案，有效改善糖尿病预后

2009 年在国际上率先开展干预脂毒性预防糖尿病的 RCT 研究，基于研究成果制定干预脂毒性的新方案，逆转了 53% 的糖尿病前期患者。牵头制定《中国成人糖尿病前期干预的专家共识》，为有效预防糖尿病提供中国方案。

制定中国糖尿病血管并发症临床风险分层管理和控制标准；建立以干预脂毒性为核心的多种危险因素综合管理技术体系；建立“健康教育 – 高危筛查 – 早诊早治”的三级防治体系，使糖尿病危险因素综合管理率提高 42.3%、并发症新发病率降低 21.2%。牵头制定糖尿病管理临床指南 / 专家共识 6 项，为推动糖尿病防治作出重要贡献。

Awardee of Medical Sciences and Materia Medica Prize, Zhao Jiajun

Zhao Jiajun was born in Zoucheng City of Shandong Province in May 1961. He serves as the Chairman of the Endocrinology Chapter of the Chinese Medical Association, the Academic Leader for the National Health Commission’s Key Clinical Discipline, and the Director of the Ministry of Education’s Key Laboratory. Dr. Zhao has received numerous prestigious awards, including two Second-Class National Science and Technology Progress Awards, and the National Innovation and Excellence Award.

Prof. Zhao focused on lipid metabolism disorders, which are one of the most common risk factors for chronic diseases. Upon the work frame of “Cause-Harm-Intervention”, he proved that abnormal levels of specific pituitary hormones are the causes of lipid metabolism disorders and further proposed the innovative concept of the "non-classical pituitary-target gland axis", thereby pioneering a new field of research into pituitary hormone functions and providing evidence to guide clinical interventions. He also revealed the new mechanism by which lipid metabolism disorders damage multiple organs, known as lipotoxicity, which leads to endocrine metabolic diseases. Specifically, he identified lipotoxicity as a new cause for hypothyroidism, resolving the mystery behind its high prevalence and advocating for lipid screening as a new preventative measure. Furthermore, he clarified the key mechanism by which lipotoxicity leads to diabetes and was the first internationally to conduct a Randomized Controlled Trial for intervening in lipotoxicity to prevent diabetes, offering new strategies for early prevention. These contributions have made significant contributions to the prevention and treatment of metabolic diseases, such as hypothyroidism and diabetes, and promoted the development of endocrinology.

机械电力技术奖获得者

李德才

李德才，1965年12月出生于河北省沧州市。1996年获北方交通大学（今北京交通大学）工学博士学位。1992—2015年在北京交通大学机械与电子控制工程学院工作。2001—2002年、2004—2005年先后前往德国不来梅大学、英国曼彻斯特大学访学。2015年至今在清华大学机械工程学院工作，现任摩擦学国家重点实验室副主任。曾任中国机械工程学会流体传动与控制分会第七届委员会密封专业委员会主任、第十二届国际磁性液体学术委员会委员、白俄罗斯国立科技大学兼职教授等。

李德才是我国磁性液体领域著名专家，长期致力于密封、传感器、减振器等基础零部件研发，取得的原创性技术成果解决了我国载人空间站工程、首次火星探测任务、国家级大科学装置、单晶硅炉、生物反应器等的密封难题，为国家重大工程、国家重点研发计划、国家重大科技基础设施建设等作出了突出贡献。曾荣获国家技术发明奖二等奖2项、省部级科学技术奖一等奖5项、机械工业科学技术奖技术发明奖一等奖1项，以及日内瓦国际发明展金奖2项、评审团特别嘉许金奖1项（金奖前3%～5%）和纽伦堡国际发明展金奖2项。

一、提出磁性液体与其中磁性颗粒相互转化的密封新原理，发明了耐宽温域零泄漏高性能密封技术，攻克了载人航天工程、火星探测任务、单晶硅炉等我国重大工程中的“卡脖子”难题

发现磁性液体中纳米磁性颗粒实现高温密封的机理，揭示了高温下纳米磁性颗粒增强换热机理和低温下磁性液体固液相变机制，提出了磁性液体与其中磁性颗粒相互转化实现可靠密封的新原理；攻克了纳米磁性颗粒表面完整包覆氧化石墨烯及在基载液中长期稳定悬浮的难题，发明了耐宽温域高性能磁性液体制备方法，拓宽了磁性液体密封耐温域范围；发明了原位生成磁性液体和密封间隙大小随温度变化自动调节的耐宽温域零泄漏高性能磁性密封结构，设计了冷却和加热系统，解决了低温密封起动力矩大、高温密封耐压能力下降的难题。

上述研究成果解决了我国空间站、“祝融号”火星探测器等重大工程关键装备的宽温域循环工况密封难题。同时打破国外技术封锁，在国内率先突破单晶硅炉的宽温域密封难题并实现产业化，占据了国内市场，获国家级新产品奖。

二、提出无齿密封新原理，发明了耐酸碱、旋转轴大径向跳动零泄漏长寿命动密封技术，解决了国家级大科学装置、生物反应器、高端反应釜等的密封难题

提出无齿磁性液体密封新原理：用多层极靴和多层磁源精准控制磁路，解决了原“有齿”表面耐酸碱差、极齿易破坏的难题；攻克了在 Fe_3O_4 纳米磁性颗粒表面完整包覆不同厚度金的难题，发明了饱和磁化强度超国内外公开报道最高值的全氟聚醚油基磁性液体，能够耐酸碱溶液、耐活性气体；发明柔性连接的组合密封结构，使磁性液体动密封在酸碱旋转轴大径跳动下长期可靠运行。

上述研究成果解决了 KDP 类晶体生长装置的强酸密封难题，首次解决了国家重大科技基础设施中微子大科学装置在强酸、旋转轴大径向跳动下零泄漏密封的难题，为我国惯性约束核聚变系统发展作出了重要贡献，使我国在同类装置的国际竞争中占据优势地位。

三、提出强自修复阶梯式密封新原理，发明零泄漏高可靠动静密封技术，解决了国家重大专项等的“卡脖子”难题

Awardee of Machinery and Electric Technology Prize, Li Decai

Li Decai was born in Cangzhou City of Hebei Province in December 1965. He is a famous expert in the field of magnetic fluid in China. He has long been committed to the research and development of basic components such as seals, sensors and shock absorbers. In particular, on the basis of the intersection of fluid mechanics, electromagnetics, physical chemistry and other disciplines and mechanics, the zero leakage sealing technology system of magnetic fluid under extreme working conditions has been established. The new sealing principle of mutual transformation between magnetic fluid and magnetic particles has been put forward, and the high performance magnetic sealing technology with wide temperature range has been invented. A new principle of toothless sealing has been proposed, and a long-life magnetic fluid dynamic sealing technology with acid and alkali resistance has been invented. A new principle of strong self-healing stepped seal has been proposed, and a high reliable magnetic fluid dynamic and static sealing technology has been invented, which has realized the breakthrough of zero leakage magnetic fluid seal from scratch. The original technical achievements have been widely used in more than 300 units at home and abroad, which have solved the sealing problems of China's manned space station project, the first Mars exploration mission, national large scientific devices, bioreactors, etc., and have made outstanding contributions to national major projects, key research and development plans, and major scientific and technological infrastructure construction.

He has won 2 second prizes of national technological invention, 5 first prizes of provincial and ministerial science and technology, and 1 first prize of mechanical industry science and technology prize. He has won 2 gold medals in Geneva International Invention Exhibition, 1 gold medal in special recognition by the jury, and 2 gold medals in Nuremberg International Invention Exhibition.

机械电力技术奖获得者

廖 文 和

廖文和，1965年1月出生于江西省万安县。1996年获南京航空航天大学工学博士学位。1985—2010年先后在南昌飞机制造公司、南京航空航天大学工作。2010年9月起任南京理工大学副校长，2021年任南京理工大学校党委副书记。兼任中央军委科技委先进结构专业组组长，科技部工业软件重大专项总体组专家，装备发展部先进制造专业组专家，中国宇航学会常务理事，中国航空学会常务理事，数控成形技术与装备国家地方联合工程实验室主任。

廖文和长期从事微纳卫星设计、制造理论与技术、装备研究，取得了系统的开创性成果。

一、主持研制并成功发射我国第一颗隐身卫星，实现我国隐身微纳卫星从无到国际先进的突破

针对隐身卫星低RCS（雷达散射截面积）构型与承载、布局、热控、通信、能源等设计相制约的难题，建立隐身性、材料与构型参数之间的关系，创立了卫星偶对称、多棱面异构融合构型与宽通带、低插损共形天线罩设计方法，提出隐身卫星在电磁、光学、力热、能量等多场耦合设计约束下的总体设计方法，实现了天线、散热面、通信与强散射源的共形雷达隐身。主持研制并成功发射我国第一颗隐身卫星“天巡一号”，首次完成卫星雷达隐身在轨试验，填补了我国隐身微纳卫星技术空白，隐身性能达到4～8GHz和被探测距离缩短44%的国际先进水平。成果荣获江苏省专利发明人奖。

二、发明微纳卫星宽频吸波超结构隐身设计方法，实现我国从单一构型隐身到构型吸波一体超宽频隐身的升级换代

发明力热融合晶格支撑的宽频吸波二维叠层超结构隐身新原理，揭示了二维超结构

阻抗匹配及谐振吸波机理、夹层晶格结构的隔热规律，使吸波频率从4～8GHz提升到2～18GHz的国际先进水平。

发明了具有隐身、力、热功能的超宽频晶胞三维超结构，揭示了光子晶体微结构亚波长尺度上的特征参数与电磁吸波性能之间的关联规律，阐明了基于生物微结构的电磁吸波晶胞三维结构损耗机理，结构吸波性能具有各向同性，实现了微纳卫星自适应隐身晶格结构轻量化设计，实现了结构材料密度降至 $0.203 \times 10^3 kg/m^3$ 的同时，吸波能力从2～18GHz提高到2～40GHz、探测角度60°不敏感的国际领先水平。提出大深度比陷光微结构+超黑镀膜的光学隐身设计方法，卫星对地面光学特性达报导的国际最高星等。揭示了固体推进剂在复杂空间环境下的性能演化规律，自主研制新型空间固体推力器，实现了从毫牛到百牛级的推力调控和在轨应用验证。突破了附着式多烈度攻击载荷等关键技术，使我国微纳卫星具有攻防一体能力，有望实现高轨对地、对空目标隐身能力的升级换代。成果获江苏省科学技术奖一等奖。

三、提出机器人加工误差相似度精度补偿理论与抑振方法，为航空航天复杂结构装配、微纳卫星低成本制造奠定了理论和技术基础

机器人高端制造装备是欧美发达国家长期对我国禁运的航空航天先进制造技术，我国工业机器人±2mm的绝对定位精度、1/50的机床刚度难以应用于航空航天高精度制造。提出并证明了机器人定位误差空间相似性及其精度补偿理论，突破了机器人精度补偿控制等技术，将国产工业机器人加工绝对定位精度由±2mm提高到±0.1mm的国际领先水平。揭示了刚度影响机器人加工系统振动的规律，发明了基于刚度辨识、超声辅助的机器人加工颤振主动抑制方法，稳定加工阈值提高100%。据此，主持研制成功钻、铆、铣等六大类机器人高端制造装备，并被航空航天等30余家龙头企业用于解决空间站、歼20战机、WS10C发动机等10余项重大型号的批产研制。上述理论与技术为微纳卫星低成本批量制造奠定了基础。

发展细分曲面建模理论，研制超人CAD/CAM软件，解决了当时我国三维曲面造型与数控编程软件缺失的急需；发展人眼屈光矫正理论体系，成功研制出我国第一台准分子激光人眼像差矫正系统并临床应用，使我国与美、德、日共同成为当时全球仅有的四个能设计制造大型高精度眼科医疗装备的国家，并应用该装备在全国成功施行10万多例人眼屈光矫正手术，成果获国家科学技术进步奖二等奖、三等奖各1项。

Awardee of Machinery and Electric Technology Prize, Liao Wenhe

Liao Wenhe was born in Wan'an County of Jiangxi Province in January 1965. He is the deputy secretary of the Party Committee of Nanjing University of Science and Technology, a leading talent of the National Ten Thousand Talents Plan, a winner of the National Innovation Excellent Award, and a member of the National Outstanding Scientific and Technological Workers. He has been engaged in micro–nano satellite design and manufacturing theory, technology, and equipment research for a long–term. Facing the major strategic needs of national space security, he created a theoretical system for the design of attack–defense stealth micro–nano satellites and robot processing accuracy compensation. He presided over the development and launch of China's first stealth satellite Tianxun–1, achieved a breakthrough in China's stealth micro–nano satellites from scratch to internationally advanced level, led the development of China's space target stealth technology, and independently developed new solid thrusters and high–specific impulse air conditioners, which enabled China's micro–nano satellites to have integrated attack and defense capabilities. He successfully developed six categories of robotic high–end manufacturing equipment for aerospace complex large–component, effectively ensured the rapid development and mass production of major national models such as the space station, J–20, WS10C engine, etc., and laid the technical and equipment foundation for the mass manufacturing of micro–nano satellites. He creatively combined CAD/CAM technology with human eye aberration correction and successfully developed China's first internationally advanced excimer laser human eye aberration correction system, broke the foreign technology monopoly, and brought China to the only four countries with the United States, Germany, and Japan in the world that could develop large–scale high–precision ophthalmic medical equipment. More than 100000 refractive correction surgeries across the country have been successfully performed using the system. He has won 4 national awards and 7 first–class provincial and ministerial science and technology awards, including 1 second–class and third–class National Science and Technology Progress Award and 2 second–class National Teaching Achievement Awards.

电子信息技术奖获得者

江 碧 涛

江碧涛，女，1967 年 8 月出生于安徽省六安市。2007 年获中国科学院空间科学与应用研究中心工学博士学位。1997 年至今在中国人民解放军 61646 部队工作，为国家高分辨率对地观测系统重大专项专家委员会地面系统专家组组长，军委科技委某重点方向专家组组长，中国光学工程学会常务理事、中国人工智能学会智能融合专委会副主任委员，北京理工大学顾问教授、航天工程大学博士生导师。

江碧涛长期从事航天遥感技术研究与工程研制，在多星多传感器协同探测与应用等方面作出一系列开创性工作，在减灾救灾、国土安全、海洋维权等方面发挥了重大作用。

一、构建电子 / 光学 / 雷达等多类卫星协同探测技术体系，推动我国航天遥感技术发展和工程建设

提出“高低轨搭配、光 / 电 /SAR 协同”的航天遥感手段体系和面向多类多级用户的服务体系，构建高分辨率卫星详细探测能力模型，设计多类异构卫星协同运用和星座自主运行模式，论证提出了高分辨率对地观测技术发展路线图，主持完成我国首个高分辨率成像卫星系统、首个遥感卫星星座系统等重大工程，推动我国高分辨率空间对地观测进入世界先进水平。

二、攻克高分辨率数据处理与应用系列关键技术，研制建成具有国际先进水平的航天遥感信息系统

一是针对单一传感器信息精度和维度有限、地物状态探测难的问题，提出多传感器信息协同处理及应用方法，构建了地物 – 波谱显著性模型和多传感器协同处理与应用技术架构，提出双向梯度连续谱段信息增强方法，信噪比提升 10dB；提取高光谱敏感谱段计算同步大气参数，支撑单通道红外温度反演，反演精度提升 50% 以上；提出基于关注度的典型地物多特征自适应变化检测方法，利用多源特征联合抑制虚警，变化检测率提升 20% 以上。主持研制首个光学多传感器协同探测信息系统，实现了航天遥感从单一特性描述到全面准确感知的历史性跨越，成果获 2016 年国家科技发明奖二等奖。

二是针对光学卫星平台颤振带来的图像畸变问题，提出仿真分析与在轨图像时频谱联合验证方法，发明高低频姿态数据融合处理方法，在卫星姿态测量精度低于国外 1 个数量级的情况下，将整星定姿精度提升到与国际最好水平相当。针对 SAR 卫星信号带宽大、合成孔径时间长等带来的图像精准复原难题，提出并建立 SAR 成像误差溯源映射模型，攻克全链路强耦合幅相误差校准技术，构建误差传递模型，幅相校准由典型波位拓展至全部波位，相关成果应用于高分辨率光学、SAR 数据处理，图像质量达到国际先进水平。主持研制光学 /SAR 多传感器协同的高分辨率成像卫星系统，为实现我国航天遥感的历史性跨越提供了有力的技术支撑，成果获 2020 年国家科技进步奖二等奖。

三是面向我国由大向强过程中维护国家权益的迫切需求，针对有关国家船只侵权行为复杂动态给探测、识别与定位带来的难题，提出了多手段协同的“引导 – 搜索 – 识别 – 定位”方法，建立对抗博弈下多约束任务规划模型，攻克多类异构卫星协同船只快速探测技术，探测概率提高 1 倍以上。主持开展航天遥感智能化技术攻关和转化应用，突破典型地物智能检测识别、多源遥感影像智能解译等关键技术，提出多源信息深度特征融合和编码方法，有效提高典型目标识别率，推动了航天遥感信息保障和应用服务能力提升。

Awardee of Electronics and Information Technology Prize, Jiang Bitao

Jiang Bitao, female, was born in Liu’an City of Anhui Province in August 1967. She graduated from the Space Sciences and Applied Research Center of the Chinese Academy of Sciences with a Doctor engineering in 2007. From 1997 to now, she has been working in Chinese People’s Liberation Army 61646 Unit. She is the Leader of High Resolution Earth Observation System Major Special Project Expert Committee on Ground System Group, and the leader of Military Science and Technology Commission on a key research direction. Executive Director of Chinese Society of Optical Engineering, Deputy-chief member of intelligent Integration Committee of Chinese Association for Artificial Intelligence, Consultant professor of Beijing Institute of Technology, doctoral supervisor of University of Aerospace Engineering.

She has long been engaged in the research and engineering development of space remote sensing technology, and has made a series of pioneering research work in the collaborative detection and application of multi satellites and sensors.

Firstly, she established electronic/optical/radar and other types of satellite cooperative detection technology system, which promotes the development and engineering construction of space remote sensing technology in China. Secondly, she has overcomed a series of key technologies for high-resolution data processing and application, built an internationally advanced space remote sensing information system.

电子信息技术奖获得者

贾　焰

贾焰，女，1960 年 4 月出生于四川省成都市。1978 年进入国防科技大学计算机科学与技术专业学习，先后获学士、硕士和博士学位。1985 年进入国防科技大学计算机学院工作，先后担任网络与信息安全研究所副所长、基础软件工程中心首席科学家。2018 年 4 月至今任鹏城实验室大型科学装置“鹏城靶场”项目负责人 / 研究员，2020 年 10 月至今任鹏城国家实验室新型网络研究部网络空间平台研究所所长 / “鹏城靶场”国家重大项目负责人 / 研究员。中国中文信息处理学会副理事长，国际未来数据和大搜索高峰论坛 FFD 发起人 / 指导委员会主任，IEEE 网络空间数据科学国际会议 IEEE DSC 发起人 / 指导委员会主任。

贾焰是我国网络空间安全态势感知领域的学术带头人，长期从事本领域理论技术研究和工程系统建设工作，在网络空间安全事件准确识别和实时量化评估等方面作出了系统性和开创性的工作。曾荣获国家科技进步奖二等奖、省部级科技进步奖一等奖各 4 项。

一、提出网络空间安全事件多维关联认知模型 MDATA，为网络空间安全事件安全、准确、实时研判奠定了理论基础

提出 MDATA 认知模型，该模型针对安全事件的 3 大特性（巨规模、多维关联、时空演化）模拟人类认知方法，即知识获取、存储管理和知识利用，构建了活化的网络安全知识库及其利用方法，并通过基于知识图谱叠加时空属性的 MDATA 图谱知识表示方法、一组面向网络空间大数据（文本、行为、结构 / 半结构等）的归纳算子和演绎算子、一组面向 MDATA 时空大图的可达路径、子图匹配的高效计算方法等关键技术的突破，全面支撑了系统级的实现。

基于该理论，成功研制网络安全态势感知系统 YHSAS、网络舆情分析系统 YHSNAS、大型科学装置“鹏城联邦靶场”、开源情报分析系统“天箭”等系统。MDATA 相关技术

成果获国家科技进步奖二等奖 2 项、省部级科技进步奖一等奖 1 项。

二、成功研制网络系统安全态势分析系统，在网络安全事件准确研判和实时量化评估发明中作出开创性工作

提出基于轻载软构件技术的异构设备 / 探针封装集成技术，采用接口描述语言零编程集成和部署设备 / 探针，并基于构件容器的远程通信进行数据采集和传输，实现了全网安全状态的全面感知；提出网络安全状态实时评估指标体系，给出了各种安全要素提取方法和量化算子及其一个可定制、层次式的流数据聚集计算框架，实现了大规模网络安全态势的多维度、多层次和多粒度实时量化评估并形成行业标准。

成功研制网络系统安全态势感知系统 YHSAS，率先实现了面向超大规模网络管理域（千万级节点）的攻击事件全面、准确、实时研判和评估，攻击事件检测全面性、准确性（无误报）和实时性方面的技术指标世界领先。已在全国电子政务外网上部署应用，保障了我国政府办公业务安全开展；在我国互联网国际出入口上成功应用，实时检测、研判和遏制来自境外的攻击；在遍布全国 22 个省市的 16 种行业私有云上成功部署应用，全面提升了我国云平台的安全防护能力。相关技术成果获 2018 年国家科技进步奖二等奖。

三、成功研制舆情分析系统 YHSNAS，在舆情话题准确检测和传播影响量化分析方面作出开拓性工作

提出面向自媒体内容的话题检测方法，该方法基于短文本会话合成、关键词语义扩展，结合用户属性及其社区分析，准确识别话题及其演化；提出基于 MDATA 理论的舆情事件传播分析方法，该方法基于话题实时检测以及已知的用户、话题、社区三维关联关系，基于可达路径的随机游走结合概率计算，实现了舆情事件传播影响的实时分析。

成功研制舆情分析系统 YHSNAS，并形成成果转化系统“鹰击”和“鹰眼”，融合了 10 万通道媒体大数据，在国内率先实现了自媒体舆情话题准确检测、群体互动和传播影响分析，并在全国范围内向 30000 余个机构用户提供在线云服务。本系统舆情事件全面准确监测和传播分析方面的关键技术指标居世界领先水平，已在网信、公安、安全和军地等职能部门全国性成功应用。相关技术成果获 2015 年国家科学技术进步奖二等奖。

四、成功研制网络安全大型科学装置“鹏城联邦靶场”，在目标网络仿真、系统安全评估方面作出开拓性工作

提出包含四维互通、目标网络跨域互联及其场景感知的应用部署在内的一组关键技术，实现了超大规模目标网络灵活、逼真复现；提出基于网络靶场，面向攻击技战术自动编排以及基于攻击检测的效果评估方法，实现了信息系统全生命周期安全性评估。

成功研制“鹏城联邦靶场”。该靶场由 1 个主靶场、81 个分靶场组成，分布在 28 个省 35 个城市，行业覆盖互联网、汽车、通信、电力、金融和能源等重要领域。本系统在我国产学研用管等领域广泛成功应用，支撑冬奥会、载人航天、探月工程等信息系统的评测、护网等活动600余次，极大提升了我国网络安全的保障能力，产生了重大的社会效益。相关技术成果获2022年广东省科学技术进步奖一等奖。

Awardee of Electronics and Information Technology Prize, Jia Yan

Jia Yan, female, was born in Chengdu City of Sichuan Province in April 1960. In 1978, she entered the Computer Science and Technology program at the National University of Defense Technology (NUDT) and obtained her bachelor's, master's, and doctoral degrees. From 1985 to 2014, she served as a lecturer, associate professor, and professor at the National University of Defense Technology, where she also held the position of Deputy Director of the Institute of Network and Information Security at the School of Computer Science.

Since April 2018, she has been the Project Director/Researcher of the "Pengcheng Cyber Range" Project at PengCheng Laboratory. Since October 2020, she has been the Director of Platform Research Institute, Department of New Networks at the PengCheng National Laboratory and the Project Director/Researcher of the "Pengcheng Cyber Range" National Major Project. She is also the Deputy Chairman of the Chinese Information Processing Society of China, the Initiator/Chairman of the Steering Committee of the International Future Data and Big Search High-Level Forum (FFD), and the Initiator/Chairman of the Steering Committee of the IEEE Data Science in Cyber Space International Conference (IEEE DSC). She has published 306 SCI/EI papers, authored 8 monographs, obtained 83 authorized invention patents and 93 software copyrights, led the formulation of 16 industry standards, and won 4 Second-Class National Science and Technology Progress Awards and 4 First-Class Provincial and Ministerial Science and Technology Progress Awards.

Jia Yan is a leading academic figure in the field of cyber situational awareness for China's cyberspace security. Situational awareness is vital for cyber security event analysis and serves as the foundation for ensuring cyber security. Yan Jia has been engaged in both theoretical and technical research and engineering system development in this field, making systematic and groundbreaking contributions to accurate identification and real-time quantitative assessment of cyber security events. She has led the development of systems such as the Network Security Situational Analysis System (YHSAS), the Network Public Sentiment Situational Analysis System (YHSNAS), and the large-scale cyber security scientific facility "Pengcheng Federated Cyber Range," filling the gaps in these areas in China. These systems have been successfully applied nationwide in national functional departments such as information and communication, public security, security, and the military, greatly enhancing China's cyber security capabilities.

电子信息技术奖获得者

王 耀 南

王耀南，1957 年 11 月出生于云南省龙陵县。1977 年进入华东地质学院电子计算机专业学习，毕业后留校任教。1992 年和 1995 年分别获湖南大学工业自动化专业硕士和博士学位，并在湖南大学自动化系从事教学科研工作。1997 年从国防科技大学自动控制系博士后出站。1998—2004 年赴德国不来梅大学开展国际科研合作。现任机器人视觉感知与控制技术国家工程研究中心主任。兼任中国图象图形学学会理事长、全国智能机器人创新联盟副理事长、国家自然科学基金委员会专家咨询委员等。中国工程院院士，中国自动化学会会士、中国计算机学会会士、中国人工智能学会会士。

王耀南长期从事机器人感知与控制技术及工程应用方面的教学科研工作，在重大工程装备研制、机器人精密制造、多机器人协同制造等方面作出一系列开创性工作，率先提出了集群机器人协同控制基础理论与关键技术体系，开辟了集群机器人协同智造的新领域。相关成果获国家技术发明奖二等奖 1 项、国家科技进步奖二等奖 4 项、省部级一等奖 12 项。个人荣获全国五一劳动奖章、全国先进工作者、全国创新争先奖等荣誉。

主持研制国家重大工程和国防装备制造高性能成套控制系统等，成功应用于电力、航空、舰船、电子等高端制造业，解决了我国工业制造领域中多项关键“卡脖子”技术难题，取得良好的社会经济效益，推动了我国制造业智能化转型升级。

一是在重大工程装备研制方面，开创了大型发电机组优化调度与高效运行智能控制技术体系，主持研制出自主可控的大规模高性能自动化成套控制系统，成功应用于国家西电东送、南水北调等重大工程，使发电机组运行效率提高 30.2%、能耗降低 23.2%、运行成本降低 20.7%，实现了我国大型水电站和泵站的经济高效运行，保障了国家重大工程安全可靠。

二是在机器人精密制造方面，攻克了机器人精密制造的测量与加工控制关键技术，主持研制出我国第一条航空发动机精密制造自动化生产线控制系统，成功应用于中国航发集团等大国重器企业，使涡轮加工误差从 0.15mm 降低到 0.1mm、合格率从 65% 提高到 87%，为我国航空制造提供了核心技术支撑。

三是在多机器人协同制造方面，突破了多机器人高效协同制造分布式控制关键技术，主持研制出我国第一条大型舰船制造自动化生产线控制系统，成功应用于中船重工等企业的 6 种型号螺旋桨加工，加工尺寸误差从 0.2% 降低到 0.14%、加工效率提高 31.8%，满足了我国大型舰船等国防装备制造的迫切需求。

四是在集群机器人协同智造方面，提出“互操作性、人机协同性、智能自主性、网络安全性”四大关键核心问题，开创了面向航空航天、海洋舰船、轨道交通等领域重大装备制造的集群机器人协同作业新模式，推动我国重大装备制造技术变革。

2015 年，他主持创建了我国机器人领域的第四个国家级科研基地——机器人视觉感知与控制技术国家工程实验室，推动机器人系统产业化应用。在 2021 年国家科技创新基地优化整合中，该工程实验室成功转型升级为机器人视觉感知与控制技术国家工程研究中心，成为国家创新体系的重要组成部分，为我国“制造强国”战略提供核心技术支撑和科技人才储备。

2008 年我国南方冰雪灾害，电力线路经济损失严重，王耀南带领团队研制出系列输电线路巡检除冰特种机器人，代替电力工人完成各种复杂危险的除冰巡检任务，为我国南方电网的安全稳定运行提供保障。2020 年年初，他带领研究团队历时一个月，研制出医用室内消毒、医用室外喷洒消毒、医用测温、医用物资配送 4 种防疫机器人，投入使用并捐赠给湖南省人民医院等多家医院，大大减轻了新冠疫情期间医护人员的工作负担和交叉感染风险。

Awardee of Electronics and Information Technology Prize, Wang Yaonan

Wang Yaonan was born in Longling County of Yunnan Province in November 1957. In 1977, he majored in the electronic computer at East China College of Geology and taught in the school after graduation. He obtained his master's degree and doctorate degree in industrial automation from Hunan University in 1992 and 1995 respectively. Then he has engaged in teaching and research work in the Department of Automation of Hunan University. After that, he finished postdoctoral work in the Department of Automatic Control, National University of Defense Technology in 1997. From 1998 to 2004, he carried out scientific research and international cooperation projects at the University of Bremen in Germany. He is currently the director of the National Engineering Research Center for Robot Vision Perception and Control Technology. He is also the chairman of China Society of Image and Graphics, the vice chairman of the National Intelligent Robot Innovation

Alliance, and the expert Advisory member of the National Natural Science Foundation.

He devoted to the teaching and research of robot perception and control technology with engineering applications for a long time. He has done a series of pioneering research work in major equipment development, robot precision manufacturing, and multi-robot collaborative manufacturing. He took the lead in proposing the basic theory and key technology system of cluster robot collaborative control. It opened up a new field of cluster robot collaborative intelligent manufacturing. He has been an academician of the Chinese Academy, a fellow of the Chinese Society of Automation, the Chinese Computer Society, and the Chinese Society of Artificial Intelligence.

He has carried out many national major projects and completed sets of high-performance control systems for national defense equipment. These control systems have been successfully applied to high-end manufacturing industries such as power, aviation, ships, electronics, etc., which achieved good social and economic benefits. His contributions have played a role in promoting the intelligent transformation and upgrading of China's manufacturing industry.

For the past few years, he led a research team to build the Robot Vision Perception and Control Technology National Engineering Laboratory to promote the industrial application of robot systems in intelligent manufacturing, which is China's fourth national scientific research base in the field of robotics. Moreover, his laboratory has developed a variety of robots, including special robots for transmission line inspection, medicine dispensing robots, security robots, medical surgery robots, epidemic prevention robots, automated guided vehicles, and unmanned aerial vehicles. In 2021, the engineering laboratory was successfully transformed and upgraded to the National Engineering Research Center for Robot Vision Perception and Control Technology, which has become an important part of the national innovation system and provided a large number of core technologies and scientific and technological talents for China's manufacturing power strategy.

电子信息技术奖获得者

杨 晓 波

杨晓波，1964 年 5 月出生于四川省南江县。1990 年获电子科技大学通信与电子系统专业工学硕士学位，后留校工作至今，先后担任微波中心主任、电子工程学院副院长、科技处处长、学校副校长。兼任教育部科学技术委员会 GF 学部委员，中央军委科学技术委员会、中央军委装备发展部专业组成员，中国电子学会常务理事及会士。曾获国家技术发明奖二等奖、国家级教学成果奖一等奖和第三届全国创新争先奖状等荣誉。

杨晓波作为我国雷达技术专家，一直从事雷达技术领域的教学科研工作，是我国严苛条件雷达成像探测新体制、新方法与工程实现的开拓者之一，其系统性、开创性的工作推动了雷达成像新系统及其集成前端新技术的发展，为中国雷达成像探测技术发展作出重要贡献。

一、提出太赫兹小转角高分辨成像雷达新体制，解决了空间目标隐蔽精细成像的基础理论方法与工程实现技术难题，为我国太赫兹波雷达技术发展和应用奠定了基础

杨晓波研究发现：太赫兹波性质独特，不仅能全天候工作，在物理机理上还支持在小转角条件下获得远高于微波的目标细节成像识别能力，不易被侦收，是实现对空间目标隐蔽精细成像较理想的选择。但由于空间目标结构复杂，而太赫兹波长极短，目标散射闪烁强烈，经典匹配方法难以真正实现高分辨。

1. 提出太赫兹空间孔径渐进最优生长成像模型与方法，从基础理论方法上解决了太赫兹雷达小转角成像问题

首先通过建立的孔径可重构最优分解模型，实现子孔径划分；然后通过导出的散射相位与本征位置定量关系进行重排与归位，实现孔径的合成与生长。在 0.4 太赫兹频段上，仅用近 7 度的转角便可获得毫米级分辨，图像分辨率达到 3 毫米级，优于代表国际领先水平的德国 FHR。

2. 提出太赫兹双源非对称相参高性能雷达前端技术，解决了太赫兹雷达成像面临的工程实现核心难题，打破了国外的长期封锁

提出一种双源非对称相参收发新架构，使发射功率提升3分贝；通过建立太赫兹半导体三维电磁精准模型，结合提出的悬浮无衬底发射倍频、点接触大跨度接收混频和垂直互联集成工艺，有效提升了成像信号质量。基于以上创新，研制出国内首批多频段、系列化、高性能太赫兹固态器件、集成前端和首部太赫兹成像雷达，获得了小转角高分辨二维图像。

3. 提出低失真高帧率太赫兹雷达信号处理技术，有效提升了对目标状态变化的实时感知能力，拓展了雷达成像技术的应用范畴

通过提出的持续极坐标帧间增量关联处理方法，既解决了帧间空时畸变问题，还实现了数据降维处理，成像帧率达7赫兹，突破了传统雷达通常获得静态图像而无法获得动态视频的传统认识。上述成果已在航天科技、科工及中国电科等单位的多个重点型号中应用，核心关键元器件技术还被国内从事太赫兹领域研究、生产的单位广泛使用。相关成果获2020年国家技术发明奖二等奖。

二、创建低频可控步进合成超宽带雷达新体制，解决了隐蔽目标透视探测的基础理论方法与工程实现技术难题，为取得新时期反恐维稳斗争胜利作出贡献

1. 提出低频可控步进合成超宽带雷达新体制，从系统体制和工程实现方法上解决了复杂多样墙体的有效穿透问题

提出一种针对穿墙应用的全新雷达架构。通过数字逐点锁相可控步进频技术，突破了低杂散快跳频大带宽信号产生技术瓶颈，实现了低频超宽带信号高质量合成；利用提出的未知墙体参数实时自主估计和超宽带频点功率自适应预失真技术，解决了回波幅度和相位严重失真校正难题。

2. 提出多视角反投影小波融合高分辨成像新方法，解决了柔性人体的三维成像难题，为墙后遮蔽目标状态的精准感知奠定了基础

利用合成的超宽带，解决成像所需的距离高分辨问题；采用提出的多视角合成孔径协同探测及小波系数分解与融合方法，重构出三维高分辨雷达图像。

3. 提出墙体透视人体生命迹象稳健检测新方法，将穿墙透视雷达从反恐维稳推广应用到灾害救援中

在高分辨穿透探测基础上，通过双通道协同熵互相关探测，找到呼吸振动相位调制的特有规律，解决了穿墙微弱生命迹象的稳定检测问题。

杨晓波主持研制的穿墙雷达已在新疆、浙江、四川等十多个省的多家单位和部门得到应用，参与反恐维稳、执法抓捕等行动均获好评。相关成果获2014年国家技术发明奖二等奖。

三、提出并实现分置运动平台雷达空间与时间同步工程实现方法，为平台分置运动严苛条件下雷达协同成像探测的工程应用奠定了关键技术基础

成果应用于多型机载雷达装备，提升了我国主力战机的目标精确指示能力。相关成果获 2017 年国家技术发明奖二等奖。

Awardee of Electronics and Information Technology Prize, Yang Xiaobo

Yang Xiaobo was born in Nanjiang County of Sichuan Province in May 1964. He graduated from the University of Electronic Science and Technology of China in 1990 with a master's degree in communication and electronic systems. Since graduation, he has been teaching at the University of Electronic Science and Technology of China, holding various positions including Director of the Microwave Center, Vice Dean of the School of Electronic Engineering, Director of the Science and Technology Department, and Vice President of the university. He also serves as a member of the Science and Technology Committee of the Ministry of Education of the People's Republic of China, GF Faculty Committee, member of the Science and Technology Committee of the Central Military Commission, and member of the Professional Group of the Equipment Development Department of the Central Military Commission. Additionally, he is an Executive Council Member and Fellow of the China Electronics Society. He has received three national second-class awards for technological inventions, a national first-class award for teaching achievements, and the Third National Innovation Award certificate.

As an expert in radar technology in China, Yang Xiaobo has been engaged in scientific research and talent development in the field of radar technology for over 30 years. He is one of the pioneers in the development of new systems, new methods, and engineering implementation in radar imaging and detection under severe conditions in China. Through systematic and innovative work, he has promoted the development of new radar imaging systems and integrated front-end technologies, making significant contributions to the development of radar imaging and detection technology in China.

交通运输技术奖获得者

王　平

王平，1969 年 7 月出生于湖北省宜昌市。1994 年、1998 年分别获得西南交通大学道路与铁道工程系工学硕士、博士学位，后留校任教至今，先后担任道路与铁道工程系主任、高速铁路线路工程教育部重点实验室主任，2020 年起任科学技术发展研究院院长。曾兼任科技部国家重点研发计划先进轨道交通重点专项总体专家组成员，川藏铁路科技攻关联合行动总体专家组成员，中国铁道学会高速铁路委员会、工务委员会、工程分会委员和轨道交通工程分会副主任委员，中国国家铁路局技术标准委员会委员，中国国家铁路集团有限公司技术委员会专家组成员。2017 年获詹天佑铁道科学技术奖成就奖。

王平从事高速铁路轨道工程科技研究，在高速铁路轨道结构动力学设计方法突破、维护理论创新与关键结构自主研制等方面作出了一系列开创性工作。

一、高速铁路道岔动力学设计方法及装备

创建了可考虑轮轨多点接触关系的道岔动力学设计理论与方法，相关专著入选国家“三个一百”原创出版工程，并受邀参与制定车辆 – 道岔多体动力学模型国际基准，验证了相关动力学模型的计算精度与多款商业软件相当。创新了缩短尖轨轮载过渡范围、轮载过渡前移、心轨水平藏尖等高速道岔轮轨关系低动力设计，大幅缩短了道岔新产品的研发周期，相关成果纳入国际铁路联盟《高速铁路道岔技术条件》。主持研制了时速 250km/h、350km/h 的系列高速道岔，形成了道岔设计、制造、铺设、养护成套技术条件和成套标准图，打造了中国高速道岔品牌，满足了我国高速铁路大规模建设的需要，实现了在役道岔 1.2 万组，市场份额达到 90% 以上，节约直接投资上百亿元，填补了我国时速 350km/h 系列高速道岔的空白，全面提升了我国道岔行业的整体技术水平，打破了德、法两国对国际市场的垄断和技术封锁，使我国高速铁路保持国际领先地位。以高速道岔轮轨滚动接触理论和列车 – 道岔 – 基础耦合系统动力学为支撑，牵头启动了时速

400km 及更高速度铁路道岔的研制，提出了道岔制造、运输、铺设及养护维修技术要求。进一步发展和完善了无缝道岔设计理论和设计方法，成功解决了道岔上桥这一世界性技术难题，突破了大温差地区、大跨度桥梁、高架车站等高速道岔的铺设禁区。所编制的桥上无缝线路与桥上无缝道岔计算软件已成为各铁路设计院校的专用设计软件；所提出的设计原则、分析模型、计算方法已纳入《铁路无缝线路设计规范》。相关成果获 2009 年四川省科技进步奖一等奖、2011 年教育部科技进步奖一等奖。

二、高速铁路轨道平顺性保持技术及应用

提出高速铁路轨道几何测量控制网建立原则、误差控制与精调标准制定的理论依据，提出了几何不平顺敏感波长分布特征及评价方法，相关成果纳入《高速铁路无砟轨道线路维修规则》（送审稿）。提出一类改进 N 点弦测法，建立其测量、反演及误差模型，从根本上解决了单点弦测法传递函数失真的缺陷；以相对测量提升检测效率，引入静态绝对测量数据平差以控制整体精度，取得了轨道几何精确、高效检测的突破性成果。研制高速铁路轨道几何状态多功能检测小车，可进行轨道长波不平顺、轨道短波波磨及钢轨光带的检测，应用于南广、渝贵等高铁，结果表明该检测技术抗干扰能力强，检测精度、效率已超越国外同类产品。建立了高速铁路轨道几何快速精调方法，开发了轨道几何精调软件，实现了轨道几何高效精调、近零偏差，大幅提升了我国高速铁路轨道几何平顺性的测控能力，全线范围内轨道单项几何平均偏差仅为 0.3mm。所建立的轨道平顺性保持技术体系，解决了高速铁路建设与运营过程中轨道平顺状态诊断与高平顺性长期保持的技术难题，在武广、沪昆等高铁线路的建设与运营中获得成功应用。相关成果获 2012 年中国铁道学会铁道科技奖一等奖、2016 年国家技术发明奖二等奖。

三、高速铁路轨道结构长寿命安全保障技术及应用

提出考虑结构变形的多点滚动接触分析方法，揭示了多点滚动接触与结构振动耦合作用机制，探明了轮轨接触界面行为与多体系统宏观动力特性的跨尺度联系，提出了多点滚动接触高效算法，突破了非赫兹精确接触算法在轮轨系统动力学中的应用局限，制定了“铁路多体系统动力学国际基准”。提出基于均良匹配的轮轨接触界面性态评价方法，实现了轮轨多体系统高速滚动接触界面的有效调控。指导高速铁路 60N 钢轨廓形以及复兴号动车组 LMD 型面的多目标优化设计，制定了在役钢轨打磨、车轮镟修、道岔尖轨摩擦改性等维护策略，形成了高速轮轨滚动接触界面调控成套技术。发明了钢轨裂纹波动辨识技术，提出了钢轨伤损非线性超声实时监测方法。发明了宽频疲劳试验技术，编制了轨道疲劳随机载荷谱，提出了磨耗与疲劳竞争失效预测方法，实现了长期服役条件下轨道疲劳寿命的预测。发明轨道隐蔽损伤高精辨识、预知精修与断轨前兆预警技术，实现了高速铁路轨道结构长寿命安全服役。发明钢轨非一致磨耗均良控制及廓形预知性精磨技术，延缓了轮轨接触关系的退变速率。应用于京沪、沪宁等高铁，消除了行

车失稳现象且各项指标优异，延长寿命一倍以上。上述研究成果成功构建了面向工务维护及实时反馈的高速铁路轨道平顺性检测评估和长效保持体系，从根本上实现了高速铁路轨道服役性能的提升与长寿命安全保障。相关成果获2019年四川省自然科学奖一等奖、2022年教育部技术发明奖一等奖。

Awardee of Communication and Transportation Technology Prize, Wang Ping

Wang Ping was born in Yichang City of Hubei Province in July 1969. He obtained a master's degree in engineering in 1994 and continued working there as a teacher after graduating from the Department of Road and Railway Engineering at Southwestern University of Transportation. In 1998, he received his Ph.D. in engineering from the same department, and become the head of the Department of Road and Railway Engineering. Since 2012, he has also held the position of director of the Key Laboratory of High Speed Railway Engineering, Ministry of Education. He has served as the dean of the Research Institute of Science and Technology Development of Southwest Jiaotong University since 2020. Wang has also held various positions in national and international organizations, including being a member of the general expert group of the "Advanced Rail Transit" key special project of the National Key R&D Plan of the Ministry of Science and Technology and a member of the general expert group for the technological challenges of the Sichuan-Tibet Railway project. He has been a member of the High-Speed Railway Committee, Infrastructure Committee and the Engineering Branch Committee of the China Railway Society, and the Deputy Director of the Rail Transit Engineering Branch Committee of Chinese Railway Society. Additionally, he has been a member of the Technical Standards Committee of the China National Railway Administration and the Expert Committee of the Technical Committee of China National Railway Group Limited Company.

Wang Ping focuses on high-speed railway track engineering and has made a series of groundbreaking contributions in the areas of dynamic design method of high-speed railway track structures, innovative maintenance theory and the independent development of key track structures.

冶金材料技术奖获得者

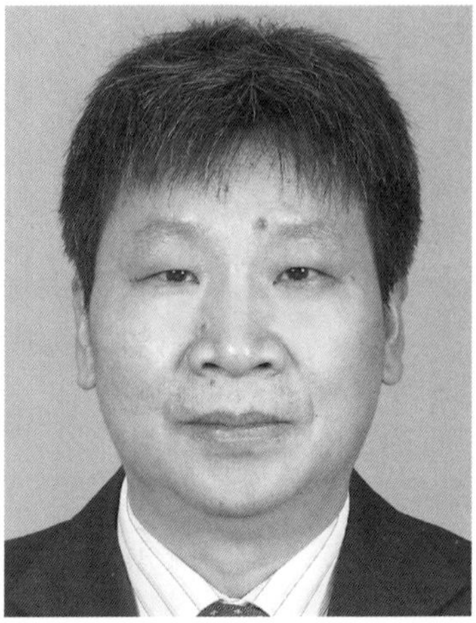

冯 志 海

冯志海，1965 年 1 月出生于浙江省绍兴市。1986 年本科毕业于北京航空学院，1989 年硕士毕业于航空航天部一院，2015 年获中南大学材料学博士学位。1989 年至今在中国航天科技集团航天材料及工艺研究所工作，历任事业部主任助理、副主任、主任、研究发展处处长、科技委副主任。现任航天材料及工艺研究所科技委常务副主任、先进功能复合材料技术重点实验室副主任，兼任中国复合材料学会副理事长。

冯志海一直致力于航天防热复合材料应用基础及工程应用技术研究，是我国航天防热复合材料技术带头人之一，也是中国航天科技集团学术技术带头人。他创建了以轻质烧蚀维形防隔热一体化复合材料、高导热碳 / 碳复合材料等为代表的新型高速飞行器用先进防热材料技术体系；发展了航天国产碳纤维复合材料制造与应用技术体系，牵引实现了宇航级碳纤维国产化，为我国新型高速飞行器自主创新、关键原材料自主可控、航天高新装备研制批产等国家重大工程作出突出贡献。曾荣获国家技术发明奖二等奖 1 项、国家科学技术进步奖二等奖 3 项、国防科技奖 8 项，以及全国杰出工程师荣誉称号。

一、发明系列轻质烧蚀维形防隔热一体化复合材料并实现工程应用，解决了高速飞行器千秒级有氧防隔热难题，保障了首型高速飞行器成功

揭示树脂基防热材料长时有氧防隔热机理，建立了基于热耗散机制的长时烧蚀防热材料设计方法。建立了高速飞行器防热材料的氧化烧蚀模型，揭示了氧化烧蚀、“碳层”疏松弱化、机械剥蚀的材料烧蚀机制；阐明了“以辐射热耗散为主体、热解气体热阻塞等多机制协同”的长时热耗散设计机理；提出了抗氧化基体与气体引射抑氧相结合的抗氧化设计方法，建立了高发射抗氧化表面和微纳多孔结构的烧蚀防热材料模型，为轻质烧蚀维形防隔热材料的突破奠定了理论基础。

发明系列轻质烧蚀维形防隔热一体化复合材料及制备方法，解决了高速飞行器千秒级有氧环境防隔热难题。发明了系列含硅、硼多元杂化抗氧化耐高温树脂，有氧烧蚀“碳层”强度提升 8 倍，实现烧蚀维形；突破特种有机无机纤维杂化技术，烧蚀气体引射效应提升 63%，热耗散和抗氧化效应大幅提高；建立基体微孔结构精细控制方法，热导率降低 60% 以上；研制出系列轻质烧蚀维形材料，密度降低至 0.3～0.9g/cm^3，综合防隔热效率提升 3 倍以上。

攻克轻质烧蚀维形防隔热一体化复合材料构件成型及工程化应用技术。发明大尺寸防热 / 缓冲 / 承载结构一体化低压液体成型方法，解决了长程均匀浸渍、大型结构件与防热层间热匹配调控等关键问题，研制出大尺寸典型防热部件，实现了防热结构减重 50% 以上。

二、攻克国产高导热碳 / 碳复合材料制备与应用关键技术，破解了新一代高速飞行器 3000℃ 疏导防热瓶颈

构建多尺度碳 / 碳复合材料传热模型，提出碳基体及界面的高导热结构调控方法。构建多尺度碳 / 碳复合材料传热模型，探明了高导热碳纤维、基体碳及界面相结构随热处理温度的演变规律，提出了超高温石墨化调控微晶尺寸 / 取向 / 孔隙率等高导热结构调控方法，为高导热碳 / 碳设计与工程应用奠定理论基础。

发明系列高导热碳 / 碳复合材料制备方法，攻克了国产高导热碳 / 碳复合材料工程应用关键技术。发明的高导热碳 / 碳材料热导率高达 750W/（m · K），3000℃区域降温 200℃以上；提出碳化纤维预制体 / 基体碳共石墨化方法，解决了高导热碳纤维脆性大、加工易损伤、材料热导率与高温力学强度协同实现难的工程应用技术瓶颈；研制的高导热碳 / 碳翼前缘、防热板等典型构件已应用于新一代高速飞行器及卫星。

提出国产高导热碳纤维全流程制备技术方案，指导实现了高导热碳纤维国产化。指导建立低灰分中间相沥青合成方法，提出非均相成核深度脱灰、双螺杆连续脱泡等技术方案，带领团队突破连续纺丝、氧化碳化石墨化等全流程制备工艺及成套装备技术，实现了高导热碳纤维连续稳定制备和成套装备的国产化。

三、建立国产宇航级碳纤维标准和评价方法，发展航天国产碳纤维复合材料研制与应用技术体系，实现航天装备用碳纤维的自主保障

创建宇航级碳纤维评价方法，支撑了系列碳纤维国产化。首次建立涵盖本征性、指纹性、离散性和工艺性等指标的宇航级碳纤维标准和评价表征方法体系，保证了纤维性能评价与制备迭代的科学性和有效性；辨识了国产碳纤维离散大、灰分高、毛丝多的主要成因，支撑了碳纤维工程化技术突破，强度离散由 10% 降至 5% 以下，灰分由 1% 降到 0.1% 以下，应用性能显著提升。

发展国产碳纤维复合材料研制与应用技术体系，实现了航天装备用碳纤维的自主保障。提出碳纤维编织损伤 / 断丝抑制的低捻度方案，解决了国产碳纤维立体织物的成型难题，建立碳纤维/酚醛界面调控方法，实现了碳/酚醛烧蚀性能稳定；研制的国产T300碳/碳、碳/酚醛、碳/环氧三类复合材料及构件性能达到国际同类产品先进水平，研制的强界面国产T700复合材料和高压缩国产T800复合材料，层剪强度和压缩强度较国外同类材料分别提高10%以上，实现了升格替代。

Awardee of Metallurgy and Materials Technology Prize, Feng Zhihai

Feng Zhihai was born in Shaoxing City of Zhejiang Province in January 1965. He received his bachelor's degree from Beijing Institute of Astronautics in 1986. He then completed his Master's degree from the First Institute of the Ministry of Aeronautics and Astronautics in 1989. He obtained his Ph.D. degree in Materials Science from Central South University in 2015. Since 1989, he has been working at Aerospace Research Institute of Materials & Processing Technology (ARIMPT). He used to be chief technologist at China Academy of Launch Vehicle Technology. Currently, he is working as ARIMPT's executive deputy director of the Science and Technology Commission. He received the national outstanding engineer award and aerospace innovation award with State Council special allowance.

Feng Zhihai has always been devoted to the fundamental research and engineering practices of aerospace thermal protection materials. He created advanced technical systems for thermal protection materials based on lightweight ablative heat protection and insulation integrated composites with dimensional stability, and high thermal conductivity carbon/carbon composites, realizing successful application in the new high-velocity aircraft.

冶金材料技术奖获得者

张 晓 宏

张晓宏，1967年1月出生于陕西省宁强县。1989年、1992年先后获得北京航空航天大学本科及硕士学位，1996年获北京理工大学博士学位。1996—1998年在中国科学院感光化学研究所从事博士后研究工作。1998—2001年、2003年作为博士后访问学者、高级访问学者分别在香港城市大学COSDAF研究中心、英国剑桥大学Cavendish实验室从事研究工作。2000—2013年任中国科学院理化技术研究所研究员，中国科学院－香港功能材料与器件联合实验室主任。2014年起任苏州大学功能纳米与软物质研究院教授。现任苏州大学校长，教育部苏州纳米科技协同创新中心常务副主任，江苏省先进负碳技术重点实验室主任。英国皇家化学会会士。

张晓宏主要从事新型光电功能材料研究，在有机及微纳结构光电材料研究方面取得了系列重要创新性成果，为该类材料的设计与性能调控以及器件效率的改善提供了重要科学依据。曾获国家自然科学奖二等奖1项、省部级科学技术奖一等奖3项。

一、高效光/电转换有机材料分子结构

提出通过分子氧化还原电势、三重态能级以及构筑多个逆向系间窜越上转换通道设计高效激基复合物第三代OLED材料的普适性策略，实现了接近理论极限的高效材料体系，促进了第三代OLED材料的研究和应用。

二、高效光/电转换有机材料聚集体结构

提出利用界面及图案化衬底诱导制备有机单晶光电微纳材料定向及图案化结构的普适性策略，实现了较大面积（晶圆级）有机单晶光电微纳有序结构制备，促进了该类高性能有机光电材料的研究和应用。

三、高效光 / 电转换有机 / 微纳复合结构

发展了金属离子刻蚀控制制备一维硅微纳有序阵列结构，以及温和条件高效制备有机 / 硅微纳复合径向 p/n 结有序结构的策略，实现了其光电性能的调控及高性能光电器件，促进了该类新型光电材料的研究和应用。

Awardee of Metallurgy and Materials Technology Prize, Zhang Xiaohong

Zhang Xiaohong was born in Ningqiang County of Shaanxi Province in January 1967. He is currently a Distinguished Professor at Institute of Functional Nano & Soft Materials (FUNSOM), and President, Soochow University. He received both his Bachelor's (1989) and Master's (1992) degrees from Beihang University, and his PhD degree (1996) from Beijing Institute of Technology. After two years of research as a postdoctoral fellow at the Institute of Photographic Chemistry of Chinese Academy of Sciences, he was a senior visiting scholar at the Center of Super-Diamond and Advanced Films (COSDAF) at the City University of Hong Kong from 1998 to 2000. In 2000, he became a Professor at the Technical Institute of Physics and Chemistry of Chinese Academy of Sciences. In 2003, he was a senior visiting scholar at the Cavendish Laboratory, Cambridge University. He joined Soochow University as a Distinguished Professor in 2014.

Zhang Xiaohong is an internationally recognized outstanding scientist in the field of optoelectronic functional materials. In three thrusts of this research area, including efficient functional organic materials for optoelectronics; efficient assembly, arrays, and patterns of functional organic materials for optoelectronics; and efficient organic/micro-nano composite structures for optoelectronics, he has come up with original, internationally recognized and highly appraised achievements.

With his contributions recognized, he has been awarded numerous prestigious honors and awards internationally and nationally, such as Second-Class Prize in State Natural Science Award, and Fellow of the Royal Society of Chemistry (2019), etc.

化学工程技术奖获得者

叶 国 安

叶国安，1964 年 9 月出生于安徽省南陵县。1986 年毕业于四川大学化学系放射化学专业，同年进入中国原子能科学研究院工作至今。2002 年获得核燃料循环与材料专业博士学位。2007 年担任中国原子能科学研究院副院长，2017 年被聘为中核集团核燃料后处理工艺首席专家。兼任中国核学会核化工分会理事长、国际原子能机构核燃料循环技术工作组委员、中核集团科技委常委等。

叶国安从事锕系元素化学与核燃料后处理工艺技术研究，在锕系元素分离与核电站乏燃料后处理工艺研究领域作出了一系列开创性工作。

一、揭示强辐射场中钚价态调控和稳定性机理，建立我国钚材料电化学溶解 – 溶剂萃取纯化工艺并实现工程应用

研究提出硝酸体系中亚硝酸氧化三价钚的自催化机理，设计了二甲基羟胺 / 甲基肼高效无盐还原剂反萃钚工艺。该工艺在快速还原四价钚的同时，快速清除亚硝酸，切断其自催化链，将钚稳定在三价，突破了高浓钚无法有效还原反萃的重大技术瓶颈。

针对高晶格能氧化钚溶解难题，研制了在线电解制备强氧化性高价银离子催化氧化钚溶解的工艺和装置，实现了常温常压下氧化钚的安全高效溶解。建立了基于新萃取剂的多级逆流萃取新工艺，提高了萃取容量，解决了高浓钚萃取过程易生成第三相的难题。

在上述基础上，集成创立首个钚材料纯化工艺并实现工业应用。相关成果获国家科技进步奖二等奖。

二、攻克铀钚镎分离、净化等核心技术，建立我国核电站乏燃料后处理先进工艺并工业应用，形成规模化后处理能力

揭示硝酸体系中锝的循环氧化还原消耗铀钚分离还原剂机理，设计了还原剂的使用

工艺，解决了锝对铀钚分离的干扰难题，建立了强化锝等杂质去除的铀钚共去污分离工艺。建立了钚的无盐回流萃取工艺，使每处理 1 吨钚可少产生 8 吨固体核废物。

研究确定了硝酸、肼及其衍生物与镎的氧化还原反应机理和动力学方程，设计了镎提取工艺并成功获得镎产品，首次为规模化制备钚 –238 准备了原料。

建立乏燃料溶解、铀钚镎共去污、分离与纯化工艺，并经热实验验证，用于后处理厂设计建造。中试厂于 2010 年完成核电站乏燃料后处理热调试，放射性杂质净化系数大于 1×10^7，成果获国家科技进步奖二等奖。

三、突破高放废液酰胺荚醚分离、钚 –238 提取等关键技术，建成我国唯一核燃料后处理放化实验设施，实现研发技术跨越提升

基于乏燃料中铀钚镎镅锔等锕系元素全分离理念，攻克了全分离技术并集成提取工艺，将其作为设施建造的设计思想，解决了原理设计和初步设计缺乏基础数据等重大难题，为设施适应多源项、多种同位素提取的建设目标奠定了科学技术基础；成功研制 I 级密封放射性工作箱、热室专用乏燃料溶解与模块化萃取等系列工艺设备。实现了强放射性化工设备灵活操作与设施对放射性全包容，2014 年建成核燃料后处理放化实验设施。

立足锕系元素分离前沿，在国际上较早系统开展了酰胺荚醚类三官能团萃取剂萃取锕系元素热力学研究，揭示了其与锕系元素配位化学规律；建立了软配体反萃镅锔工艺，解决了从高放废液中分离锕系元素关键技术，并作为设施设计基础参数。2021 年在设施内用真实高放废液完成工艺热实验验证，铀钚镎镅锔及锶铯回收率均达到 99.9%，建立了高放废液酰胺荚醚分离工艺。

攻克二氧化镎 – 铝弥散体靶件溶解、镎钚分离纯化等关键技术，完成钚 –238 提取关键技术攻关，建立了钚 –238 提取工艺，在设施内用真实辐照镎靶完成全流程热实验验证，成功提取出钚 –238。

该设施是我国目前唯一可采用真实乏燃料开展放射化学研究的甲级实验室，是面向国家重大需求、突破放射化学前沿的综合性研究设施。建成后，完成了特种同位素分离、特种反应堆乏燃料后处理、后处理示范厂工艺热验证等技术研发，取得重大效益。相关成果获国家科技进步奖二等奖。

Awardee of Chemical Engineering Technology Prize, Ye Guoan

Ye Guoan was born in Nanling County of Anhui Province in September 1964. He graduated in 1986 with a degree in Radiochemistry from Sichuan University, earned his master's and doctoral degrees from the China Institute of Atomic Energy in 1992 and 2002, respectively.

Starting in 1986, Ye Guoan has been working at the China Institute of Atomic Energy. He has held various positions, including Deputy Director and Director of the Radiochemistry Institute, and Vice President of the China Institute of Atomic Energy. Since 2017, he has served as the Chief Expert of Spent Fuel Reprocessing Technology at China National Nuclear Corporation (CNNC), and in May 2018, was appointed Deputy Chief Designer of the Subproject for the National Science and Technology Major Project on Spent Fuel Reprocessing.

Ye Guoan has also held part-time teaching positions at universities such as Tsinghua University and the University of Science and Technology of China. He has been a member of the 4th and 5th sessions of the CNNC Science and Technology Committee, and the Chairman of the 8th and 9th Councils of the Nuclear Chemical Engineering Branch of the Chinese Nuclear Society. He has also been a member of the Teaching Guidance Committee for Nuclear Engineering Majors in Higher Education Institutions under the Ministry of Education, and a member of the IAEA Technical Working Group on Nuclear Fuel Cycle Options and Spent Fuel Management (TWG-NFCO) since 2017.

Ye Guoan has achieved the following significant accomplishments in the field of spent fuel reprocessing, and received the Second-Class National Science and Technology Progress Award four times.

He successfully tackled core technologies related to the separation and purification of uranium, plutonium, and neptunium, established advanced processes for nuclear power plant spent fuel and implemented them on an industrial scale.

He elucidated the mechanisms governing the valence state control and stability of plutonium in high-radiation environments, developed an electrochemical dissolution-solvent extraction purification process for plutonium oxides in China, which has been successfully applied in engineering applications.

He made breakthroughs in critical technologies, including the separation of high-level liquid radioactive waste using amine podands. He also built China's only experimental facility for nuclear fuel reprocessing and radiochemistry, which has become a core platform for various national strategic projects and has led to significant advancements in research and technology development.

资源能源技术奖获得者

范 维 澄

范维澄，1943 年 1 月出生于贵州省福泉市。1965 年毕业于中国科学技术大学近代力学系喷气动力热物理专业，后留校工作。1979 年 11 月—1982 年 4 月赴英国帝国理工学院访学。1995—2014 年担任中国科学技术大学火灾科学国家重点实验室主任、中国科学技术大学副校长；2003 年至今在清华大学公共安全研究院工作，担任研究院院长；2013 年主持创建清华大学合肥公共安全研究院并担任院长。先后担任国务院学位委员会“安全科学与工程”一级学科首届评议组召集人、“国家安全学”一级学科评议组召集人、国家中长期科技发展规划（2021—2035 年）战略研究公共安全专题专家组组长、“十三五”国家重点研发计划重点专项“公共安全风险防控与应急技术装备”和“科技冬奥”专家组组长、住建部城市安全与防灾减灾专业委员会主任、工信部安全产业联盟理事长、全国公共安全基础标准化技术委员会主任委员。中国工程院院士，公共安全科学技术学会名誉理事长，亚太公共安全科学技术学会主席。

范维澄是我国火灾科学学科方向的开创者，也是我国安全学科创立的主要带头人，在火灾动力学与防治技术、公共安全动力学演化、风险评估、预测预警与应急管理等方面作出了一系列开创性工作。他创建的火灾科学国家重点实验室已成为位居国际领跑行列的火灾安全研究中心和我国火灾安全高层次人才培养的主要基地；创建了亚澳火灾科学技术学会和亚太公共安全科学技术学会，并获得亚澳火灾科学技术学会首届终身成就奖、国际火灾研究机构主任论坛 Sjolin 奖等重要国际学术奖项。

一、火灾科学与安全

提出火灾规律双重性理论，建立湍流与燃烧耦合作用的火灾动力学演化模型，创建大空间火灾探测、定位与联动控制技术和火灾风险评估与性能化防火设计技术，解决了我国复杂建筑防火技术难题，应用于人民大会堂、国家奥林匹克主体育场等近 100 项标志性建筑和重大工程，获国家科技进步奖二等奖。

二、公共安全科技

创立公共安全科技体系的“三角形”基础理论，解构了公共安全“突发事件”“承灾载体”和“应急管理”三个核心要素的内涵及其相互作用。以该成果为科学基础，为国家中长期科技发展规划（2021—2035 年）公共安全专题战略研究、“十四五”国家应急体系规划等国家规划工作、全国公共安全基础标准化以及“十三五”国家重点研发计划两个重点专项的顶层设计和任务部署发挥战略科学家和学术带头人的作用。

三、应急管理科技

创建事件链 - 预案链综合预测预警和决策指挥技术，研发国家应急平台核心软件和成套应急装备以及“应急一张图”协同会商技术和系统，在国务院、31 个省、10 多个部委、200 多个地市县应用，引领支撑“纵向到底、横向到边”的国家应急平台体系建设，在玉树地震等国家重大突发事件应对中发挥重要作用，获国家科技进步奖一等奖。

四、科技冬奥

作为“科技冬奥行动计划”专家委员会主任、“科技冬奥”重点专项实施方案和指南编制专家组组长、专项实施总体专家组组长，提出专项的主要框架和核心方向，带领专家组确定了攻关方向，指导编制专项实施方案并亲自答辩通过。深入一线调研北京冬奥组委、国家体育总局等科技需求，审定相关指南和项目立项。

Awardee of Resources and Energies Technology Prize, Fan Weicheng

Fan Weicheng was born in Fuquan City of Guizhou Province in January 1943. He studied Jet Power Thermophysics in the Department of Modern Mechanics at the University of Science and Technology of China (USTC), and graduated from there in 1965. He served as the Vice-President of USTC from 1996 to 2003. He was elected an academician of the Chinese Academy of Engineering in 2001. He has been working at Tsinghua University since 2003, where he is currently the dean of the Public Safety Research Institute.

Fan Weicheng founded the fire science discipline direction in China and is a prominent leader in establishing the safety science discipline. He founded the Asia-Oceania Association for Fire Science and Technology (AOAFST) and the Asia-Pacific Public Safety Science and Technology Association, and received the First Lifetime Contribution Award issued by AOAFST as well as the Sjolin Award issued by the International FORUM of Fire Research Directors.

He has conducted groundbreaking research in fire dynamics and prevention technology, public safety dynamic evolution, risk assessment, prediction and early warning, and emergency management.

He proposed the duality theory of fire laws and established a fire dynamic model that couples turbulence and combustion. He also created technologies for large-space fire detection, location, and linkage control as well as fire risk assessment and performance-based fire prevention design.

He established the "Triangle" theory of public safety technology systems and decomposed the three core elements of public safety: "emergency events," "disaster-affected entities," and "emergency management."

He created a comprehensive prediction, warning, and decision-making command technology for the event chain and contingency chain. He also developed core software for national emergency platforms, a series of emergency equipment, and "emergency map" collaborative consultation technology and systems.

He was the director of the "Sci-Tech Winter Olympics Action Plan", the director of the "Sci-Tech Winter Olympics" key special project implementation plan and guide development expert group, and the overall expert group leader for project implementation. He led the expert group to determine research directions, conducted in-depth research on the Beijing Winter Olympics Organizing Committee, the National Sports Administration, and other scientific and technological needs, and reviewed relevant guidelines and project approvals.

资源能源技术奖获得者

胡 振 琪

胡振琪，1963年5月出生于安徽省蚌埠市。1991年获中国矿业大学测量物探系工学博士学位，1989—1991年在美国南伊利诺伊大学学习，1996—1997年在英国埃克塞特大学进行客座研究。1997年回国至今在中国矿业大学（北京）工作，先后担任矿山生态安全教育部工程研究中心主任、煤矿生态环境保护国家工程实验室主任。兼任国际土地复垦家联合会协调委员会委员，中国煤炭学会土地复垦与生态修复专业委员会主任委员，中国岩石力学与工程学会矿山采动损害与生态修复专委会主任委员。

胡振琪长期从事煤矿土地复垦与生态修复研究与实践，针对传统矿山生态修复存在耕地恢复率低、矸石山复燃率高、治理后土壤质量差等技术挑战作出了一系列开创性研究工作，为我国矿山生态修复事业创建创新和国际化作出突出贡献。曾荣获国家科技进步奖二等奖3项，以及中国青年科技奖、美国采矿与复垦学会Barnhisel奖、生态修复先锋奖等多个奖项。

一、揭示井工开采对地表生态损伤机理与规律，发明边采边复和黄河泥沙充填的耕地复垦技术，解决了高潜水位采煤塌陷区耕地保护修复的世界性难题

发明了“星－空－地－井”感知技术，精准获取地上地下信息，通过数据融合，考虑岩体分层异质性，构建了井下开采逐层向地表传递形变的非均质动态预测方法，建立了井上下多要素耦合的地表生态损伤诊断模型，揭示了煤粮复合、耕地损伤、动态裂缝自修复等地表生态损伤机理与动态演变规律，为矿山生态修复提供了理论基础。

针对高潜水位塌陷区耕地恢复难的问题，首创与开采过程相协同的边采边复和黄河泥沙充填的两种耕地复垦新技术。①传统技术多为稳沉后治理，耕地深度积水难以恢复。基于井上下耦合的地表生态损伤模型，精准预测耕地损伤发生的时空分布及减产程度，提出了基于临界积水阈值加约束条件的复垦时机优选方法，攻克了顾及未来下沉的水陆

布局优化和动态施工技术，创建了与采矿过程协同的边采边复技术，成果在山东新巨龙、济宁三号井、安徽刘桥二矿等应用。与稳沉后治理相比，多恢复耕地15%～40%，实现了避水保土和煤粮兼得，是治理理念与方法的重大突破。②针对煤矸石、粉煤灰等充填复垦存在污染风险的问题，创新性利用黄河泥沙为充填材料，攻克了动水、长距离条件下高浓度取输沙技术，提出了土工布拦截、絮凝剂加暗管排水的泥沙快速固结技术，发明了间隔条带交替式多层多次充填的连续施工工艺，首创了黄河泥沙绿色充填复垦技术，成果在山东邱集、赵官等矿应用，耕地恢复率达95%以上。与传统固废充填复垦技术相比，无污染风险，耕地生产力可提前3年达原有水平，为充填复垦提供了新方法。成果获2004年和2012年国家科技进步奖二等奖、2021年安徽省科学技术奖和2016年测绘科技进步奖一等奖。

二、发明自燃煤矸石山安全灭火与长效防火技术，创建阻燃型生态修复技术，解决了治理难与易复燃的普遍性重大难题

在深入研究矸石山自燃机理的基础上，发现传统治理技术复燃的主要原因是没有精准识别并扑灭内部燃点，且缺乏有效防灭火措施。据此，他发明了自燃诊断－安全灭火－长效防火－植被恢复一体化的阻燃型生态修复新技术，包括：①攻克热红外与空间信息的四维耦合，构建多孔非连续介质条件下内部燃点位置反演模型，实现了由表及里的自燃位置立体定位，满足了精准靶向灭火要求；②提出远距离浅层喷浆控火降温、深部交替注浆间隔排气、梯级冷却式灭火方法、材料和装备，灭火效率提升近3倍且能保障人员安全；③首次提出杀菌剂和还原菌联合抑制氧化、阻隔层隔绝氧气相结合的长效防火方法，并筛选出杀菌剂、还原菌、阻隔层材料及其配比、施用量和施用工艺。成果在山西潞安、阳泉和河南平顶山等矿区推广应用，治理自燃矸石山73座，植被覆盖率超80%，至今未复燃。成果获2019年国家科技进步奖二等奖。

三、提出以“土层生态位”和“土壤关键层”为核心的土壤重构理论框架与技术体系，填补了矿山生态修复基础理论空白，解决了修复后土壤质量差的难题

揭示土壤分层特征及不同土层生态功能与作用的差异性，创新性提出“土层生态位”“土壤关键层”概念和高质量土壤重构方法：①构建了面向不同土地利用方式的土层生态位优化定量模型和土壤生产力综合评价方法，揭示土壤关键层质地、位置、厚度对土壤系统功能提升的作用机理，实现土壤重构剖面的优选；②模拟地质成土过程，提出基于多材料混配、生物化学改良的土壤关键层快速成土技术；③首创非充填复垦双表土层、充填复垦土壤与充填材料有机镶嵌夹层、矸石山自燃阻隔层、干旱风沙区海绵营养层等重构土壤剖面构型；④创立了“分层剥离、交错回填、关键层构建”的土壤重构数学模型和技术工艺。与传统技术相比，耕地生产力水平提高15%以上，可在1—3年内达原有水平。该矿山生态修复独特的基础理论与方法达国际先进水平，并纳入矿山生态修复领域行业标准和高校教材。成果获 2004 年国家科技进步奖二等奖。

Awardee of Resources and Energies Technology Prize, Hu Zhenqi

Hu Zhenqi was born in Bengbu City of Anhui Province in May 1963. He got his Ph.D. degree in Science and Engineering from the Department of Surveying and Geophysical Exploration at the China University of Mining and Technology in 1991. During1989 to 1991, he studied at Southern Illinois University at Carbondale in the United States. From 1996 to 1997, he worked at Exeter University, UK as a visiting scholar. From 1997 to 2018, he worked at the China University of Mining and Technology (Beijing) . Since 2006, he has been serving as the Director of the Engineering Research Center of the Ministry of Education for Mining Environment and Ecological Safety, China University of Mining and Technology (Beijing) . In 2018, he started to work at the China University of Mining and Technology and has been serving as the Director of the National Engineering Laboratory for Coal Mine Ecological Environment Protection since 2022. He has successively served as a member of the Coordination Committee of the International Affiliation of Land Reclamationists, the Chairman of the Land Reclamation and Ecological Restoration Professional Committee of the China Coal Society, and the Chairman of the Mining Damage and Ecological Restoration Special Committee of the China Rock Mechanics and Engineering Society.

Hu Zhenqi has been engaged in the research and practice on coal mine land reclamation and ecological restoration for a long time and has made a series of groundbreaking research work to solve the technical challenges in the traditional mining ecological restoration, such as low farmland restoration rate, high coal gangue hill burning rate, and poor soil quality after treatment. The achievements have won 3-second prizes in the National Science and Technology Progress Award, and won 5 first prizes from provincial, ministerial, and industry associations. He has won the Barnhisel Award and Ecological Restoration Pioneer Award from the American Society of Mining and Reclamation, and the China Youth Science and Technology Award.

生态环保技术奖获得者

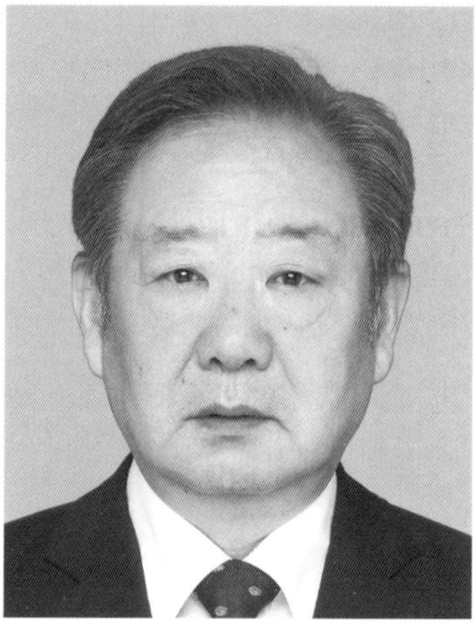

张 远 航

张远航，1957 年 7 月出生于重庆市。1990 年获北京大学环境科学中心理学博士学位，后留校工作至今，先后担任环境科学中心主任、环境学院常务副院长、环境科学与工程学院院长、信息与工程学部副主任等职。现兼任中国科协生态环境产学联合体副主席、中国环境科学学会臭氧污染控制专业委员会主任、教育部区域污染控制国际合作联合实验室主任等。中国工程院院士。

张远航长期专注于研究城市与区域大气复合污染形成机制、环境影响及控制对策，以大气氧化性为主线，贯通监测技术、理论探索、决策支持和区域实践，在自由基化学理论创新、臭氧和 $PM_{2.5}$ 成因量化上取得突破，构建区域污染防控技术体系，支撑了珠三角和成渝等地污染防控的长期实践和空气质量快速改善，为国家大气污染攻坚提供了典型案例。

一、构建大气复合污染研究方法体系

针对 $PM_{2.5}$ 和臭氧（O_3）快速增长的核心科学问题，提出定量检验科学假设的闭合实验新思路，设计以揭示 $PM_{2.5}$、O_3、大气氧化和大气消光之间本质关系为目标的区域空气质量研究计划，制定外场测量、实验室模拟和数值模型相互印证的技术路线。自 2004 年起，组织国内外一流科研机构百余人的国际化团队，在珠三角、京津冀和成渝地区开展系列大型外场综合观测实验，实现 $PM_{2.5}$ 和 O_3 及二次污染前体物 – 反应中间体 – 产物的精细在线测量，探究核心参数的闭合测量问题，获得区域污染和气象过程三维立体表征。结合多模型印证，掌握了 O_3 和 $PM_{2.5}$ 等污染物区域分布特征，揭示了 O_3 与前体物强非线性关系，定量解析了二次气溶胶、黑碳及相对湿度的致霾作用，量化了长距离输送对城市和区域空气质量的影响。基于长期实践，主持构建大气复合污染防治的研究方法体系，包括区域观测网络技术、污染机制诊断技术、控制方案设计技术，并在此基础上发起组

建中国大气超级观测站联盟，研究成果支撑了全国城市空气质量监测站实现在线联网、空气质量状况的实时发布和预警。

二、深化大气氧化性与二次污染基础研究

2006 年在我国首次实现自由基外场实测，发现珠三角和北京大气羟基自由基（OH）浓度是迄今全球报道的最高值、大气 OH 变化滞后于紫外辐射、高浓度气态亚硝酸（HONO）光解对 OH 的贡献远远超过 O_3、颗粒物表面光催化和土壤释放 HONO 等新现象，为自由基理论创新提供了数据基础。在精细观测数据约束下，定量分析 OH 浓度演变、生成与去除过程，揭示传统理论低估 OH 浓度 3～5 倍，发现高挥发性有机物（VOCs）大气中存在未知的 OH 重要再生新机制，异戊二烯降解中间体是新机制的关键物种，进而构建 OH 归一化模型，成功模拟了全球 12 个观测实验结果，揭示区域大气氧化能力已达峰值，证明新机制具有全球普遍性。厘清了大气氧化性内涵和构成，发现新机制的主要构成包括新型 VOCs 氧化衍生的过氧自由基氢转移及自氧化和硝酰氯光解等，揭示了夏季自由基高浓度、冬季自由基快速循环和夜间活性氮高效转化是我国大气强氧化性的特征。采用多技术相互印证，量化了 O_3 和二次 $PM_{2.5}$ 污染与前体物的强非线性，提出区域 / 城市 VOCs 总量控制和氮氧化物（NOx）承载力，揭示 VOCs 和 NOx 快速氧化及二次污染区域输送是重霾污染的关键因素。构建日照时数与 $PM_{2.5}$、重霾日数与气候因子之间的量化模型，发现我国东部具有连续干旱日增加的趋势，揭示其与 O_3 和 $PM_{2.5}$ 污染及排放的复杂关系，提出了“双碳”战略背景下强化污染减排的新思路。

三、开展大气污染联防联控区域实践

2002 年提出建立粤港监测网方案，得到政府采纳并于 2005 年建成全国第一个业务化区域监测网。“十一五”期间，对粤港监测网监测点位、功能和属性进行区域化布局，制定广东大气超级站选址方案、总体规划和技术配置，提出强氧化性和高颗粒物条件下多模型集成预报系统的技术设计。主持研究珠三角空气质量立体监测预警业务化系统，实现区域监测、源清单、数值模型、决策支持等技术环节的高效联动，成为国家区域空气质量监控的范例。主持研究并量化粤港城市间污染输送，支撑粤港政府 2002 年发布《改善珠三角空气质量的联合声明》，研究和编制区域大气科学中心建设方案、区域协调决策机制和多污染物协同减排方案，支撑广东省建成珠三角联防联控技术示范区，推动珠三角 2015 年 $PM_{2.5}$ 率先达标和持续改善。随后，提出区域视野 – 城市行动的联防联控机制新思路，指导广东和成渝地区持续开展臭氧污染防治行动，遏制了污染恶化势头，支撑 2023 年成都世界大学生运动会期间 O_3 全面达标。2018 年，主持在京津冀地区建设了国际上迄今为止规模最大、功能最全的星空地一体化大气污染科研区域监测网，推动首次构建了区域综合污染源解析方法和排放 – 气象 – 化学对污染贡献的解耦分析方法，厘清了京津冀地区大气重污染的来源成因和主控因子，回应了国家对大气重污染成因的关切。

参与和承担大气污染防治科技规划顶层设计，牵头编制科技部“十二五”以来的蓝天工程重点专项和国家重点研发计划大气专项实施方案，并担任总体专家组长或常务副组长、国家大气攻关中心副主任，致力于引领“双碳”背景下大气污染防治科技的创新和跨越。

Awardee of Ecology and Environmental Protection Technology Prize, Zhang Yuanhang

Zhang Yuanhang was born in Chongqing City in July 1957. He received his Ph.D. in the Center for Environmental Sciences (CES) at Peking University (PKU) in 1990. At PKU, he has successively served as the director of CES, executive dean of the College of Environment, dean of the College of Environmental Sciences and Engineering and vice director of the Division of Information and Engineering. He currently serves as chair of the ozone pollution control committee of CSES, and director of the international joint lab of regional pollution control of MOE. In 2015, he was elected as member of the Chinese Academy of Engineering.

His major research field is atmospheric environmental chemistry, with a long-term focus on understanding the formation mechanism, environmental impacts, and control strategies for urban and regional air pollution complex. With the atmospheric oxidative capacity as the main line, he has made breakthroughs in the radical chemistry theory, the quantification of ozone and $PM_{2.5}$ source and formation schemes, and the establishment of a regional pollution prevention technical system, by integrating monitoring technology, theoretical exploration, decision support and regional practice. His major scientific achievements include: establishing a new research methodology for the air pollution complex by the integration of regional monitoring network, development of multiple diagnostic techniques, and designment of comprehensive mitigation strategies; discovering unrecognized OH regeneration scheme and fundamental causes of strong atmospheric oxidation capacity in China, based on both direct radical measurements and closure studies; promoting the synergy control strategy of regional air pollution with a new concept of “regional vision, city action” .

Additionally, he has authored multiple monographs and textbooks, and edited the Blue Book on Ozone Pollution Control in 2020 and 2023. He has led the China's top-level design team for science and technology initiatives in air pollution protection since the 12th five-year plan, making significant contributions to the advancement of atmospheric pollution control technology in China.

工程建设技术奖获得者

贾 金 生

贾金生，1963 年 1 月出生于河南省民权县。1990 年获中国水利水电科学研究院结构所工学博士学位并留在单位工作，先后任结构所副所长、所长、研究院副院长，兼任中国大坝工程学会副理事长、秘书长。2003—2006 年当选国际大坝委员会副主席，2009—2012 年任国际大坝委员会主席，成为首个任此岗位的中国专家，并兼任世界水理事会董事；2016—2022 年任中国大坝工程学会专职秘书长。现任中国水利水电科学研究院流域水循环模拟与调控国家重点实验室副主任、中国大坝工程学会副理事长、国际大坝委员会荣誉主席和国际大坝委员会胶结坝专业委员会主席。

贾金生长期从事水库大坝建设研究，是我国水工结构学术带头人，在大坝安全和新坝型研究等关键技术方面作出了一系列开创性工作，为促进我国筑坝技术在世界上实现从跟跑到并跑和领跑作出重要贡献。

一、创立高混凝土坝性能优化理论，为我国高混凝土坝技术发展作出突出贡献

揭示 200 米以上特高坝开裂、劈裂等破坏机理是结构细观上的损伤导致中观上的失衡和宏观上的失稳，首次揭示了高压水劈裂破坏机理并建立了设计准则，创立了静、动荷载作用下考虑开裂、劈裂等影响的性能优化理论。该成果应用于 294.5 米小湾拱坝，节省投资 8%，漏水量为世界同类工程最小；应用于拉西瓦等 100 多座拱坝，每个工程节省投资 5%～15%。

带领团队提出性态精细模拟方法和细观损伤与宏观性能定量关系等模型，实现了特高坝性态的精准预测，发现了混凝土多元胶凝粉体的紧密堆积效应和大坝混凝土配置等新方法。成果在三峡大坝工程应用，很好地解决了三峡大坝二期及之后的混凝土高质量施工问题，不仅混凝土抗裂指标提升 13% 以上，还节省投资 2 亿多元，创造了大坝最大体积混凝土高质量浇筑的奇迹。

针对南水北调丹江口大坝加高这一世纪工程的安全问题，带领团队通过准确模拟大坝建设过程和大坝中裂缝的性态，提出科学的大坝安全状态评估方法，最后得出大坝加高后安全运行没有问题的结论并被决策部门采纳。此外，带领团队先后分析论证丰满、陈村等一系列工程的重大安全问题，为这些工程的重大决策提供了科学依据。

二、研发高面板堆石坝安全防控关键技术，解决世界级工程建设难题

带领团队揭示高面板坝挤压破坏的机理在于大坝变形大、变形不协调；提出止水结构和材料一体化优化方法，实现了高面板坝止水设计由定性到定量的跨越；提出混凝土面板耐久性定量设计方法，解决了低温、冻融循环、高压水等严酷条件下面板抗裂和耐久性问题。

研发高坝柔性防渗、淤填自愈体系和面板动态稳定止水结构，能承受300米水头作用下最大张开5厘米、沉降10厘米、剪切5厘米的三向变位，实现特高面板坝止水防渗设计由定性到定量的跨越。

上述成果对于我国面板坝技术实现由跟随到引领贡献突出，并为233米的世界最高坝水布垭面板坝、世界第二高的马来西亚巴贡面板坝等工程的成功建设运行作出创造性贡献。成果还应用于国内外100多座面板坝工程。

三、首创胶结坝新坝型，开创了新的筑坝体系

针对土石坝漫顶易溃问题，提出功能梯度结构设计和广源料配合比设计方法，首创利用少量水泥、粉煤灰、外加剂胶结广源料筑坝，开创了新的筑坝体系，破解了当地材料筑坝遇洪水漫顶速溃的世界难题。新型胶结坝的提出是世界筑坝理论的一项重大创新，一改过去大坝建设主要坝型均由欧美等西方国家提出的历史。被国际大坝委员会赞誉为“大坝发展史上的重要新进展，具有里程碑意义”。

为加快新坝型的推广应用，带领团队发明胶结坝专用施工设备和质量快速测定仪器，解决了200毫米大粒径、高离散、用水量大波动的非连续骨料高效拌和难题；研发了智能加浆振捣设备，实现防渗层加浆量的精准控制；开发了专用外加剂和阻泥剂；研发了基于超宽带定位的数字化质量监控系统，实现施工质量全过程数字监控、动态调整和实时预警。编制了水利部胶结坝技术标准与设计、施工等团体标准。

胶结坝技术和成套施工装备成功应用于我国西江水库、金鸡沟水库等国内外40多座水利水电工程，充分彰显了就地取材造价低、施工简单工期短、漫顶不溃安全高、减少弃渣环保好的优势。据初步分析统计，胶结坝比混凝土坝节省投资10%～20%。

四、推动中国坝工走向世界，不断扩大国际影响

倡导设立国际大坝委员会胶结坝专业委员会并担任主席，负责组织在世界范围内的研究和推广。牵头组织编制国际大坝委员会技术公报，合作编制完成《胶结土坝》技术公报，正在编制《胶结砂砾石坝》技术公报。这是国际大坝委员会的核心产出，是世界各国水利水电工程招投标的技术参考文件，标志着由中国专家首创发明的胶结坝筑坝技术标准体系已开始成为世界各国建设胶结坝的重要依据和准则。倡议并推动设立了大坝国际里程碑工程奖和国际大坝杰出工程师奖，先后有 21 个国家的 40 多座大坝工程获奖。

在担任中国大坝工程学会秘书长期间，积极搭建中外学术交流平台，主办 15 届水库大坝与水电可持续发展圆桌论坛，联合主办 11 届中日韩坝工学术交流会等各类国际会议。成功获得 2025 年第 28 届国际大坝委员会大会暨第 93 届年会在我国的举办权；组织设立国际大坝委员会青年论坛，为年轻人成长搭建学习交流平台。同时，先后推荐多位中国专家任国际大坝委员会专委会主席，有力提升我国坝工领域在国际上的话语权和影响力。

贾金生先后获国际大坝创新奖 1 项，国家科技进步奖一等奖 1 项、二等奖 4 项，省部级特等奖、一等奖 13 项。获首届国家创新争先奖、光华工程科技奖、科技部青年科技创业奖以及巴西和印度颁发的国际奖。2022 年荣获第五届“杰出工程师奖”。

Awardee of Engineering and Construction Technology Prize, Jia Jinsheng

Jia Jinsheng was born in Minquan County of Henan Province in January 1963. In 1990, he obtained a doctoral degree in engineering from the Institute of Structural Engineering of the China Institute of Water Resources and Hydropower Research and became employed by the institute upon graduation. He successively served as deputy director and director of the Institute of Structural Engineering, and vice president of the China Institute of Water Resources and Hydropower Research, as well as vice chairman and secretary-general of the China National Committee on Large Dams (CHINCOLD). From 2003 to 2006, he was elected as vice chairman of National Committee on Large Dams (ICOLD). From 2009 to 2012, he served as chairman of the ICOLD, becoming the first Chinese expert to hold this position. During this period, he also served as a director of the World Water Council. From 2016 to 2022, he served as full-time secretary general of CHINCOLD. At present, he is deputy director of the State Key Laboratory of Simulation and Regulation of Water Cycle in River Basin of the China Institute of Water Resources and Hydropower Research, vice chairman of the CHINCOLD, honorary president of the ICOLD, and president of the Technical Committee on Cemented Material Dams of ICOLD.

Jia Jinsheng has long been engaged in research on the construction of reservoirs and large dams, and is an academic leader in hydraulic structure engineering in China. He has done a series of pioneering jobs in key technologies such as the safety of large dams and research on new dam types, making important contributions for China to catch and keep up with other countries and take a leading position in dam construction technologies.

工程建设技术奖获得者

李　东

李东，1967年6月出生于陕西省延安市。1989年获北京航空航天大学飞机设计专业学士学位，1992年获中国运载火箭技术研究院导弹设计专业硕士学位，并留在单位工作至今，历任结构设计室副主任、总体设计室主任、总体设计部副主任、研发中心主任；型号主任设计师、副总设计师、总设计师。其间，于2020年在北京航空航天大学获先进制造专业博士学位。中央军委装备发展部航天运输与发射技术专业组成员、国防科技工业战略火箭创新中心专家、北京航空航天大学未来空天技术学院特聘导师。

李东是我国运载火箭专家和长征五号、长征五号B两型大型火箭总设计师，长期工作在运载火箭总体、结构的研究与设计一线。主持研制了我国运载能力最大的火箭，在高效总体构型、大型轻质结构和先进低温动力等方面有重大创新，为我国火箭从中型到大型的跨代发展、运载能力和总体技术水平跃升至国际前列作出了系统性、开创性贡献。曾荣获国家科技进步奖特等奖1项、国防科技进步奖特等奖2项，以及全国创新争先奖状、全国五一劳动奖章、航空航天月桂奖等奖项和荣誉。

一、构建国际在役火箭独有的总体构型，攻克减少级数时运载效率难以提升的难题，使我国火箭运载能力、运载效率和可靠性跃居国际前列

率先提出氢氧芯级+液氧煤油助推器的全新火箭构型，利用高密度比冲的液氧煤油动力有效扩大火箭规模，利用高性能比冲的氢氧动力提供高效速度增量，攻克助推与芯级推重比、级间比匹配难题，实现了两种动力低空和高空工作效能的最佳组合，火箭运载能力大幅提升，高、低轨能力是我国上一代火箭的2.5倍和2.9倍，居国际前列。

提出高性能氢氧级小推重比、长时工作方案，攻克重力转弯效应最优适配技术，成功使火箭整体减少一级，使运载效率比我国上一代火箭提高33%，比国外常用的氢氧+固体方案提高19%，同时减少了一种发动机的研制和全箭16%的部件，设计可靠性提升至国际先进水平。二级半的长征五号可完成传统三级半火箭的高轨任务，一级半的长征五号 B 可替代传统二级半火箭，是迄今国际唯一实现一级半直接入轨的火箭。使我国成为国际上第二个同时拥有高轨 14 吨、低轨 25 吨火箭的国家。

二、创新助推传力路径设计和贮箱受力形式，突破千吨级集中载荷力扩散结构技术，显著提升结构效率和可靠性，实现我国火箭 5 米大直径轻量化箭体结构技术的重大突破

长征五号相比我国上一代中型火箭直径增大 49%、轴压和弯矩增大 1.8 倍和 1.4 倍，综合结构效率却需提升 20%，轻质化与高承载矛盾突出。面临大推力助推高效传力、薄壁结构安全承载等难题，他颠覆传统下捆绑点传力模式，提出通过上捆绑点将助推千吨级推力传递到芯级的方案。国内首创芯级主结构悬挂连接技术，降低芯级轴向载荷 90%，创新性地将强非线性的轴压失稳问题转化为内压强度问题，攻克长期制约薄壁贮箱结构效率提升的低应力轴压失稳难题，结构许用应力提高 1 倍以上，实现火箭主结构受力形式由受压到受拉的重大创新。成功研制超大液氢贮箱，容积是我国上一代氢箱的 8 倍，厚径比降低 37%，结构效率提高 57%，达到国际先进水平。发明力与力矩定向解耦、传力路径刚度分配等薄壁结构安全承载技术，实现了集中力传递路径定向导引，降低捆绑结构应力水平 60%，攻克千吨级集中载荷在薄壳结构有限空间内安全承载与高效力扩散难题，大幅提升火箭运载能力。

三、提出窄窗口多弹道发射、行星际双曲线逃逸轨道设计与控制、故障自适应应急飞行程序设计等全新技术，圆满完成天问一号、嫦娥五号、天宫空间站等国家重大航天任务的发射

深空探测任务发射窗口窄，发射机会珍贵，如火星探测每 26 个月才有一次发射机会。确保窄窗口甚至零窗口发射是对大型低温火箭的重大挑战。他首次提出多轨道预装订 + 实时自主选择方案，将 10 分钟的发射窗口大幅拓展到 50 分钟。攻克双曲线轨道设计与控制技术，国内首次将逃逸能量 C3 作为行星际轨道制导特征量，解决了制导参数畸变难题，将全球最重的火星探测器天问一号送入奔火轨道，首次使我国拥有了行星际探测器发射能力；成功发射嫦娥五号月球采样返回探测器，实现我国首次地外天体采样返回；突破大型低温火箭零窗口发射技术，成功发射空间站天和核心舱、问天和梦天实验舱，圆满完成中国空间站的建造。

Awardee of Engineering and Construction Technology Prize, Li Dong

Li Dong was born in Yan'an City of Shaanxi Province in June 1967. In 1989, he graduated from the Aircraft Design Department of Beihang University with a bachelor's degree in aircraft design. In 1992, he obtained a master's degree in missile design from the China Academy of Launch Vehicle Technology. In the same year, he joined the Beijing Institute of Aeronautical System Engineering at the China Academy of Launch Vehicle Technology. He has held positions such as Deputy Director of the Structural Design Laboratory, Director of the General Design Laboratory, Deputy Director of the General Design Department, and Director of the Research and Development Center. He has also served as the Director of Launch Vehicle Engineering, Deputy Chief Designer, and Chief Designer. In 2020, he earned a Ph.D. degree in Advanced Manufacturing from Beihang University. He is a member of the Aerospace Transport and Launch Technology Professional Group in the Equipment Development Department of the Central Military Commission. He is also an expert at the National Defense Science and Technology Industry Strategic Rocket Innovation Center and a distinguished mentor at the School of Future Aerospace Technology, Beihang University. He has won one special National Science and Technology Progress Award and two special National Defense Science and Technology Progress Awards. He has received the National Innovation Award, the National Greatest Science and Technology Worker Award, the National Labor Medal, and the Aerospace Laureate Award.

Li Dong is an expert in China's launch vehicle technology and serves as the chief designer of the Long March 5 and Long March 5B. For over 30 years, he has been involved in researching and designing launch vehicle systems and structures. He led the team to achieve breakthroughs in the development of China's large rocket program, taking it from zero to one. As a result, the rocket's carrying capacity has reached the international advanced level. The Long March 5 series represents the highest level of technological innovation in China's launch vehicle industry. It fills the gap in China's large thrust non-toxic and non-polluting liquid rockets, enabling China to achieve an internationally advanced rocket carrying capacity. He has made systematic and pioneering contributions to the rapid development of China's rockets, particularly in the transition from medium to large sizes. His work has also focused on improving payload capacity and technological advancements, positioning China at the forefront of international rocket technology.

工程建设技术奖获得者

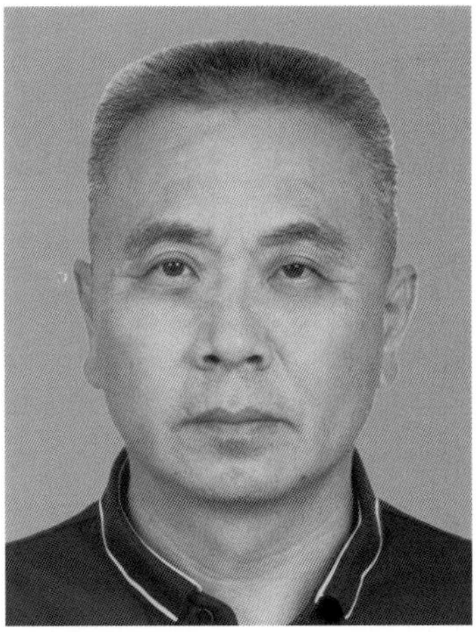

刘清宇

刘清宇，1968 年 4 月出生于河南省商丘市。1989 年毕业于哈尔滨船舶工程学院水声工程专业，后进入海军装备论证研究中心工作，历任某研究所助理工程师、工程师、室主任、副所长，海军研究院某研究所所长 / 研究员、中国工程院院士。

刘清宇作为我国分布式声呐系统领域的学术带头人，开拓发展基于目标固有特征的分布式声呐系统理论技术，担任分布式被动声呐系统、分布式主动声呐系统和体系集成运用工程总设计师，为我国水下预警探测的能力跃升和持续发展作出了突出贡献。曾荣获全国优秀科技工作者、全军优秀科技创新工作者荣誉称号；并获得国家技术发明奖二等奖 1 项，国家科技进步奖二等奖 2 项，军队科技进步奖一等奖 6 项、二等奖 7 项，以及全国首届创新争先奖状、中国青年科技奖等诸多奖项；5 次荣立个人二等功。

一、创建“低频特征 + 探测控制”的分布式声呐系统技术体制

针对潜艇隐身带来的重大挑战，发现航船螺旋桨特征的非线性增强检测特性，验证了航船极低频辐射线谱特征的远程检测特性，提出分布式声呐系统探测控制概念方法，奠定分布式声呐系统理论基础。

二、围绕远海水下预警探测，突破特征信息分布处理技术，研制分布式被动声呐系统

针对远海隐蔽探潜难题，基于多目标特征的差异性和可分离性，实现不依赖空间指向的多目标分辨；突破多节点特征融合处理技术，实现强干扰抑制和弱目标辨识；主持研制小孔径分布式无人声呐系统，实现远海大洋水下声监测。

三、围绕舰艇编队水下预警探测，突破声呐探测分布控制技术，研制分布式主动声呐系统

针对多声呐协同探潜和环境适配难题，建立海洋声场、目标散射、背景干扰等物理数学模型，提出多基地动态效能计算和探测控制方法，研制编队探测控制系统，成倍提高探潜范围和跟踪时间。

四、围绕广域水下预警探测，突破分布式系统集成技术，构建水下预警探测体系

针对水下、水面、空中异构节点大区域探测难题，开展海洋声学调查，突破节点部署优化、信息综合处理、体系运用筹划、信息交互协议等技术，主持某集成运用工程，实现整体能力大幅提升。

Awardee of Engineering and Construction Technology Prize, Liu Qingyu

Liu Qingyu was born in Shangqiu City of Henan Province in April 1968. He graduated from the College of Shipbuilding Engineering, Harbin Engineering University, majoring in hydroacoustic engineering in 1989. A full-time employee of the Naval Equipment Demonstration Research Center, he has successively served as associate engineer, engineer, department director and deputy director of a research institute, director/researcher of a research institute of the PLA Naval Research Academy, and academician of the Chinese Academy of Engineering.

As an academic leader in the field of distributed sonar system in China, Liu Qingyu has pioneered the development of distributed sonar system theory and technology based on the inherent feature of the target, and serves as the chief designer of distributed passive sonar system, distributed active sonar system and system integration application engineering, making outstanding contributions to the improvement and sustainable development of China's underwater early warning and detection capability. The honors and titles he has won include National Outstanding Science and Technology Research Worker and Outstanding Science and Technology Innovation Worker of the PLA; one second prize of the State Technical Invention Award, two second prizes of the State Scientific and Technological Progress Award, six first prizes and seven second prizes of the Military Science and Technology Progress Award of the PLA, the First State Scientific Innovation and Pioneer Award, the China Youth Science and Technology Award and others; as well as five individual second-class merit citations.

I. Create a technical system for distributed sonar system with "low frequency feature+ detection control"

In response to the major challenges to submarine stealth, he discovered the nonlinear enhanced detection feature of ship propeller characteristics, verified the remote detection feature of ship extremely low frequency radiation spectrum characteristics, and proposed the concept and method of detection and control of distributed sonar system, laying a theoretical foundation for distributed sonar system.

II. Develop a distributed passive sonar system with a focus on the open-sea underwater early warning and detection and a breakthrough in the feature information distribution processing technology

To tackle the difficulty in open–sea covert submarine detection, he realized multi–target resolution independent of spatial orientation based on the difference and separability of multi–target features; made breakthrough in the multi–node feature fusion processing technology and realized suppression of strong interference and identification of weak targets; presided over the development of a small–aperture distributed sonar system and realized underwater acoustic monitoring in the open sea.

III. Develop a distributed active sonar system with a focus on the underwater early warning and detection of ship formation and a breakthrough in the distributed sonar detection and control technology

To tackle the difficulty in multi–sonar collaborative submarine detection and environmental adaptation, he established physical and mathematical models such as ocean acoustic field, target scattering and background interference, proposed a multi–base dynamic efficiency calculation, detection and control method, and developed a formation detection and control system to double submarine detection range and tracking time.

IV. Create an underwater early warning and detection system with a focus on the wide-area underwater early warning and detection and a breakthrough in the distributed system integration technology

To tackle the difficulty in detecting heterogeneous nodes in large areas under the water, on the water surface and in the air, he carried out marine acoustic investigation, made breakthrough in node deployment optimization, comprehensive information processing, system application planning, information interaction protocol and other technologies, and presided over an integrated application project, realizing a significant improvement in overall capabilities.

何梁何利基金科学与技术创新奖获得者传略

PROFILES OF THE AWARDEES OF PRIZE FOR SCIENTIFIC AND TECHNOLOGICAL INNOVATION OF HO LEUNG HO LEE FOUNDATION

青年创新奖获得者

陈　　鹏

陈鹏，1979 年 6 月出生于甘肃省兰州市。2002 年本科毕业于北京大学化学与分子工程学院，2007 年获美国芝加哥大学化学博士学位，随后在美国 Scripps 研究所从事博士后研究。2009 年 7 月回到北京大学化学与分子工程学院工作至今，先后任北京大学前沿交叉学科研究院副院长、北京大学研究生院副院长、北京大学学科建设办公室主任。现任北京大学化学生物学系主任、北京大学合成与功能生物分子中心主任、生物有机与分子工程教育部重点实验室主任、北京大学交叉学位分会主席。兼任中国化学会化学生物学专业委员会主任、国家自然科学基金委“生物大分子动态修饰与化学干预”重大研究计划专家组副组长等。

陈鹏长期致力于化学生物学研究，潜心探索利用化学反应推动生命科学研究的原创路径并取得系统性创新成果，引领了“活细胞化学反应”这一交叉科学前沿的发展，推动了我国在以生物正交反应为代表的化学生物学领域进入国际前沿。

一、提出并发展生物正交剪切反应，开拓生物正交化学新方向

陈鹏潜心探索在活细胞内原位调控蛋白质功能的化学方法，在国际上率先提出并发展了基于“断键”思想的生物正交剪切反应，实现了生物大分子的原位激活。他所报道的基于钯催化剂和炔丙基碳酸酯以及基于逆电子需求狄尔斯－阿尔德反应的“剪切－脱笼”组合，能够利用非天然氨基酸将保护性官能团引入蛋白质关键位点，将其活性中心“锁在笼中”；然后通过生物正交剪切反应，实现活性中心的“化学脱笼”。这一策略突破了活细胞内原位研究蛋白质的瓶颈，实现了激酶等关键信号转导蛋白的原位激活与功能研究。

二、系统开展活细胞化学驱动的蛋白质底物解析，揭示生物学新机制

在活细胞内发现和解析蛋白质机器的生理底物，是揭示其功能机制的关键途径，也是生物学研究的难点所在。陈鹏紧盯这一核心科学问题，在蛋白质“活性位点脱笼”的基础上，进一步发展了针对整个活性口袋的“邻近脱笼”策略。通过与合作者开发计算机辅助的脱笼位点选择方法，仅利用一个氨基酸残基的脱笼化学即可实现活细胞内各类酶家族蛋白的原位调控，建立了普适的蛋白质激活平台。该方法还首次在活细胞内实现了 Caspase 3 水解酶的实时激活，发现其在触发细胞程序性死亡过程中的多个未知底物，为癌细胞耐药机制的产生提供了新的解释，也为药物靶标发掘提供了新的契机。

针对染色质、分子伴侣等非酶类分子机器的生理底物，他还发展了一系列基于双吖丙啶的光交联探针，可通过原位生成卡宾中间体实现底物蛋白的高效捕捉，已先后为国内外 60 多家实验室提供了该光交联系统或开展合作研究。通过捕获抗酸伴侣 HdeA 的 30 多种生理底物，与生物学家合作揭示了肠道病原菌利用“伴侣保护”突破宿主胃酸屏障的独特机制。最近，设计开发带有酰化修饰的“双功能光交联”探针及活细胞内“关联解析”染色质相互作用蛋白质组与基因组的“单位点－多组学”技术 SiTomics，与合作者建立了二者之间的信息关联，揭示了细胞如何利用染色质酰化修饰调控代谢与转录的分子机制。

三、发展活体动物正交反应，探索活体化学驱动的生物创新药技术变革

陈鹏克服活体动物环境对生物正交反应更为严苛的要求，成功发展了一系列活体正交反应，探索了在活体化学驱动的生物新技术引领下，从基础研究向实际应用的转化贯通。他发展的生物正交剪切反应可用于在活体动物内原位释放“生物正交前药”，成功构建了生物正交抗体偶联前药。提出基于活体 SuFEx 反应的膜蛋白靶向降解策略，通过将共价反应基团引入合作者筛选的抗体，使之与免疫检查点蛋白 PD-L1 发生原位交联，实现了 T 细胞的特异激活和实体肿瘤的有效清除。

发展细胞邻近标记技术 EXCELL 和 PhoXCELL，其中 EXCELL 被作为“化学方法表征免疫细胞相互作用的代表性技术”写入最新出版的国际化学生物学教材，相关专利已转让生物技术企业，用于新一代红细胞治疗技术的开发。与合作者开发 PhoXCELL 技术，实现了患者体内肿瘤特异性 T 细胞的捕获，揭示了这一特殊细胞亚群在助力肿瘤免疫疗法创新上的潜力。这些活体化学驱动的生物技术创新为新药研发提供了新思路、新途径。

Awardee of Youth Innovation Prize, Chen Peng

Chen Peng was born in Lanzhou City of Gansu Province in June 1979. He obtained BS degree in Chemistry at Peking University in 2002, and Ph.D in Chemistry at The University of Chicago in 2007. After a postdoctoral training at the Scripps Research Institute, he started his independent career at Peking University since 2009. He is currently Professor and Chair of the Department of Chemical Biology at the College of Chemistry and Molecular Engineering, Peking University. He is also the Director of Synthetic and Functional Biomolecule Center at Peking University, Fellow of the Chinese Chemical Society, and Division of Chinese Chemical Society, etc.

Chen Peng's research interest is at the interface of Chemistry and Biology. He has developed bioorthogonal reactions and probes to study protein functions and interactions in living systems. He employed this toolkit to study how the spatial–temporal organized human proteome is rewired during cancer and immune signaling, and his lab also exploited the potential of these new reactions in protein–based therapy. His lab is a leading group in developing bioorthogonal cleavage reactions for chemical controlled protein activation and profiling in living systems. He also developed a series of genetically encoded protein labeling, crosslinking and proximity–tagging tools for monitoring biomolecule interactions as well as cell communications during various biological processes.

青年创新奖获得者

刘　诚

刘诚，1981年10月出生于安徽省蚌埠市。2010年博士毕业于德国海德堡大学物理系，随后在美国哈佛大学从事博士后研究。2015年回国至今在中国科学技术大学工作，现任精密机械与精密仪器系执行主任，同时担任国家重点研发计划“臭氧及前体物多源卫星高分辨率遥感与集成解析技术”项目负责人、“地球观测与导航”专项总体专家组成员。

刘诚致力于发展我国自主可控的温室气体和污染气体天空地一体化超光谱遥感技术，研发了国产卫星在轨超光谱定标与多组分气体反演技术，实现了我国首个污染气体卫星载荷EMI和首个温室气体卫星TanSat的精准遥感；研发地基超光谱遥感技术，推动了我国自主可控温室/污染气体超光谱遥感的科技创新。

一、研发国产超光谱卫星遥感技术

刘诚针对国产超光谱卫星载荷发射后性能随时间衰变给光谱反演带来的不利影响，研发了在轨超光谱实时定标技术，修正了国产EMI载荷和碳卫星载荷的波长漂移、光谱形变和辐亮度失真，为实现温室/污染气体的准确反演创造了必不可少的条件。基于校正后的卫星超光谱，进一步研发了低信噪比下的多组分气体反演技术，实现了基于国产超光谱卫星载荷EMI的高精度污染气体反演；同时，在太阳耀斑观测模式下实现了国产碳卫星的CO_2反演，满足了全球CO_2监测的精度要求。超光谱卫星遥感技术成果获安徽省科学技术奖一等奖，并入选2021年度中国生态环境十大科技进展。

卫星在轨超光谱定标技术被生态环境部卫星环境应用中心用于国产超光谱卫星载荷的在轨测试，为太空环境下性能剧烈变化的国产卫星提供了长期稳定观测的基础。基于自主研发的遥感技术，实现了对国产超光谱卫星载荷观测光谱的当天反演，突破了欧美卫星不提供近实时光谱的制约，大幅提升了国产卫星遥感的时效性，被生态环境部卫星环境应用中心、上海市生态环境局等部门用于北京冬奥会、中国国际进口博览会的空气质量保障工作，实现了我国重大活动的空气质量保障用国产卫星观测支撑。由于遥感结果的准确性和在大气污染防治工作中的实用性，受邀提供自主研发的卫星遥感成果，作为生态环境部卫星环境应用中心大气环境遥感监测和分析应用的标准产品，遥感技术的工程化编码程序已在卫星中心完成整体部署，并被生态环境部、中国环境监测总站、国家大气污染防治攻关联合中心和20余家地方政府部门应用于我国的减污降碳工作，实现了工业园区有毒有害气体的遥感监测，相关成果获国家科学技术进步奖二等奖。

二、研发超光谱地基垂直遥感技术

针对我国长期缺乏高分辨地基遥感技术的不利现状，刘诚开展地基超光谱遥感技术研究工作，研发了干涉条纹成像硬件定标技术和基于太阳散射光谱的多元梯度回归超光谱定标算法，获得了准确的地基观测光谱；研发了增益权数先验迭代技术，通过融合卫星遥感和空气质量模型等多源数据，弥补了传统最优估计算法受先验信息约束过大的缺陷，实现了多组分污染气体和温室气体垂直廓线的精准反演，从垂直演化的新视角提出了对大气污染来源和成因机制的新认识。在此基础上，突破了从时效性差、只能在稳定环境条件下运行的实验室研究到在野外复杂环境下落地应用的瓶颈，实现了长期稳定的业务化观测，建立了我国具有完全自主知识产权、能够同时观测多组分气体垂直结构的超光谱地基遥感网络和我国首个达到全球总碳柱网观测质量标准的高分辨率傅立叶变换遥感站点，验证了美国OCO-2、日本GOSAT等国际卫星对我国温室气体浓度观测的准确性，研究成果获中国青年科技奖。自主研发的温室/污染气体垂直廓线被欧空局、美国大气海洋局等多个国际机构的卫星产品研发团队用于卫星结果的准确性验证，提升了我国在大气环境监测领域的国际话语权；牵头制定超光谱遥感领域团体标准2项，并受邀与生态环境部卫星环境应用中心合作构建我国大气环境卫星遥感地基验证技术体系，为多个省市政府部门解决臭氧污染垂直交换影响评估、大气污染物高空传输溯源等环保工作中的实际难题。温室/污染气体天空地一体化超光谱遥感领域的研究成果获国家发明专利授权10余项，并获中国专利优秀奖等奖励。

在学术研究基础上，建立了向科研院校、环保部门免费共享的温室/污染气体遥感数据库，数据下载量已超110万TB；关键核心技术在多家上市公司实现成果转化，推动了我国环境监测产业的发展。

Awardee of Youth Innovation Prize, Liu Cheng

Liu Cheng was born in Bengbu City of Anhui Province in October 1981. He completed his doctoral studies in 2010 at Heidelberg University in Germany in the Department of Physics. Subsequently, he conducted postdoctoral research at Harvard University in the United States.

In 2015, he returned to China and worked at the University of Science and Technology of China (USTC) . Since 2019, he has been appointed the Executive Director of the Department of Precision Machinery and Precision Instruments at USTC. Liu Cheng also serves as the project leader for the National Key Research and Development Program of China on "High-Resolution Remote Sensing and Integrated Resolution Technology for Multi-Source Satellite Observation of Ozone and Its Precursors" and is a member of the overall expert group for the National Key Research and Development Program of China on "Earth Observation and Navigation" .

Cheng Liu has long been dedicated to advancing autonomous and controllable hyperspectral remote sensing technology for greenhouse gases and pollution gases in China. He developed calibration and multi-component gas retrieval techniques for domestic satellites in orbit, achieving precise remote sensing for China's first pollution gas satellite payload EMI and the first greenhouse gas satellite TanSat. Additionally, he pioneered ground-based hyperspectral remote sensing technology, which enabled China to meet Global Total Carbon Column Observing Network (TCCON) quality standards for vertical observation of greenhouse gases. These accomplishments represent a departure from the long-standing reliance on foreign satellite payloads and has fostered technological innovation in China's autonomous and controllable hyperspectral remote sensing of greenhouse gases and pollution gases.

青年创新奖获得者

刘　洋

刘洋，女，1978 年 10 月出生于河南省郑州市。特级航天员。2018 年获清华大学社会科学学院法学博士学位。2010 年 5 月入选中国第二批航天员。2012 年 6 月执行神舟九号载人飞行任务，在轨飞行 13 天。2019 年任中国航天员科研训练中心高级工程师。2022 年 6 月执行神舟十四号载人飞行任务，在轨飞行 183 天。

刘洋是我国首位执行载人航天飞行任务的女航天员，长期从事载人航天相关技术工作，在航天员选拔训练、航天食品研制、环控生命保障、空间医学实验等方面作出一系列工作，解决了航天员长期在轨飞行面临的部分难题，为载人航天事业作出了重大贡献。曾荣获国家科技进步奖特等奖、载人航天飞行任务特殊贡献奖等奖项，以及二级航天功勋奖章、三级航天功勋奖章、“英雄航天员”等荣誉称号。

一、执行神舟九号、神舟十四号两次载人飞行任务

突破航天员手控交会对接地面训练技术，飞行乘组圆满完成首次在轨手控高精度交会对接，解决了我国空间站建设舱段在轨组装难题，成果应用于后续航天员训练及在轨飞行任务，实现空间手控交会对接技术的重大突破；突破真空、低重力、强辐射等特殊环境下防护和极端训练要求，实现我国女性航天飞行零的突破，进一步扩大了载人航天工程的社会影响，向全世界展示了中国女性的良好形象；神舟十四号任务在轨飞行 183 天，天地协同配合完成了九种组合体构型试验、五次交会对接试验、两次分离撤离和两次太空转位试验，为我国空间站组装建造奠定了坚实基础；首次利用气闸舱实施出舱活动，并使用组合臂支持两次出舱活动，为后续出舱活动奠定了技术基础；在轨飞行期间，完成了国家级太空实验室的建设，并成功开展百余项多学科复杂空间科学与技术实 / 试验。

二、参与环境控制与生命保障系统研制

参与大小便收集装置等十余种产品研制，解决了空间微重力、复杂人机接口界面、高装配集成度等约束条件下操作工效学、防误操作、安装维护可靠性等多目标平衡与优化难题，确保了微重力条件下多舱段的环境舒适性；参与二氧化碳还原系统总装集成、维修性设计、在轨操作流程设计等环节的研制工作，并完成在轨组装及验证工作，使水资源的物质闭合度提高到90%以上，大幅降低通过地面携带消耗品的上行补给负担，成果应用于空间站飞行任务，保证了二氧化碳还原系统在轨运行和关键技术验证的顺利完成。

三、完成多项技术攻关任务

结合自身飞行体验，为载人航天工程各系统提出空间结构布局、人机交互操作等技术优化和改进建议50余项；参加航天食品研制、环控控制与生命保障、空间医学实验等科研攻关20余项，突破了菜肴类食品超长时间保藏、双标记水法能量代谢测量优化、物化再生生保性能提升、座舱环境应急生理限制等关键技术四项。相关研究成果成功应用于空间站任务，为我国空间站安全、长期、高效运行作出重大贡献。

Awardee of Youth Innovation Prize, Liu Yang

Liu Yang, female, was born in Zhengzhou City of Henan Province in October 1978. In 2018, she graduated from School of Social Sciences, Tsinghua University with a Juris Doctor degree, now is a special-class astronaut. In May 2010, selected as the second batch of Chinese astronauts. In June 2012, flew in orbit for 13 days during Shenzhou-9 manned spaceflight mission. In October 2012, granted the honorary title of "Heroic Astronaut", and awarded a third-grade Space Service Medal. In 2019, appointed as a senior engineer in China Astronaut Research and Training Center. From June 2022, she experienced a 183 days spaceflight during Shenzhou-14 manned spaceflight mission, and awarded a second-grade Space Service Medal in 2023. Additionally, she also awarded the Medal for Special Achievements to Manned Spaceflight Mission in 2012, and National Science and technology progress award-special award in 2013.

As the first Chinese female astronaut participating in a manned spaceflight mission, Liu Yang has been constantly engaged in tasks related to manned spaceflight technologies, executed a series of research work involving astronaut selection and training, space food research & development, environmental control and life support and space medical experiments, solved several problems faced by astronauts in long-term orbital flight, and made significant contributions to the cause of manned spaceflight.

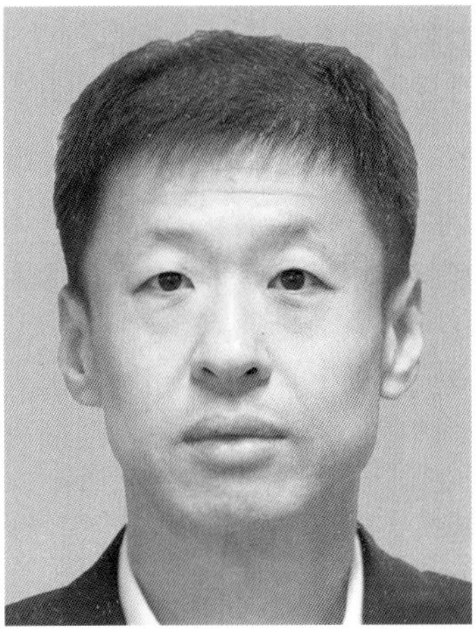

青年创新奖获得者

娄智勇

娄智勇，1980 年 1 月出生于天津市。2002 年获清华大学物理系学士学位，2007 年获清华大学生物系博士学位，后留校工作。现任清华大学医学院教授、研究员，兼任中国生物物理学会常务理事等职务。

娄智勇从事分子病毒学研究，在高致病性病毒感染、复制、与宿主相互作用的分子机制以及抗病毒抑制剂研究等方面作出了系列创新性成果。围绕冠状病毒、布尼亚病毒、流感病毒等，系统研究了冠状病毒转录复制过程，揭示了 RNA 合成、复制校正、加帽等核心步骤的机制，发现了新的药物靶点，为抗病毒药物研发提供了关键科学基础；揭示了布尼亚病毒、流感病毒等的转录复制机制。曾获谈家桢创新奖、树兰医学奖等。

一、冠状病毒转录复制机制的系统性研究

自 2003 年“非典”疫情后，娄智勇长期从事冠状病毒转录复制机制研究，明确了转录复制复合体在病毒生命周期各阶段的功能形式，揭示了 RNA 合成、复制校正、加帽等核心步骤的分子机制，发现了新的药物靶点。该系列工作是国际上迄今为止在新冠病毒转录复制领域最系统的工作之一。

1. 新冠病毒 RNA 合成与延伸机制研究

在国际上首次解析了病毒核心转录复制复合体的结构，阐明了聚合酶合成 RNA 的机制，提出瑞德西韦等核苷类药物的作用机制和可能的局限性，为抗病毒药物研发提供关键信息；发现解旋酶与聚合酶的直接耦合，阐明了解旋酶驱动的 RNA 链延伸机制。

2. 新冠病毒错配矫正机制研究

首次发现新冠病毒“反式互补”的复制校正机制，揭示病毒通过该途径逃逸核苷类抗病毒药物的机制，为发展新型抗病毒药物提供关键信息。该成果被评为 2021 年度中国生命科学十大科技进展和 2021 年度中国科学十大进展。

3. 新冠病毒加帽机制研究

发现聚合酶 NiRAN 结构域是合成病毒 RNA 帽结构的关键酶分子，回答了冠状病毒领域近 30 年的未解之谜，证实其作为药物靶点的潜力。在此基础上，进一步发现新冠病毒特有的由 NiRAN 结构域催化发生 RNAylation 蛋白质修饰以及由 RNAylation 介导的 RNA 加帽新途径，是首次在自然界中发现该类型的蛋白质修饰和加帽机制，并阐明了药物抑制该过程的机制，提出 induce-and-lock 的药物设计思路。这一工作更新了对病毒生命过程的理解，为进一步发展全新机制的抗病毒药物提供了新的靶点和独特思路。

二、布尼亚病毒家族转录复制机制的系统性研究

娄智勇团队系统研究了发热伴血小板减少综合征病毒、布尼维尔病毒、克里米亚－刚果出血热病毒、汉塔病毒等代表性布尼亚病毒核蛋白复合体的组装机制以及病毒转录复制的分子机制，系统揭示了布尼亚病毒核蛋白复合体的形成、功能机制、演化规律，为理解负链 RNA 病毒的复制机制提供了系统、完整的范例。

Awardee of Youth Innovation Prize, Lou Zhiyong

Lou Zhiyong was born in Tianjin City in January 1980. He received Bachelor of Science degree in Academic Talent Program, Department of Physics, Tsinghua University, in 2002. After graduation, Lou commenced his Ph.D. studies in structural biology and molecular virology at School of Medicine in Tsinghua University, and received Doctor of Science degree in 2007.

Lou's research is focused on understanding the molecular mechanisms underlying the life cycle of virus, and in the development of novels antiviral inhibitors. As a molecular virologist, he has revealed fundamental mechanistic insights into the structure and the function of the replication-transcription complexes of coronaviruses (including SARS-CoV and SARS-CoV-2), assembly and function of ribonucleoprotein complex of highly pathogenic bunyavirus and influenza virus. Since the early days of COVID-19 pandemic, he has been dedicated to the systematic study of the assembly and the working mechanisms of SARS-CoV-2 Replication-Transcription Complex, leading to the in-depth understanding of the life cycle of SARS-CoV-2 and the discovery of new therapeutic targets and inhibitors.

Lou is awarded C.C. Tan Life Science Innovation Award in 2020, Shu-Lan Medicine Award for Young Scientist in 2014, and etc. His scientific achievements are selected as 10-Major National Scientific Progress (2021), 10-Major Scientific Progress in Life Sciences (Association for Science and Technology, 2021 and 2017), 10-Major Scientific Progress of MOE Universities (Ministry of Education, 2016 and 2009), Science and Technology Award of Beijing (2011) .

青年创新奖获得者

陆 朝 阳

陆朝阳，1982年11月出生于浙江省东阳市。2004年获中国科学技术大学学士学位，2011年获英国剑桥大学博士学位。2011年回国任中国科学技术大学教授，2021年起兼任中国科学技术大学上海研究院执行院长，2022年起任上海量子科学中心副主任，2023年起任合肥国家实验室量子计算部执行主任。

陆朝阳致力于量子信息科学的数理基础交叉领域研究，在国际上首次实验阐明了虚数在量子力学中的必要性这一基础数学问题，研制了国际最高品质和效率的半导体量子点单光子源和纠缠光源作为量子技术的核心物理资源，实现“多自由度量子隐形传态”，开拓了多自由度量子调控新方向；负责完成“九章光量子计算机”国家重大任务，使我国首次成功达到“量子计算优越性”历史性里程碑。系统性工作确立了我国该领域在国际上的引领地位。陆朝阳是首位入选美国光学学会阿道夫隆奖章、美国物理学会量子计算奖、IUPAP-ICO光学青年科学家奖、CLEO高登讲席的中国科学家。其研究成果五次入选中国科技十大进展新闻，并获国家自然科学奖一等奖、中国物理学会黄昆奖、日本仁科芳雄亚洲奖、欧洲物理学会菲涅尔奖、全球华人物理学会亚洲成就奖等诸多国内外奖项。

一、证明虚数 *i* 在量子力学中的必要性，阐明量子算法的数学基础

通过高精度的量子操控技术，首次开展了对实数形式下标准量子力学的定量实验检验，在无探测漏洞和严格满足爱因斯坦定域条件下，以43个标准差的实验精度证明了复数在标准量子力学中的必要性，回答了这个古老而基础的问题。

成果阐明了量子信息的数学基础问题，对量子算法设计具有基础和深远的意义。该工作与激光聚变跨越盈亏点、詹姆斯韦布空间望远镜等成果一起入选美国物理学会“国际物理学年度十大进展”。

二、实现高品质的单光子和纠缠光源，奠定可实用化量子技术的物理基础

系统揭示了影响半导体量子点单光子相干性退化和效率低的物理机制，首创脉冲共振激发方法、高 Purcell 微柱腔耦合技术、双色共振相干激发、原位非对称微腔耦合量子点等理论和实验，在国际上首次成功研制出同时具备高纯度、高全同性和高效率的量子点单光子源。发展起来的半导体量子点单光子源系列原创性方法被包括哈佛大学、斯坦福大学、剑桥大学、牛津大学、麻省理工学院在内的全球 180 多个研究组采用。四次入选美国光学学会“国际光学年度重要进展”。

在非线性光学方面，提出相位匹配、共线参量转换、频率解关联等，首次实现 6 光子纠缠、8 光子纠缠、10 光子纠缠、12 光子纠缠、多自由度 18 比特超纠缠态制备，五次刷新光量子纠缠的国际记录。作为国际上光量子计算实验的早期开拓者，率先开展利用光子演示 Shor 分解、容失编码、线性方程组和量子机器学习。

三、光量子信息技术的里程碑式突破：多自由度隐形传态和九章量子计算

1. 多自由度量子隐形传态开辟了多自由度量子调控新方向

未来量子计算机互连组网的主要方式是通过量子隐形传态。然而，自 1993 年量子隐形传态理论（获沃尔夫奖）和 1997 年实验演示（获诺贝尔奖）以来，一个根本的局限是：只能传输基本粒子的单一自由度。

面对该挑战，陆朝阳提出单光子非破坏测量理论，使得可以感知到单个光子而不破坏它，从而打破了笛卡尔奖得主 Kwiat 关于多自由度无法隐形传态的论断，在国际上首次实现多自由度量子隐形传态，从基本原理和关键技术上把量子隐形传态提升到一个新的水平，为可扩展量子计算网络奠定了物理基础。该工作入选 2015 年英国物理学会评选的“年度突破”（Breakthrough of the year）。每年在全球范围内仅选一项，属中国本土成果首次入选。

2. 光量子计算原型机“九章”确立我国量子计算方向的国际领先地位

自 1981 年费曼提出量子计算概念以来，整个领域 40 年追求的一个重大里程碑目标就是“量子计算优越性”，即真正造出量子计算原型机，在对特定问题的求解上展示出超级计算机无法比拟的算力。

自主发展高性能量子光源和高精度锁相干涉线路，研制了 76 光子的量子计算原型机“九章”，实现了对高斯玻色取样任务的快速求解，在国际上首次用光子实现了“量子计算优越性”里程碑。提出量子压缩光受激放大的新实验方法，研制 113 光子 144 模式的量子计算原型机“九章二号”，并演示在具有实用价值的图论问题求解方面带来的量子加速。该成果入选美国物理学会“国际物理年度十大进展”、联合国教科文组织“全球十大数字创新”，并入藏中国国家博物馆。

Awardee of Youth Innovation Prize, Lu Chaoyang

Lu Chaoyang was born in Dongyang City of Zhejiang Province in November 1982. He obtained a bachelor's degree from the University of Science and Technology of China in 2004 and a Ph.D. from the Cavendish Laboratory at the University of Cambridge, United Kingdom, in 2011. Returning to China that same year, he became a professor at the University of Science and Technology of China. Since 2021, he has served as the Deputy Director of the Science and Technology Sector of the National Youth Federation and the Executive Dean of the Shanghai Research Institute of the University of Science and Technology of China. Starting in 2022, he assumed the position of Deputy Director of the Shanghai Center for Quantum Sciences, and in 2023, he became the Executive Director of the Quantum Computing Division at the Hefei National Laboratory.

His accomplishments have been selected five times for the annual Top Ten Progresses in Chinese Science and Technology. Internationally, his work on "Multi-Degree-of-Freedom Quantum Teleportation" was chosen as the Breakthrough of the Year by the Institute of Physics in 2015, marking the first domestic Chinese achievement to receive this accolade. Lu Chaoyang has received numerous awards and honors, including the First Prize of the National Natural Science Award, the Huang Kun Prize of the Chinese Physical Society, the Nishina Asian Award, the Fresnel Prize by the European Physical Society, and the Asian Achievement Award, etc. He is the first Chinese scientist to be awarded the Adolf Lomb Medal by the Optical Society of America, the Ralf Landauer and Charles H. Bennett Award in Quantum Computing by the American Physical Society, the IUPAP-ICO Young Scientist Prize in Optics, and the James P. Gordon Memorial Speakership at CLEO.

Lu Chaoyang's groundbreaking experiments have shed light on the necessity of complex numbers in quantum mechanics, addressing a fundamental mathematical question. He has developed semiconductor single-photon sources and entangled light sources as crucial physical resources for quantum technology. His achievements include multi-degree-of-freedom quantum teleportation, pioneering new directions in multi-degree-of-freedom quantum control. Notably, he led the project of the "Jiuzhang Optical Quantum Computer", marking a historic milestone for China's successful attainment of "quantum computing supremacy". Through his systematic work, China has established its leadership position in this field internationally.

青年创新奖获得者

张 阿 漫

张阿漫，1981 年 3 月出生于江西省武宁县。2003 年获大连理工大学工学学士学位，2007 年获哈尔滨工程大学工学博士学位，2011 年赴英国伦敦大学学院访学。2006 年起在哈尔滨工程大学工作，现任哈尔滨工程大学科学技术协会秘书长，兼中国船舶力学学术委员会副主任。

张阿漫从事水下气泡动力学研究，在气泡理论方程、模型算法、工业软件、试验技术、服务国家重大型号等方面作出一系列开创性工作。

一、创立气泡统一方程，同时计入边界、多气泡、可压缩迁移等条件和因素，破解了气泡理论难题，提出了近边界气泡多涡环模型与方法，揭示了气泡脉动与射流形成机制，实现了水下冲击载荷定量评估与设计

构造波动方程移动点源基本解，同时计入气泡可压缩脉动和迁移效应，建立了气泡统一方程，将不同源 / 尺度 / 环境下的气泡力学行为统一到方程中，Rayleigh-Plesset 方程、Keller 方程为该方程的特例，学术界称为“Zhang 方程”，破解了边界效应、多气泡等条件下气泡理论难题，发现了气泡之间复杂波系相互作用及能量传递新规律；提出气泡三维密度势边界元理论模型和算法，解决了近边界气泡动力学特性精确模拟难题；建立近边界气泡多涡环理论模型与方法，预测精度达 95%，揭示了近边界气泡脉动和高速射流形成机制，实现了近场水下冲击载荷定量评估与设计。

成果有力支撑了我国大型船舶等多型船舶冲击环境预报、评估与设计，有效提升了船舶抗冲击载荷预报能力；为航行体空泡载荷异常分析提供依据，支撑某航行体水下航行；应用于深海勘探新型低频高压气枪阵列研发并实现国产化，且反演算法优于国外。相关成果获国家技术发明奖二等奖、科学探索奖等奖项。

二、提出水下冲击强非线性瞬态气液固全耦合模型与算法，解决了近场接触冲击大密度比、强间断计算难题，主持开发了水下冲击流固耦合 FSLAB 基础工业软件，打破了封锁，在船舶高效能量传递与防护领域获得广泛应用

提出水下冲击强非线性瞬态气液固全耦合模型，建立了适用于近场水下冲击模拟的高精度高效率数值算法，解决了冲击波、气泡与后期涌流作用下船舶沉没全过程力学分析难题；开发水下冲击流固耦合 FSLAB 基础工业软件并获得广泛应用，核心算法精度显著优于通用软件；解决了近场接触冲击大密度比、强间断计算难题，揭示了波浪等环境下水下冲击流固耦合规律，为船舶高效能量传递与防护设计提供了基础。

成果为我国海上实船试验工况设定提供了方法，协助完成了大型船舶海上试验结构性能评估；直接支撑我国某水中航行体的评估系统研制，解决了某海洋装备力学分析难题。相关成果获教育部自然科学奖一等奖、国家科技进步奖二等奖等奖项。

三、建立水下气泡高效能量传递方法和多相多介质防护技术，创建大当量功能先进的水下特种试验设施，研制了新型多舱防护结构，在大型船舶高效能量传递与防护设计中发挥重要作用

建立水下气泡高效能量传递方法，发现复杂界面下气泡脉动和射流增强效应，探明了气泡高效能量传递机制，给出了气泡高效能量传递的临界条件；主持创建大当量功能先进的大型特种试验设施，形成大尺度模型试验技术，解决了大尺度和实尺度试验难题，开展系列模型试验，揭示了船舶高效能量传递与防护机制；形成近场水下冲击多相多介质防护技术，自主研制新型多舱防护结构，为提高大型船舶防护能力提供了方法和依据。

成果有力支撑了我国多型船舶抗冲击评估、改进与设计，以及多型舰用大型设备抗冲击能力提升、新型水中航行体评估与设计、航行体高速入水构型设计等研制任务，实现了大型船舶防护能力大幅提升，在我国大型船舶的研制任务中发挥了重要作用。相关成果获全国创新争先奖、省部级科技进步奖一等奖等奖项。

Awardee of Youth Innovation Prize, Zhang Aman

Zhang Aman was born in Wuning County of Jiangxi Province in March 1981. He graduated from Dalian University of Technology in 2003 with a Bachelor Degree in Engineering and earned a Doctoral degree in Engineering from Harbin Engineering University in 2007. He began working at Harbin Engineering University in 2006 and became the Secretary-General of the Harbin Engineering University Science and Technology Association in 2022. He also served as the Vice Chairman of the China Ship Mechanics Academic Committee.

Zhang Aman has been extensively engaged in the study of underwater bubble dynamics, contributing to a series of groundbreaking research efforts in various aspects, including bubble theorical equations, model and algorithms, industrial software, experimental techniques, and national major projects.

He proposed the unified bubble equation, referred to as the "Zhang's equation" in academia, which simultaneously incorporates the effects of boundaries, multiple bubbles, compressible migration, etc., and successfully resolved longstanding challenges in bubble theory. He proposed a near-boundary multi-vortex ring bubble model and method, unveiled the mechanism of bubble pulsation and jet formation, and realized the quantitative evaluation and design of underwater impact loads.

He proposed a fully coupled strong nonlinear model and algorithm for solving the Gas-Fluid-Structure Interaction in underwater impact, which effectively addresses the formidable computation challenges of intense density contrast and strong discontinuities in near-field contact impacts. He led the development of the underwater impact Fluid-Structure Interaction basic industrial software FSLAB, which shattered the technological blockade and found wide-ranging applications in the fields of efficient energy transfer and protection for ships.

He established efficient underwater bubble energy transmission methods and multiphase, multimedium protection technology, established high-capacity advanced underwater specialized test facilities, conducted a series of experiments, and developed innovative multi-compartment protection structures, which played a crucial role in the design of high-efficiency energy transmission and protection for large vessels.

青年创新奖获得者

郑 海 学

郑海学，1979 年 4 月出生于河南省淮滨县。2007 年获中国农业科学院研究生院农学博士学位。2008—2009 年在英国 Pirbright 研究所任科研助理。2009 年回国后工作于中国农业科学院兰州兽医研究所，先后任家畜疫病病原生物学国家重点实验室研究员、实验室主任、所长。2021 年 10 月至今任兰州大学动物医学与生物安全学院院长。中国农业大学、南京农业大学和河南农业大学等兼职教授，农业部第七届兽药评审委员会评审专家，中国兽医协会学术委员会主任，中国畜牧兽医学会口蹄疫学分会理事长。

郑海学从事重大动物疫病基础理论与防控技术研究，在重大动物疫病病原流行变异、感染致病和免疫机制研究及防控产品创制等方面作出了一系列开创性工作，有力推动了口蹄疫和非洲猪瘟等重大动物疫病理论创新，为疫苗设计创制、国家重大动物疫病防控和畜牧业健康发展作出了突出贡献。先后获得国家科技进步奖二等奖、全国创新争先奖状、中国专利优秀奖等国家及省部级奖项 12 项。

一、立足临床防疫一线，发现我国的 O 型口蹄疫毒株发生宿主嗜性改变，揭示其嗜性改变的分子基础，为我国口蹄疫防控产品的创制和防控策略的优化调整提供重要科学依据

首次揭示非编码区可调控 FMDV 宿主嗜性改变，这一结论改变了“受体位点突变和 3A 蛋白编码区缺失致 FMDV 嗜性改变”的传统认知。阐明了猪口蹄疫形成原因，为研制猪用 O 和 A 二价疫苗提供理论依据，为农业农村部调整全国免疫政策提供了重要依据，增加了对猪同时免疫 A 型和 O 型口蹄疫疫苗。

二、面向病毒理论前沿，在全基因组水平上系统鉴定 FMDV 免疫抑制蛋白，揭示了其抑制Ⅰ型干扰素信号通路活化的机制，深化了对 FMDV 免疫抑制与逃逸的理论认知，为设计免疫抑制消除性疫苗提供了新靶点

在全基因组水平上系统筛选并鉴定了 FMDV 免疫抑制蛋白 9 个，进一步阐明了其免疫抑制机制，从病毒和宿主两个层面揭示了 FMDV 引起免疫抑制和促进病毒复制、增强致病性的机理，深化了对 FMDV 免疫抑制和逃逸的理论认知，拓宽了宿主抗感染免疫的生物学认知。研究结果为下一步疫苗种毒设计构建、生产细胞改造、疫苗免疫效力提升提供了理论依据。

三、围绕国家重大需求，发明单质粒 FMDV 拯救系统，理论指导疫苗设计创制，突破了流行病毒自然属性缺陷限制疫苗发展的技术障碍

国际首创 FMDV 单质粒拯救系统，为疫苗种毒定向设计构建提供了技术平台。借助上述平台建立设计构建疫苗种毒的方法，创新疫苗种毒制备技术，实现国际首例构建的口蹄疫疫苗种毒应用于生产，解决了 A/Sea-97 谱系毒株防控的世界难题，被 OIE/FAO 口蹄疫参考实验室推荐使用。实现国际首例猪用重组口蹄疫二价高效疫苗、一类疫苗，是我国口蹄疫防控的主导产品。

先后获新兽药注册证书 3 项，其中一类新兽药证书 1 项，转让企业生产和全国推广应用，引领了动物重大疫病疫苗行业发展，对我国“Asia1 型免疫根除、A 型免疫 4 年无疫、O 型有效控制”的国家防疫大局发挥关键性和决定性技术支撑作用，有力保障了我国畜牧业健康发展，推动了行业科技进步和企业国际竞争力提升。该成果是“十三五”健康养殖领域五个标志性成果之一，获国家科学技术进步奖二等奖、甘肃省技术发明奖一等奖、神农中华农业科技奖一等奖、甘肃省工业优秀新产品奖一等奖。

四、响应国家重大急需，攻关完成非洲猪瘟病毒（ASFV）全基因组天然免疫调控基因的筛选和鉴定，阐明了调控宿主免疫应答机制；攻关非洲猪瘟亚单位疫苗，突破有效免疫保护世界难题，建立了疫苗生产线并通过 GMP 静态验收，有望为我国实现非洲猪瘟净化提供有力、有效的核心“武器”

带领团队在全基因组层面筛选出有效抗非洲猪瘟病毒的重组蛋白，优化组合配制非洲猪瘟 7 组分亚单位疫苗，有效抑制非洲猪瘟病毒复制和增殖，成功解决了非洲猪瘟亚单位疫苗无法提供有效免疫保护的世界难题，完成了实验室和中间试制等所有疫苗申报所需的试验，并建立该疫苗生产线，通过 GMP 静态验收，正在推进疫苗应急评价，加紧推进产业化，将为实现我国非洲猪瘟防控和净化提供最核心的疫苗技术支撑。

Awardee of Youth Innovation Prize, Zheng Haixue

Zheng Haixue was born in Huaibin County of Henan Province in April 1979. He gained his Ph.D. degree at Graduate School of Chinese Academy of Agricultural Sciences in 2007. From 2008 to 2009, he worked in Pirbright institute as a research assistant. In 2009 he came back to Lanzhou Veterinary Research Institute and successively served as the director of the State Key Laboratory on Veterinary Etiological Biology, the director general of Lanzhou Veterinary Research Institute, and later as the dean of College of Veterinary Medicine and Biosecurity, Lanzhou University.

He developed his interests in academic and translational research on major animal disease and achieved a serial of pioneering breakthroughs, especially in uncovering viral diversity and evolution, infection, pathogenesis and immunity as well as developing preventive animal health products.

He discovered the host tropism shift of FMD serotype O and revealed the molecular basis for FMD host tropism variation, providing key academic basis and evidence for designing preventive products and optimizing prevention and control measures. He identified the FMD immunosuppressive proteins at the whole genome level, revealed the mechanism–of–action of suppressing type I interferon pathway and deepened the understanding of immune inhibition and evasion of FMD, providing new therapeutic target for developing non–immunosuppressive vaccines. He developed the FMDV single–plasmid rescue system, serving as a theoretical framework for vaccine design and development. This breakthrough has effectively overcome the technical obstacles presented by the inherent limitations of epidemic strains. Additionally, Zheng's lab has completed the screening and identification of natural immune regulatory genes in the entire genome of African swine fever virus (ASFV), elucidating the mechanism of regulating the host immune response. They has broken through the world challenge of effective immune protection by tackling the subunit vaccine of ASF. It is expected to provide a powerful and effective core weapon for China to combat with ASF.

青年创新奖获得者

赵 立 东

赵立东，1979 年 3 月出生于黑龙江省哈尔滨市。2009 年获北京科技大学材料学博士学位，2009—2014 年先后在法国巴黎第十一大学和美国西北大学从事博士后研究。2014 年入职北京航空航天大学，现任北京航空航天大学材料科学与工程学院副院长，兼任中国材料研究学会热电材料及应用分会理事。

赵立东长期从事热电材料的开发与应用，致力于利用各向异性解耦热传输和电传输的矛盾，开发宽温域高效热电材料，在温差发电和半导体制冷领域作出了一系列开创性工作。曾获教育部自然科学奖二等奖、中国材料研究学会科学技术奖二等奖等奖项。

一、基于强非谐振效应的低热导材料

率先开发出高性能硒化锡（SnSe）晶体热电材料，并揭示了其源于声子在热传输中偏离平衡位置产生的热振动——非谐振效应，进一步发现 SnSe 的强非谐振效应源于其特殊的层状和非对称晶体结构。借助层状结构的各向异性，通过生长高质量的 SnSe 晶体，在其层内获得优异的载流子迁移率和导电性，使 SnSe 晶体沿晶体学 b 轴方向在 923 K 的 *ZT* 值可达 2.6。在一个长期被认为不符合热电特征的宽带隙半导体中发现了其高温优异热电性能，并在此基础上先后开发了一系列具有本征低热导特性的高效热电材料，如 BiCuSeO、$K_2Bi_8Se_{13}$、$BiSbSe_3$、BiSeBr 等，极大拓宽了热电材料的研究范畴。

二、多能带协同参与的电传输增强机制

利用 SnSe 等材料的复杂能带结构，通过掺杂改性提高载流子浓度，通过激活费米能级移动促进多个能带参与电传输，实现了多能带协同参与的电传输性能优化，实现了 SnSe 晶体宽温域（300～773K）的整体性能提升。进一步发展了 SnS 材料多个价带随温度升高的动态交互作用，通过适当元素固溶促进多价带传输，在低成本、环境友好和储量

丰富的 SnS 中实现了宽温域高效热电性能；揭示并促进了 SnSe 材料多价带在动量空间和能量空间的协同效应（首次将该效应命名为 Synglisis），大幅优化了 SnSe 晶体的宽温域性能并逐步将其优异热电性能拓展至室温区域，首次开发了宽带隙 SnSe 晶体基热电器件的温差发电和电子制冷性能，打破了以往热电理论中“热电制冷材料必须是窄带隙半导体或半金属材料”的传统认知。这些成果引起了国际上对于 SnSe 等材料多能带结构特征广泛的理论和实验研究，赵立东带领团队先后为国内外数十家科研机构提供高性能 SnSe 晶体样品。

三、“二维声子－三维电荷”热电输运特性

基于 SnSe 材料层状结构的各向异性，发现材料沿层外方向的极低热传导特性（二维声子）；通过 N 型电子掺杂促进电子离域交叠杂化，得到高的层间电荷密度，实现层间电子隧穿（三维电荷），大幅提高了 N 型 SnSe 晶体沿层外方向的热电性能；进一步提出利用层状结构促进声－电解耦的性能优化思路，设计了通过引入应力提升 SnSe 晶体结构对称性以提升其声－电解耦程度的实验方案，通过降低形变势解耦层状材料电声传输耦合效应，大幅优化了 N 型 SnSe 晶体的热电性能。将“二维声子－三维电荷”热电输运特性成功拓展至多个材料体系，开发了 SnS 和 $PbSnS_2$ 等晶体热电材料的层外优异性能。

四、寻找宽温域热电材料的研究思路

提出了筛选新型高效热电材料的规则：大带宽、层状结构和低对称性晶体材料。以上筛选规则突破了热电材料长期受限于窄带半导体的禁锢，逐渐形成了在宽带半导体中寻找高效热电材料的研究思路。

五、新型热电制冷材料的探索和开发

提出基于成分－工艺调控的“栅格化”策略优化热电制冷的研究思路，通过调整材料本征缺陷和载流子浓度，实现超高的载流子迁移率和近室温热电性能，从而实现同体系的高性能 P/N 材料、开发更多传统热电材料的制冷性能，对于热电制冷技术未来的大规模应用十分关键。在此基础上发展了“晶格素化”研究策略，大幅优化了 SnSe 晶体的热电制冷性能，使其可媲美 Bi_2Te_3 的性能水平。与商用 Bi_2Te_3 相比，SnSe 晶体具有成本低、储量丰富、环境友好、可加工性能优异和运行功耗小等优势，展现了巨大的应用潜力。

Awardee of Youth Innovation Prize, Zhao Lidong

Zhao Lidong was born in Harbin City of Heilongjiang Province in March 1979. He graduated from University of Science and Technology Beijing in 2009 with doctorate degree in materials science, and engaged in postdoc research at Universite Paris-Sud and Northwestern University from 2009 to 2014. He joined Beihang University in 2014 and currently serves as deputy dean in School of Materials Science and Engineering. He is currently a council member of Chinese Thermoelectric Society, Chinese Materials Research Society. He has won the Second Prize of Natural Science Award of the Ministry of Education, and Second Prize of Science and Technology Award of China Materials Research Society.

Prof. Lidong Zhao is mainly engaged in the research of thermoelectric materials and devices, and the development of high-efficiency thermoelectric materials over wide temperature ranges by decoupling the electron and phonon transports. He has made pioneering academic achievements in the field of thermoelectric power generation and electronic cooling. He discovered a series of new thermoelectrics with intrinsic low thermal conductivity by utilizing the strong anharmonicity. He extended high-efficiency thermoelectric properties to wide temperature ranges by promoting the multiple bands transport. He developed the strategies of "two-dimensional (2D) phonon and 3D charge" transports and layered phonon-electron decoupling for out-of-plane performance enhancement. He proposed the research idea of finding high-efficiency thermoelectrics in wide-bandgap semiconductors. He presented the grid-design method and lattice plainification strategy to develop novel thermoelectric coolers with important application potential. The research team he led has made significant impact in the international thermoelectric field.

产业创新奖获得者

曹宏斌

曹宏斌，1971 年 10 月出生于江苏省南通市。2001 年获天津大学化工学博士学位。2001 年 7 月至今在中国科学院过程工程研究所工作。2013 年 10 月至今，先后担任北京市过程污染控制工程技术研究中心主任、战略金属资源绿色循环利用国家工程中心副主任、中国科学院化学化工科学数据中心主任。中国环境科学学会会士，中国环境科学学会固体废物分会副主任委员，中国环保产业协会冶金环保专业委员会主任委员。

曹宏斌长期从事重化工过程减污降碳技术及其应用研究，针对有毒难降解物质因生产工艺限制进入末端导致的资源浪费、污染排放难以达标和过程碳排放高等“卡脖子”问题，提出了以高效分离回收为重点、生产端与末端统筹的污碳协同控制技术创新模式，突破 20 余项关键核心技术。曾荣获国家技术发明奖二等奖、国家科技进步奖二等奖各 1 项，省部级一等奖 4 项，以及光华工程科技奖 – 青年奖和全国创新争先奖。

一、发明以酚油协同萃取、非均相催化臭氧氧化为核心的煤化工水污染全过程控制关键技术，解决了被发改委和环境部重点关注的煤化工高浓度难降解废水高效处理重大难题

针对煤化工水污染控制难以低成本运行、焦油回收不彻底、无法深度解毒、出水不达标等“卡脖子”难题，研制出高效减排有毒难降解有机物的分离药剂优化设计平台，指导开发出从复杂体系中协同分离回收多 / 杂环芳烃类、酚的酚油协同萃取药剂 IPE–PO，实现有毒难降解物质源头减排与资源化回收；发明梯级催化臭氧氧化技术与装备，解决了生化尾水有机物难氧化与提标排放的难题；发明了生产端到末端协同强化的煤化工水污染全过程控制集成技术，实现资源利用率提高 20% 以上、成本降低超 15%。技术在停产三年的云南先锋化工复产中发挥关键作用，并推广应用到宝武、大唐等央企在内的 30 项工程（含 4 项行业首座工程），保障近 1.2 亿吨煤 / 年安全生产。核心技术 5 次入选国家部委先进技术目录以及国家“十三五”科技创新成就展。

二、发明伯胺萃取分离钒铬、热解络合精馏深度分离重金属－氨新技术，为涉重行业污染物近零排放提供产业化技术与成套装备

针对钒铬、钴镍等冶金行业战略关键金属性质相近、分离效果差、有价资源进入末端增加处理难度等深度分离的国际难题，发明了伯胺萃取分离钒铬新技术与药剂，生产端大幅提升钒、铬回收率，精准减排重金属污染；提出热解络合精馏分离重金属－氨络合物新思路，发明了药剂强化热解络合精馏关键核心技术与成套设备，深度分离母液中的重金属与氨，实现介质回收。建立以“伯胺萃取分离钒铬－热解络合精馏蒸氨－废水处理与分质循环”为核心的钒铬渣高效利用新工艺，从生产端解决了钒铬分离、重金属和氨深度分离的难题，近零排放污染物，总资源利用率提高 30% 以上。基于以上关键技术突破完成了规模化推广，应用至 75 项工程（含 8 项行业首座工程），实现每年减排超过 1 万吨重金属和 10 万吨氨，锂电正极材料覆盖度超过 70%，为我国稀土行业秩序整顿中恢复氨皂工艺提供关键核心技术。核心技术两次入选国家部委先进技术目录。

三、发明以选择性提锂、双极膜酸碱循环等为核心的锂电固废低碳循环利用成套技术，助力我国锂电固废处置实现国际引领

针对新能源固废组成结构复杂、有机－无机多种污染物共存、面临环境－资源－安全多重风险等重大瓶颈问题，提出了基于有价资源短流程循环、复合污染协同控制、工艺全过程优化的原理，通过有价金属选择性提取耦合萃取深度分离，突破了锂电废料选择性提锂、基于活性氧强化的钒 / 铬 / 镍高效提取、含钴废料多组分高值化清洁循环利用等关键核心技术，实现有价资源的短程提取与高值化产品制备。突破了高盐废水双极膜酸碱再生循环、废水高效除油等关键核心技术，实现污染物协同控制与近零排放。研发多单元优化集成技术，指导创建了新能源固废低碳处理技术工艺包，构建了新能源固废短流程低碳高效处理与污染全过程控制技术体系。核心技术成功应用到包括全球最大废锂电池处理企业和我国最大钴生产企业在内的 11 项产业化工程（含 4 项行业首座工程），锂回收率由不足 70% 提高到 90% 以上，国内产能覆盖度超过 70%，并推广至 5 家国际企业。主持和参与 16 项相关国家 / 地方 / 行业等标准制定。

Awardee of Industrial Innovation Prize, Cao Hongbin

Cao Hongbin was born in Nantong City of Jiangsu Province in October 1971. He is a professor at the Institute of Process Engineering of Chinese Academy of Sciences (CAS), director of the Chemistry & Chemical Engineering Data Center of CAS, and director of the Beijing Process

Pollution Control Engineering and Technology Research Center. He won Guanghua Engineering Science and Technology Award in 2016, and the National Innovation and Pioneering Award in 2023.

Cao Hongbin has been engaged in the research of pollution control and carbon reduction technology and its application in industry for decades. Aiming at the problem of waste of resources, the difficulty in meeting the discharge standards, and the high carbon emission in the process caused by toxic and hardly degradable substances entering the back-end of the process, he put forward an innovative mode of synergistic whole-process control of pollution and carbon reduction, focusing on high-efficiency separation and recycling, and integrating the manufacturing process with the end governance. He won the second prize of National Technological Invention in 2013, the second prize of National Scientific and Technological Progress in 2018, one special prize of association and four first prizes of province/ministry.

产业创新奖获得者

陈 嘉 川

陈嘉川，1962 年 1 月出生于山东省诸城市。1982 年毕业于山东轻工业学院（现齐鲁工业大学）并留校工作至今。1994 年获华南理工大学制浆造纸专业工学博士学位，1994—1997 年在山东大学生物学博士后流动站开展研究工作。2003—2021 年任齐鲁工业大学校长；2017 年 8 月—2021 年 1 月兼任山东省科学院院长；2018 年 10 月至今担任生物基材料与绿色造纸国家重点实验室主任。中国造纸学会副理事长，中国发酵产业协会副理事长，广西大学和天津科技大学兼职教授。

陈嘉川从事绿色造纸技术研究，突破了制浆造纸过程酶催化等多项绿色造纸关键技术并实现工程化应用，产生了重大经济社会效益，推动了造纸工业的技术进步，拓展了绿色造纸学科领域。

一、揭示并完善绿色生物造纸作用机制

1. 揭示酶催化生物制浆作用机制

研究证明纤维二糖水解酶（CBH）和 β–1,4– 葡聚糖酶（EG）协同作用于植物纤维，操控生物酶复合体系对植物纤维进行有限降解，酶分子首先在纤维表面发生反应，进而浸入纹孔、胞间层和次生壁的非结晶区反应，导致纤维细胞壁的潜态层离，使植物纤维软化，纤维易于分离。进一步研究发现，纤维二糖脱氢酶（CDH）可以和木质素过氧化物酶或锰过氧化物酶构成协同作用关系，促进过氧化物酶对木质素的降解；通过 β– 聚糖酶类处理，有利于纤维的机械帚化和细纤维化，增加纤维结合力；通过酶催化作用定向降解去除部分半纤维素，可改善纸浆滤水性、降低纸页脆性和透明性。

2. 阐释纸浆生物漂白原理

研究发现木聚糖酶的催化作用可以降解木质素 – 碳水化合物复合体（LCC）、去除纤维表面吸附的半纤维素、打通木质素溶出通道，从而使小分子木质素溶出、漂白剂有效

接触有色物或基团；酶催化作用导致己烯糖醛酸溶出，使 -COOH 和 C=C 发色基团减少；催化作用如发生在纤维非结晶区，则纸浆结晶度提高；催化作用如发生在表面，则其氧碳比降低、木质素浓度升高，即导致木质素的裸露，促进木质素与漂白剂的优先反应。

3. 探索非纤维素组分高效转化利用的新方法

针对溶解浆预水解液半纤维素的利用，构建物理化学法协同生物酶途径分离纯化半纤维素路径，发现木聚糖类半纤维素必须在多种酶组分的联合作用下才能实现彻底降解，须构建复合酶体系以实现对木聚糖的高效降解，最终制备木寡糖、木糖和木糖醇产品。利用黑液木质素合成石墨烯量子点（GQDs），并探索了其在 GQDs/TiO_2 光催化剂领域的应用。

二、突破制浆造纸过程酶催化关键技术

1. 生物化机浆制浆技术

根据 CBH、EG 和 β–G 性质的不同和纤维原料的差异，开发出专用酶制剂复合体系。酶预处理使木片得到软化，纤维易于分离，磨浆能耗降低 20% 以上，COD 减少 15% 以上。提出秸秆生物化机浆生物反应系统、磨浆系统和生物质燃料制备系统等技术方案，构建了制备生物化机浆关键技术体系。在高浓磨浆后，针对纤维出现的扭曲潜态性缺陷，用酶促消潜工艺替代传统高温低浓加机械搅拌的消潜工艺，促进了纤维潜态力释放，使能耗降低 25%、纸浆抗张指数提高 18%。

2. 纸浆酶法改性与纯化技术

发现木聚糖酶可使非木浆纤维纯化，少量木聚糖的去除可改善纸浆脆性和强度，脆裂指数降低 20% 以上；纤维素酶具有改进纸浆滤水性的明显作用，并可提高纤维结合力，使纸浆打浆度降低 3～5° SR。针对纸机湿部存在的阴离子垃圾障碍和细小组分流失等问题，研发湿部系统生物酶助留、助滤和增强技术，酶催化处理可使浆中阴离子垃圾降低 65% 以上、抽出物含量下降 40% 以上。

3. 低二氧化氯用量 ECF 漂白技术

针对氯漂导致氯代酚类有毒物质产生且废水无法进入回收系统的问题，将生物漂白（X）、臭氧漂白（Z）应用到 ECF 漂白程序中，使二氧化氯总用量降低 50%、可吸收有机卤化物生成量减少 50% 以上。

制浆造纸过程酶催化关键技术相关成果获国家技术发明奖二等奖。

三、实现绿色造纸技术工程应用与示范

1. 秸秆浆生物漂白与秸秆生物化机浆技术应用示范

通过合作攻关，成功实现非木浆生物漂白、酶法改性的工业应用，建成年产 20 万吨全球最大规模农作物秸秆生物化机浆示范生产线。相关成果获国家科技进步奖二等奖。

2. 木浆臭氧漂白与 ECF 漂白工程应用

设计 X/Z/D 等顺序漂白单元并应用于 X/Z/D-E_{OP}-D 等漂白流程，可减少 1 个二氧化氯漂白段、用水量节省 25% 以上。相关技术在我国木浆产能最大的企业成功应用。相关成果获国家科技进步奖二等奖。

3. 废纸生产新闻纸和包装纸工程应用

对废纸原料特别是旧瓦楞箱纸板进行分级，并借助纤维素酶的细纤维化作用提高纤维结合力、降低产品定量，节省纤维资源。合作项目“废纸制浆关键技术研究”在国内最大规模新闻纸生产线上应用。相关成果获国家科技进步奖二等奖。

Awardee of Industrial Innovation Prize, Chen Jiachuan

Chen Jiachuan was born in Zhucheng City of Shandong Province in January 1962. He received his bachelor's degree from Shandong Light Industries College, and has been working here till now after graduate. He obtained his Ph.D from South China University of Technology in 1994, then worked as a postdoctoral fellow at the postdoctoral research station in biology of Shandong University from 1994 to 1997. He served as the president of Qilu University of Technology and the dean of Shandong Academy of Sciences, and is now the director of the State Key Laboratory of Biobased Materials and Green Papermaking, as well as the vice chairman of the Chinese Paper Society and other academic posts.

Chen Jiachuan has been engaged in the research of green pulping and papermaking science and technology for more than 30 years. Related achievements have won one second prize of National Technological Invention , three second prizes of National Scientific and Technological Progress, six first prizes of provincial and ministerial level.

The mechanism of green pulping and papermaking by microbiological method has been revealed, the key technologies of enzyme catalysis in the pulp and papermaking process have been invented, which has promoted the traditional pulp and papermaking technology innovation and upgrading, then the demonstration applications of green pulping and papermaking technology have been realized. The enzymatic beating, enzymatic eliminating latency, biological bleaching, biological refining and purification were proposed and successfully applied. In order to reduce pollution, save energy and improve pulp and paper properties, the developed technologies of green pulping and papermaking were widely used in the fields of pulp and papermaking engineering with wood, non-wood and waste paper as materials.

产业创新奖获得者

陈　　群

陈群，1963 年 7 月出生于江苏省苏州市。1984 年本科毕业于江苏化工学院基本有机合成专业，后留校工作，历任江苏工业学院化学化工学院院长，常州大学副校长、校长、党委书记等职务。2023 年获俄罗斯乌法科技大学名誉博士。现为中国化工学会常务理事，中国石油和化学工业联合会理事，中国高等教育学会科技服务专家指导委员会副主任委员，教育部高等教育化工类专业教学指导委员会委员。中国化工学会会士。

陈群长期致力于功能聚合物材料、绿色催化等化工清洁生产领域的创新研究，特别是在树脂功能催化材料、金属有机框架材料（MOFs）、离子交换与吸附树脂材料等技术研发和工程应用上作出了一系列开创性工作。

一、树脂功能催化材料和催化工艺

发现反应性高分子骨架和活性巯基分子结构与苯酚烷基化反应历程的构效关系，研制了具有微纳结构特征的系列功能树脂催化剂，首创多烷基酚重排转化的多段绝热固定床反应制造壬基酚工艺和苯酚烷基化清洁催化生产成套技术，自主研发的功能树脂催化剂在双酚 A 国产装置上使用率达 100%，打破了美国 Badger、日本三菱等国外公司同类催化剂的垄断地位。

发明高性能双酚 A 催化剂在线再生技术、减少异构体生成的重排反应技术、悬浮结晶与降膜结晶组合的高效分离技术以及双酚 A 喷雾造粒技术。通过质量分级、热量平衡及副产物综合利用，首创双酚 A– 环氧树脂耦合工艺和绿色制造技术，建成了全球唯一、单线规模最大的 20 万吨 / 年双酚 A– 环氧树脂协同生产装置，开发了具有自主知识产权的单线 24 万吨 / 年双酚 A 工艺包，产品质量和能耗达到国际先进水平。不断延伸拓展功能树脂催化技术应用，首创树脂载体镍基加氢催化剂，用于乙烯法制乙二醇和煤制乙二醇的加氢提质，并在国内 70% 的装置上获得应用。

二、金属有机框架材料和制造工艺

构筑和开发了适用规模化制造的对苯二甲酸 MOFs 材料新结构，首创对苯二甲酸－金属氢氧化物－水绿色反应体系，独创浆料喷射、超声辅助等强化控制技术，实现了高浓度对苯二甲酸与氢氧化钙室温快速反应。开发絮凝除杂、定向结晶、超声分散等集成工艺，形成了从印染行业“碱减量”废水中回收符合配位聚合物单体要求的对苯二甲酸新技术，为 MOFs 合成提供价廉的有机配体，生产成本降低 50%，建成了国内唯一的万吨级 MOFs 生产装置。

发明 MOFs 钙配位缺陷位控制新技术，创制多功能 PVC 材料加工助剂；发明“种子沉积法”和超声辅助微纳材料合成新工艺，开发高分散、低锌轮胎用橡胶硫化活性剂；发明 MOFs 材料双活性位点精准调控技术，研发 L 酸与 B 酸协同催化合成聚乙醇酸新工艺，提高了可降解聚酯的聚合分子量。在国际上率先建成两条 6 万吨 / 年多功能 PVC 助剂和橡胶硫化活性剂生产线、一条 200 吨 / 年低毒高效配位聚合物基催化剂生产线。

三、树脂吸附材料和植物染技术

发明长间隔臂结构大孔强碱性树脂吸附材料，开发水 / 乙醇低温超声高效分离－树脂移动床吸附纯化技术，可选择性分离粗提物中蛋白质、胶糖等杂质化合物，攻克了长期以来植物中色素与糖类杂质分离提纯的难题，制得性能稳定的植物染料粉体产品；开发了可用于数字调色的红、黄、蓝、棕、紫、黑、灰 7 个基础色系植物染料，建成 5 条植物染料粉体生产线，建立了植物染料中关键物质指纹识别方法，主导制定中国首个植物染料团体标准，首次实现植物染料批量化、标准化生产。

发明壳聚糖等天然大分子对色素表面原子结构调控的新方法和新工艺，开发非靛蓝植物染料无盐染色技术以及靛蓝植物染料非保险粉的还原染色技术，解决了色牢度、匀染性和上染率差的难题。发明植物染料聚酯色母粒制备方法和原液着色染整技术，实现合成纤维的工业化无水染色，避免了染料废水难处理问题。首次实现植物染料染色对合成纤维、蛋白质纤维和纤维素纤维的全覆盖，实现了全品类生态纺织品植物染料工程化。产品通过全球有机纺织品标准等权威机构绿色认证 9 项，并在国内 72 家企业推广应用。

Awardee of Industrial Innovation Prize, Chen Qun

Chen Qun was born in Suzhou City of Jiangsu Province in July 1963. He graduated with a bachelor’s degree in basic organic synthesis from Jiangsu University of Chemical Technology in 1984 and was awarded an honorary doctorate from the Ufa University of Technology in Russia in 2023. From 1984 to August 2023, he successively served as the dean of the School of Chemistry and Chemical Engineering at Jiangsu Institute of Technology, the vice president, president, and Party secretary of Changzhou University. Currently, he serves as the executive director of the Chemical Industry and Engineering Society of China (CIESC), the director of the China Petroleum and Chemical Industry Federation, and the vice chairman of the Science and Technology Service Expert Supervisory Committee of the China Association of Higher Education. Moreover, he is a member of the CIESC and a member of the Chemical Engineering Teaching Supervisory Committee of the Department of Higher Education in the Ministry of Education.

Chen Qun has long been committed to the innovative research of functional polymer materials, green catalysis, and other green production fields in chemical engineering. Especially in the technology development and engineering application of resin functional catalytic materials, metal-organic framework materials (MOFs), ion exchange and adsorption resin materials, etc., he has made a series of pioneering works.

产业创新奖获得者

窦　　强

窦强，1973 年 5 月出生于河北省石家庄市。2001 年获国防科技大学工学博士学位，后留校工作至 2018 年，历任计算机研究所副所长、微电子与微处理器研究所所长等。其间于 2013—2014 年赴香港科技大学访学。2018 年至今在飞腾信息技术有限公司工作，现任中国电子信息产业集团科技委副主任、飞腾信息技术有限公司首席科学家。中国计算机学会抗恶劣环境计算机专业委员会常务委员，中国计算机学会计算机工程与工艺专业委员会委员，国防科技大学、上海交通大学、西安电子科技大学兼职博士生导师，南开大学兼职教授。

窦强是我国高性能 CPU 方向的学术带头人之一，突破了多路分组交叉多线程微体系结构、高效能超标量单核微体系结构、芯片设计与境内芯片制造工艺协同优化等关键技术，推动飞腾 CPU 实现从超算专用 CPU 到通用 CPU、再到基于境内芯片制造工艺的全谱系通用 CPU 的跨越式发展，为自主 CPU 领域技术突破作出了系统性贡献；作为飞腾 CPU 总设计师，主持研制成功多代飞腾 CPU，推动其在国防重大工程、国家党政信创工程和国民经济关键行业实施大批量部署超过 600 万片，为解决我国 CPU 芯片长期依赖进口作出突出贡献。相关成果荣获国家科技进步奖特等奖 1 项、一等奖 2 项，省部级科技进步奖一等奖 6 项。其个人荣获第三届全国创新争先奖章、中国计算机学会“王选奖”。

一、突破多路分组交叉多线程微体系结构等并行设计技术，主持研制成功 FT-1000 高性能 CPU，为我国天河等系列高性能计算机 CPU 的自主可控发展奠定了坚实基础

面向超算领域，突破多路分组交叉多线程微体系结构等并行设计技术，大幅提高 CPU 执行科学计算应用的并行性能；突破基于片间直连技术的多路并行架构，解决大规模系统的可扩展性问题。主持研制的 FT-1000 CPU 获省部级科技进步奖一等奖，其中面向大规模科学计算的多路分组交叉多线程体系结构等达到同期国际领先水平。FT-1000 成

功应用于天河一号高性能计算机的自主计算阵列，在科学计算典型应用中发挥重要作用。

二、突破高效能超标量单核微体系结构等设计技术，主持研制成功 FT-1500A 高性能 CPU，实现重大应用领域批量部署，推动我国关键行业信息系统国产化进程

突破高效能超标量单核微体系结构设计技术，显著提升 CPU 单核性能；突破高主频 CPU 设计实现技术，进一步提升 CPU 工作频率和性能；突破多层次细粒度低功耗设计技术，有效降低 CPU 功耗。主持研制的 FT-1500A 高性能 CPU 在高效能超标量单核微体系结构设计方面取得重大创新，是世界上首款兼容 ARM 64 位指令集的 16 核高性能 CPU，处于国际先进。FT-1500A 高性能 CPU 荣获国家科技进步奖一等奖，这是国产 CPU 首获国家科技进步奖一等奖。

三、提出芯片设计与境内芯片制造工艺协同优化等技术，主持完成全谱系飞腾 CPU 基于境内工艺的研制与量产，为解决我国 CPU 芯片供应链安全作出贡献

提出芯片设计与境内工艺协同优化技术，提升芯片性能；提出多维度良率分析优化及仿真与寿命试验拟合的可靠性评估方法，推动境内工艺的生产良率提升，加强批量供货的可靠性保障；提出 CPU 内生安全架构技术，从硬件底层提升 CPU 安全防护能力。采用上述技术，主持完成全谱系飞腾 CPU 基于境内工艺的研制与量产，性能、良率、可靠性等指标整体上与境外同代工艺产品相当，实现了我国高性能 CPU 全流程的国产化。

Awardee of Industrial Innovation Prize, Dou Qiang

Dou Qiang was born in Shijiazhuang City of Hebei Province in May 1973. He is one of the leading academic figures in the field of high-performance CPU in China. He has achieved multiple developments in key technologies including multi-way packet cross-interleaved multi-threading micro-architecture, high-performance super-scalar single-core micro-architecture, and collaborative optimization of chip design and domestic chip manufacturing processes. These advancements have expanded Phytium CPU's marketability beyond specialized CPU for supercomputers into the market for general-purpose CPU, and subsequently to full-spectrum general-purpose CPU applications (utilizing domestic chip manufacturing processes). His contributions have been fundamental to developments within the autonomous CPU technology field. As the Chief Designer of Phytium CPU, Dou Qiang has overseen the successful development of multiple generations of Phytium CPU. He has organized the large-scale supply of 6+ million chips to major national defense projects, national party and government information innovation projects, as well as to fundamental sectors of the national economy. His contributions have been instrumental in overcoming the long-standing issue of China's previous significant dependence on imported CPU chips.

Dou Qiang has been recognized with multiple accolades, including one special prize and two first prizes for national scientific and technological advancements, six first prizes at the provincial and ministerial levels for technological advancements. In 2023, he was awarded the Third National Innovation Medal.

产业创新奖获得者

黄　立

黄立，1963 年 6 月出生于陕西省西安市。1987 年获华中科技大学通信与电子系统专业硕士学位，毕业后进入湖北省电力试验研究所工作。1996 年 11 月—1998 年任武汉中兴电器有限公司总经理，1999 年创办武汉高德红外股份有限公司。现任华中科技大学兼职教授。

黄立是我国高性能红外芯片研发及产业化的主要开拓者和奠基人，带领团队攻克了高端红外核心芯片“卡脖子”难题，成功打破西方技术封锁，扭转了我国红外核心芯片长期受制于人的局面，引领了我国红外产业体系的快速形成和跨越发展，研发产品市场占有率居国内第一、全球第三，为我国国防建设和国计民生作出了重大贡献。

一、攻克超晶格红外探测器芯片“卡脖子”难题，实现红外芯片完全自主可控，奠定我国高性能红外探测器的国际地位

黄立带领武汉高德红外股份有限公司在国内率先开展超晶格探测器芯片技术研究，首创基于 shDFT-1/2 算法能带技术，完成全红外波段超晶格结构设计；首次提出界面二维层状生长工艺，突破超晶格材料外延关键技术；首创超晶格芯片工艺制程，研制成功国内首款长波和双色大面阵超晶格红外探测器芯片，填补了国内空白，整体达到国际先进水平，其中关键指标 NETD 和像素分辨率达到国际领先水平。主持创建了国内第一条超晶格探测器生产线、碲镉汞探测器批产线和氧化钒探测器批产线，累计销售红外探测器芯片 100 余万片。相关成果获 2020 年湖北省科技进步奖一等奖。

超晶格红外探测器芯片关键技术的突破，解决了我国红外探测领域“缺芯少核”的问题，为我国在高过载图像识别、天基预警、夜视夜战、精确打击、空间遥感、航空航天等高端装备领域的应用奠定了基础。

二、研制成功新一代高超声速导弹红外探测装置、机载导弹逼近红外告警系统和第四代红外成像自寻的反坦克导弹，在主力战机、战略导弹等国之重器中得到应用

提出超晶格红外探测器高温辐射抑制、百微秒级积分时间自适应技术路线，主持研制成功新一代高超声速战略导弹红外导引头，成功应用于国之重器的新一代中远程高超声速战略导弹，大幅提升了我军精确制导武器的全天候打击能力和对航母等目标的打击精度。

攻克自适应灰度梯度抑制算法和弱小目标时空域能量累积等关键技术，主持研制成功主力战机用导弹逼近红外告警系统，实现了全空域导弹来袭告警，填补了国内空白，数百套产品已批量装备在 5 种主力战机上。

带领武汉高德红外股份有限公司成为国内唯一具有导弹总体研制生产资质的民营企业并建成国内首家民营导弹研究院，多项成果填补国内空白。开创了民营企业造导弹的先河。

解决超十倍声速气动热红外成像等难题，带领团队研制成功我国首枚第四代红外热成像自寻的反坦克导弹；采用自研探测器，使该导弹的核心性能达到世界先进水平并实现稳定批量生产，开创了我国便携式反坦克导弹的新局面，结束了我军与西方的代差。此外，还采用自研探测器研制了各类机载、弹载、单兵等 40 余种光电装备，累计交付近 30 万套。相关成果获 2012 年军队科技进步奖二等奖。

三、首次研制成功人体测温仪等红外产品，大规模应用于公共卫生、生态保护等国民经济重要领域

针对“非典”等重大疫情传染性极强等难题，首次将红外热成像技术用于人体测温，攻克非接触实时人体测温、表面温度可视化等关键技术，带领团队研制全球首套全自动红外发热人群快速筛查系统，实现了大范围人群的自动搜索与预警，在 2003 年“非典”和 2020 年新冠疫情等公共卫生事件中得到应用达 20 万台套，顺利完成国家下达的防疫产品调拨任务，受到国务院表彰，并被授予“全国抗击新冠肺炎疫情民营经济先进个人”。

针对长江水域全时、全域、全线立体化监测的行业难题，攻克目标行为自主识别定位跟踪技术、GIS 等技术难题，带领团队成功开发基于红外热成像核心技术的天地察打一体化禁捕指挥系统，打造自主、高效、智能的禁捕水域防护网络，有效解决了长江大保护中“十年禁捕”监管难题，为从根本上养护长江水域生态资源环境作出了重要贡献。

针对汽车在夜间、雾霾、强光等恶劣环境下的行车安全问题，研制成功国内首款获 AEC-Q104 国际认证的 GST612W9 车规级非制冷红外模组，基于该模组开发的车载红外夜视高级驾驶辅助系统在光线不足、强光眩光、高速团雾等复杂场景中成像清晰，可精准识别行人、车辆等障碍目标，全时全天候提升驾驶员视觉感知能力，守护行车安全，已在东风猛士 917 豪华越野、广汽埃安 Hyper GT 轿跑和 Deep Way“深向星辰”新能源重卡等车型上量产使用，助力智能驾驶迈向新征程。此外，研制的红外产品在北京冬奥会、武汉军运会等重大项目中得到应用。相关成果获 2013 年湖北省科技进步奖一等奖。

Awardee of Industrial Innovation Prize, Huang Li

Huang Li was born in Xi'an City of Shaanxi Province in June 1963. He graduated from Huazhong University of Science and Technology in 1987 with a master's degree in Communication and Electronic Systems. Then he worked at Hubei Electric Power Experimental Research Institute. From November 1996 to December 1998, he served as the general manager of Wuhan Zhongxing Electric Appliance Co., Ltd., and founded Wuhan Guide Infrared Co., Ltd. in 1999. Currently, he is an adjunct professor at Huazhong University of Science and Technology.

Huang Li, the pioneer and founder of our country's high-performance infrared chip research and industrialization, has led a team through decades of crucial technological breakthroughs. Eventually, they overcame the bottleneck of high-end infrared core chips and successfully broke through the technological blockade imposed by the West. This has reversed the longstanding situation where our country was dependent on others for infrared core chips. Huang Li has applied advanced infrared chips and technology to modernizing our national defense and promoting national economic development. This has paved the way for the rapid formation and leapfrog development of our country's infrared industry. The infrared products which developed by Huang Li ranked first domestically and third internationally in market share. Huang Li has made a significant contribution to national defense construction and the well-being of our citizens.

产业创新奖获得者

林 松 涛

林松涛，1962 年 10 月出生于辽宁省沈阳市。1986 年获冶金工业部建筑研究总院（现中冶建筑研究总院有限公司）结构工程专业硕士学位，后留在单位工作至今。自 1992 年以来，先后担任工程结构试验室主任、结构与抗震分院副院长、建筑工程检测中心副主任兼总工程师、中冶检测认证有限公司副总经理兼总工程师、总院副总工程师、总院首席专家。同时兼任中国钢结构协会核电钢结构分会秘书长等。

林松涛长期从事核电站安全壳结构检测评估技术研究与创新工作，是我国核电重大基础设施安全检测评估领域的学术带头人，在核电站安全壳结构可靠性评价理论、安全壳结构预应力长期损失监测与评估、安全壳老化评估等方面作出了一系列开创性工作，为我国核电站持续安全可靠运行、核电走出国门发挥了积极作用。曾荣获国家技术发明奖二等奖 1 项，国家科技进步奖二等奖、三等奖各 1 项，省部级科技奖 11 项。

一、核电站安全壳结构可靠性评价理论体系的建立

依托国家“九五”科技攻关项目，自主开发了全壳结构安全评估计算分析软件，明确了检测内容和验收准则。通过高温、高压等复杂环境的模拟试验，系统解决了高压、高温、高湿和强电磁干扰环境下各类安全壳结构监测仪表的可靠性、耐久性、抗干扰性及敏感度检测机理问题。建立了完善的安全壳结构整体性试验的数据自动采集和分析处理系统，解决了大型结构试验中多参数、多测点、持续时间长、环境影响复杂等关键技术难点。

由此建立了我国核电站安全壳可靠性评价技术体系，解决了安全壳整体性检测与可靠性评定的系列难题，打破了国外的技术封锁，形成了拥有自主知识产权的中国方案。已应用于我国所有已建和在建核电项目，填补了我国核电工程自主验收的技术空白。相关成果获 2001 年国家科技进步奖二等奖。

二、安全壳结构预应力长期损失监测与评估技术

创造性地开发出高温（160℃）高压注油技术，解决了预应力孔道填充油脂和石蜡的快速加热和孔道预热技术，建立了安全壳预应力孔道高温高压灌油（蜡）技术工艺流程，开发了用于监测预应力损失的高温大量程钢束力传感器，建立了安全壳无粘结预应力长期损失监测体系。

研制专用的光纤光栅传感器，发明了兼具承载能力和测量功能的智能钢绞线。在国内外首次实现了对有粘结预应力钢束应力状态的直接监测，建立了有粘结预应力损失的监测评估体系。最终形成了安全壳预应力长期损失监测与评估的成套技术，突破美、法等核电大国的技术垄断，实现了技术自主化，为核电站的安全运行提供了技术保障。相关成果获 2014 年国家技术发明奖二等奖。

三、安全壳老化评估技术

在国内率先开展安全壳系统老化机理研究，建立了基于故障树理论的安全壳结构老化状态劣化树模型。针对核电站安全壳的特殊使用环境，开展一系列加速老化模拟试验，确定了 24 项安全壳老化机理，并对每项机理的劣化状态、趋势进行研究，提出了量化的评价标准。构建了基于事故树分析法的安全壳结构性能的劣化树评价模型，确定了安全壳性能劣化发生的主要路径、劣化因素的基本事件以及劣化基本事件因素间的逻辑关系。实现了依据劣化基本事件综合作用对安全壳老化状态进行综合评价，创建了安全壳老化评估技术体系。

基于劣化树评价模型，开发安全壳结构老化管理数据库软件，创立安全壳老化管理和评估数据库平台架构，将混凝土材料、预应力系统、钢内衬和贯穿件系统的劣化和损伤程度及分级评估方法引入数据库平台；并根据我国不同技术体系核电站安全壳的实际运行情况，确定老化管理核心机制和流程，制定具有针对性的老化管理实施程序，形成了一套完整的安全壳结构老化管理技术体系，解决了核电站安全壳延期服役的技术管理难题，保障了安全壳在设计运行寿命期内的安全性，奠定了我国核电站安全壳延期服役工作基础。通过在秦山核电站延寿项目中的实际应用，为国家核安全主管部门决策提供了技术支撑，实现了我国核电设计、建造、验收、运行和延寿的全过程自主化。

Awardee of Industrial Innovation Prize, Lin Songtao

Lin Songtao was born in Shenyang City of Liaoning Province in October 1962. He has been working in Central Research Institute of Building and Construction Co., Ltd, MCC Group（CRIBC）since 1986. Over the years, he has been the director of Engineering Structure Lab, deputy director and chief engineer of the Engineering Testing Center, deputy general manager and chief engineer of Inspection and Certification Co., Ltd, MCC Group (MCC Inspection), deputy chief engineer and chief expert of CRIBC. He also served as the executive director of the Nuclear Safety Committee of Chinese Nuclear Society, and the executive director of the Nuclear Industry Structures Committee of China Nuclear Industry Exploration & Design Association. Lin Songtao has been working on the development of testing and assessment technology for containment buildings in Nuclear Power Plants (NPPs) for decades, and has made a series of pioneering progresses in this area.

He established the reliability assessment method for containment buildings, including the testing technique for structural integrity, the automatic data acquisition system, and the assessment approach. He developed long-term monitoring and assessment techniques for prestressing loss of containment buildings, including the oil/wax grouting technique under high-temperature & pressure for prestressing tendons, smart strands with load-carrying capacity and measurement function, and the evaluation method for grouted prestressing loss. He developed aging management technologies of containment buildings, including the aging management model based on fault tree analysis, the aging/deterioration mechanisms, the aging management database platform, and the aging management program.

Lin Songtao is the principal research leader in the area of testing and assessment of major structures in NPPs in China. He has won one Second Class State of Technological Invention Award, one Second Class of State Science and Technology Progress Award, one Third Class of State Science and Technology Progress Award, as well as 11 scientific and technological provincial/ministerial awards.

产业创新奖获得者

王　　琦

王琦，1967 年 10 月出生于内蒙古自治区呼和浩特市。1997 年获中国农业大学农学博士学位，之后在中国农业大学植物保护学院工作至今，现任植物病理学系教授。先后担任中国植物病理学会植病生防专业委员会主任、科技部增产菌技术研究推广中心主任、生物农药与生物防治产业技术创新战略联盟副理事长、中国农业大学植物生态工程研究所所长等职务。

王琦长期从事植物病害生物防治工作，致力于挖掘生防微生物资源，揭示其作用机理，开发防病、增产、提质的微生物菌剂，在防控作物病害、解决连作障碍、减少化学农药与肥料使用等方面效果显著，为推动我国植病生防事业发展、保障国家粮食与生态安全作出突出贡献。曾荣获 2010 年国家科技进步奖二等奖、2022 年教育部科学技术进步奖一等奖、2023 年全国创新争先奖状、2015 年全国农业科研杰出人才、2010 年全国科技优秀工作者等奖项及荣誉。

一、创建微生态系菌种资源库和高通量精准快速筛选体系

创建基于宏基因 – 微生物培养组学技术的生防微生物高通量精准快速筛选体系，筛选周期缩短 1/3，筛选效率提高 30%；建立国内最大的微生态系资源库，保藏菌种 33278 株；已获得防稻瘟病、疮痂病与线虫病等重要病害的菌种 2216 株，为生防菌剂功能与种类的多样化提供“芯片”供给保障。上述成果极大缓解了菌种资源短缺状况，有力推动了生防菌剂向多元化方向发展，相关成果获 2007 年教育部高等学校科学技术奖专利一等奖。

二、解析有效生防菌种的微生态作用机理

首次明确蔗糖介导的芽孢杆菌与植物互作，促进了根系定殖，阐明了芽孢杆菌定向塑造根际微生物群落结构增强防病效果的作用机制，为生防微生物生态机理的解析指明

了新方向；明确芽孢杆菌与哈茨木霉的组合促进假单胞菌在马铃薯根际富集，实现对疮痂病的高效防控；证实了外界信号因子影响酪氨酸激酶 / 酪氨酸激酶调节器的“交互应答”，调控生物膜形成，促进枯草芽孢杆菌根际定殖；首次揭示 PTS（磷酸转移酶系统）控制碳源利用、生物膜形成、运动性和 MnSOD 的产生，调控蜡样芽孢杆菌根系定殖。阐明生防微生物防病的生态机理，将对生防菌作用机理的认知提升至系统生物学层面。揭示了解淀粉芽孢杆菌、枯草芽孢杆菌与多粘类芽孢杆菌等防病菌种产生表面活性素、伊枯草素 A、多黏菌素等化合物抑制稻瘟病菌、马铃薯疮痂病菌、苹果轮纹病菌等；明确了枯草芽孢杆菌诱导防御基因 *PR2*、*PR3* 和 *STS* 表达与胼胝质积累，防控葡萄病害的功能。上述成果为生防微生物菌种资源高效挖掘、自主知识产权生防菌剂产品创制与精准应用奠定了坚实的理论基础。

三、建立生防菌剂的低成本无污染规模化生产工艺与产品保质增效技术

通过优化芽孢杆菌规模化生产培养基配方与原料酶解预处理工艺，生防菌剂的水溶性显著提高，有效抑制泡沫产生；基于生防菌种代谢流特征，调整发酵工艺参数，形成“一菌一工艺”精准化发酵，含菌量提高至 500 亿芽孢 / 毫升，芽孢形成率超 90%。从有效菌株的生物学特性与产品使用的便利性出发，筛选获得水溶性载体以及环保型助剂，改良剂型加工工艺，为可湿性粉剂、悬浮剂、微胶囊剂等剂型的开发提供技术保障，形成“一剂一工艺”标准化加工，货架期延长 6 个月以上，有效解决了菌体存活时间短与二次发酵等制剂生产瓶颈。创建生防菌种高效低成本无污染规模化生产工艺流程，综合成本降低超 35%。上述成果有效解决了生防菌剂产品制造成本高与货架期短的技术难题，强化了生防菌剂对病害绿色防控的支撑力，相关成果获 2011 年中华农业科技奖一等奖。

四、开发生防菌剂系列产品，开展示范试验推广应用

基于科技部“植物微生态国家级星创天地”平台，建立完整的研究成果高效转化体系，开发生防菌剂系列专用产品 91 个（在 53 家企业完成转化，72 个产品获得农业农村部登记），已在全国 31 个省 50 余种粮食与经济作物以及观赏植物上示范试验 1578 次，推广应用面积超 10 亿亩，平均防病效果超 70%，平均增产 12% 以上，化学农药及肥料的投入量降低近 30%。拥有自主知识产权的生防菌剂已具备国际竞争力，产品远销韩国与喀麦隆等国家。建立了以科研成果快速转化为发力点、高效多功能生防菌剂产品开发应用为核心的作物病害绿色防控投入品支撑体系，有力保障了国家粮食安全与生态安全。

Awardee of Industrial Innovation Prize, Wang Qi

Wang Qi was born in Hohhot City of Inner Mongolia Autonomous Region in October 1967. He got his Ph. D. degree in the department of Plant Pathology in China Agricultural University (CAU) in 1997. Then he worked in the Department of Plant Pathology, College of Plant Protection of CAU. In addition, he also has some social positions in the past decades including the director of the Biocontrol Committee of Chinese Society for Plant Pathology, the director of the National Technical Research and Extension Centre of Yield Increasing Bacteria, the vice president of the Industrial Technology Innovation Strategy Alliance for Biopesticide and Biological Control, and the director of the Plant Ecological Engineering Research Institute of CAU. In the past 30 years, he devoted himself to the biological control of plant diseases. He focuses on isolating and screening biocontrol microorganisms, revealing their modes of action and developing microbial agents for disease prevention, yield increasing and quality improvement. The microbial agents have been applied to more than 1 billion acres in China. His research work makes a great contribution to controlling crop diseases, solving the problem of crop succession and reducing the use of chemical pesticides and fertilizers. He also constructed and cultivated the innovative research team of biological control in China. All his works significantly promote the development of biocontrol of plant disease and make outstanding contributions to ensuring national food and ecological security.

产业创新奖获得者

王 曙 群

王曙群，1970 年 6 月出生于浙江省海宁县。1989 年入职中国航天科技集团第八研究院 149 厂，从事航天飞行器总装总测工作。2012—2014 年在北京航空航天大学函授学习。先后兼任江苏省产业教授，湖南省产业技能顾问，南京机电职业技术学院客座教授，上海市高技能人才培养工作评审专家，中国劳动关系学院教育研究中心特聘研究员，上海职工技术协会第八届理事会会长，上海发明协会副会长，中国国防邮电技术协会精密机械装配专业技术委员会主任委员等职务。

作为中国航天科技集团载人航天工程总装总测领域的领军人才，王曙群立足航天空间飞行器机械装备制造工艺技术领域，致力于实现航天器产品小批量总装总测技术的突破，在航天精密机构制造及非标小力值检测装备开发领域作出了一系列开创性工作，为载人航天工程顺利实施作出贡献。曾荣获国家科技进步奖二等奖 1 项、上海市科技进步奖三等奖 1 项，以及 2011 年中国载人航天工程突出贡献者、2012 年中华技能大奖、2020 年全国劳动模范等奖项和荣誉。

一、超细直径小腔检漏管路制造技术

针对两个飞行器交会对接的关键产品——对接机构研制过程中，航天超细直径小腔检漏管路制造技术工艺技术难题，通过建立超细薄管焊接工法创新交变磁场方向；找到最佳钎焊工艺参数，钎焊试样合格率达到 99% 以上；甄选出适应超细直径管路钎焊的填充焊料（在钎料中提高 Ag 含量、同时添加适量 Sn 元素），配制了一种可以降低熔点、提高润湿性能的钎焊材料，焊接质量均达到或超过航天标准 QJ1156A–96II 级焊缝要求，管路漏率满足$\leq 1\times10^{-7}$Pa · m^3/s 的产品指标；优化传统的超细管路清洗工艺路径，配制出一种分解油污能力强、自身易挥发的清洗剂，采用高压气体驱动高分子材料在导管内多次高速往复摩擦，有效去除超细管路内壁残存的油污、金属颗粒等有害多余物，产品检验合格率为100%，实现产品小批量制造的工程研制目标。形成的创新技术成果已在我国载人航天工程中得到应用，经20余次飞行试验考核，圆满完成近30次交会对接任务，技术成熟度得到验证；在X-2等新型空间飞行器及地面密封检测设备等航天产品中得到推广使用。

二、测试链刚性分配等技术

开展基于皮带移位技术路线为核心的差动组合测试链刚性分配技术研究，研发了以梯形齿带传动平行移位结合独特胀紧装置的创新方案，解决了小间距大扭矩平行轴检测的工艺瓶颈，提出磁粉制动器结合电磁离合器的技术方案，实现了对扭矩测试数据的精确控制。自主开发电子逻辑控制器，采用一个以与非门为接触的控制电路板，突破机构运动互锁控制、触发控制的技术瓶颈，电性能开关量测试≥150点、频率≥5kHz。研制成功国内唯一差动组合测试装备，属国内首创产品，基于本技术的测试系统和整体测试方案达到国内领先水平。目前，年测试产品10套以上，数据一致性差异≤0.5%，为后续深空探测任务中的同类产品研制提供了技术支撑。

三、大温差环境下复杂精密机构的性能测试技术

开展大温差环境下复杂精密机构的性能测试技术研究，建立了真空及高低温环境下多种类、多物理量、多尺度精密机构综合性能测试仪开发体系，并对驱动与传感等功能模块在极端环境下的性能变化规律进行研究；研制了具有自主知识产权、质量稳定可靠、核心部件国产化的精密机构综合性能测试仪，实现机构装配精度、静态力学、动态传动、电性能等各项关键性能参数的测量；建立极端环境下综合性能测试仪的量值溯源方法，研制测试溯源标准装置，实现关键测试参数的量值溯源。该技术推动综合性能测试仪的工程化开发研究，并结合航天型号空间机构的复杂性能测试需求进行工程化应用和产业化推广的探索，为满足我国航天工程快速发展需求、开发超前技术和进行技术储备奠定了坚实基础。

Awardee of Industrial Innovation Prize, Wang Shuqun

Wang Shuqun was born in Haining County of Zhejiang Province in June 1970. In 1989, he joined No. 149 Factory of the Eighth Research Institute of China Aerospace Science and Technology Corporation, where he engaged in general assembly and testing of spacecraft. From 2012 to 2014, he studied at Beihang University by correspondence. He has successively served as an industry professor in Jiangsu Province, an industry skills consultant in Hunan Province, a visiting professor at Nanjing Vocational Institute of Mechatronic Technology, an evaluation expert of high skilled talent training in Shanghai, a specially appointed researcher at the Education Research Center of China University of Labor Relations, president of the 8th Council of Shanghai Workers' Technical Association, vice president of Shanghai Association of Inventions, and chairman of the Precision Machinery Assembly Professional Technical Committee of China National Defense Posts and Telecommunications Technical Association.

As a leading talent in the field of general assembly and testing of manned space flight projects of China Aerospace Science and Technology Corporation, Wang Shuqun is committed to achieving breakthroughs in small batch general assembly and testing techniques for spacecraft products in the field of the manufacturing process techniques of mechanical equipment for spacecraft. He has done a series of pioneering jobs in the manufacturing of aerospace precision mechanisms and the development of non-standard small force testing equipment, contributing to the smooth implementation of manned space flight projects. He has won one second prize of the National Award for Science and Technology Progress, one third prize of the Shanghai Municipal Award for Science and Technology Progress, as well as awards and honors such as Outstanding Contributor of China's Manned Space Flight Project in 2011, China Skills Award in 2012, and National Model Worker in 2020.

产业创新奖获得者

王 喜 瑜

王喜瑜，1974年11月出生于湖南省娄底市。1998年获北方交通大学（现北京交通大学）工学硕士学位，同年进入中兴通讯股份有限公司工作，历任CDMA事业部工程师、高级工程师、开发部长、副总经理、无线研究院院长、技术规划部部长、公司副CTO兼总裁助理等职务。现任中兴通讯股份有限公司首席技术官，移动网络和移动多媒体技术国家重点实验室学术委员会常务副主任，移动专用网络国家工程研究中心常务副主任。东南大学兼职教授，美国电气和电子工程师协会高级会员。

王喜瑜长期坚守移动通信网络技术研发一线，主持了一系列技术攻关和核心产品研发，在移动通信基站的核心架构、组网、算法和芯片等方向取得了系列重要成果。曾荣获国家科学技术进步奖二等奖3项，国内省、市、相关学会科学技术奖8项。

一、软件定义无线电（SDR）软基站的技术攻关

通过对基带、射频、空口、组网、生产、制造等技术的深入研究，发现SDR技术对改变传统基站设备形态具有重要价值。为此，他与科研项目团队积极开展技术攻关工作，成功解决了SDR技术在基站系统应用的技术难题。2009年，创新性应用控制与运算分离理论，研制出软件可配置SDR芯片，并定义了兼容2G/3G/4G的基站通用架构。

SDR软基站成功改变了“一种制式一款基站”的传统模式，在解决基站重复投资的产业规模应用难题的同时，实现了基站整体技术性能的领先。

二、以太网有源数字多模室内分布式（QCell）基站的系统研发

基于广泛应用的以太网技术，创造性提出以太网有源数字室内分布式组网思想，成功突破了以太网分布式密集组网、分布式多频多模共存、密集蜂窝无线信号调度等多项关键技术瓶颈，最终实现了蜂窝组网裂变为室内以太网互联的密集小基站组网，成功研

制出以太网有源数字多模室内覆盖分布式基站系统 QCell。

QCell 基站系统实现了室内场景下最高达 1.45Gbps 的无线数据速率能力，该速率超过了网线速率，颠覆了一直以来人们认为“无线不如有线”的认知。该基站系统有效突破了“室内数据业务占比高、覆盖难”的发展瓶颈，解决了室内系统容量、信号覆盖、组网的难题，使北京冬奥场馆、乌镇互联网大会等国家重大工程的 5G 无缝、高速、超大容量连接重大需求得以解决。

三、大规模天线阵列（MIMO）基站方案的产业化应用

根据 5G 标准需求的定义，5G 通信系统迫切需要解决无线业务持续增长带来的大容量需求与无线资源日益饱和之间的矛盾。然而，受限于 4G 基站的技术瓶颈，5G 需要在无线领域采用新的技术方案解决该问题。2013 年，王喜瑜率先组织专家对相关候选技术进行评估。经过充分论证和集体决策后，认为 MIMO 技术是解决 5G 发展无线资源瓶颈的重要技术路径之一。2014 年，他组织科研团队围绕 MIMO 技术在通信基站领域的应用进行技术攻关，先后攻克了波束赋形等多项核心算法，成功解决了 MIMO 技术在通信基站领域应用的技术难题，自研了高集成度的中频芯片，推出了 64 通道基站。

MIMO 基站方案将传统基站的天线数提升一个数量级，频谱效率提升 4～6 倍，极大提升了网络覆盖能力与系统容量。该方案在 2016 年世界移动通信大会上获得了“最佳移动技术突破奖”。目前，该方案已成为 5G 标准必选技术，并在全球 5G 网络中进行了广泛部署和产业化应用。

王喜瑜在科研创新中始终坚持“一代工艺、一代芯片、一代产品”的原则，带领团队完成了通信基站基带、中频、射频全系列核心芯片的自主研发与产业化，并实现了器件国产化。同时，通过 5G 全连接和 5G 机器视觉、5G 云化 AGV、5G 云化 PLC、数字孪生等应用创新技术，带领团队打造了中兴南京全球 5G 智能制造基地。该基地具备从原材料到成品端到端的先进制造工艺能力，实现了驱动装备智联化、制造数字化和运营智能化，达到了生产要素全连接，将公司的基站交货周期（合同生效到产品发货）缩短 40% 以上，显著提升了生产能力。目前，中兴基站已全球规模商用达千万台，同步带动产业链数千家企业发展，并为通信产业发展培养了一大批青年技术骨干。

Awardee of Industrial Innovation Prize, Wang Xiyu

Wang Xiyu was born in Loudi City of Hunan Province in November 1974. He obtained a Master's Degree in Engineering from Beijing Jiaotong University in 1998. Upon graduation, he joined ZTE Corporation, and successively served as Engineer, Senior Engineer, Development Director, Deputy General Manager, Director, and Deputy CTO and Chief of Staff. Since 2018,

Wang Xiyu has been working as CTO of ZTE Corporation. He is also Part-Time Professor at Southeast University and IEEE Senior Member. So far, he has won China's State Scientific and Technological Progress Award three times.

Over the past 25 years, Wang Xiyu has been dedicated to the R&D of wireless communications technology, with significant results in technological innovation and core product development. His major achievements are as follows.

In 2009, Wang Xiyu and his team developed the SDR chip and a standardized paradigm in base station architecture that enables the coexistence of 2G/3G/4G networks. Such an innovative architecture reduces TCO in large-scale network deployment and ensures the technical performance of base stations at the top of the industry.

In 2012, Wang Xiyu pioneered the QCell system. Featuring high capacity, strong signal, and flexible networking, the system realizes high downloading rate over the wireless network indoors. Therefore, it was deployed for Beijing Winter Olympics and WIC Wuzhen Summit to ensure seamless, high-speed, and massive 5G connectivity.

In 2014, Wang Xiyu and his team proposed the Massive MIMO solution, and developed the highly-integrated IF chipset and the 64T64R base station, increasing spectrum efficiency by 4 to 6 times. In 2016, the Massive MIMO solution was granted "Best Mobile Technology Breakthrough Award" at the MWC Barcelona. As an essential technology for 5G, it has been widely deployed in the world.

Committed to the principle of continuous and independent innovation, Wang Xiyu contributes a lot to mass production of full-series chipsets. With the philosophy of "Intelligent Manufacturing Powered by 5G", he promoted the establishment of ZTE Global 5G Intelligent Manufacturing Base in Nanjing, greatly increasing the annual output of base stations. Currently, over 10 million ZTE base stations have been put into commercial use globally, bringing about significant economic benefits and powering the whole industry chain.

产业创新奖获得者

吴 一 弦

吴一弦，女，1967 年 2 月出生于福建省莆田市。1986 年、1989 年先后获得北京化工学院学士学位和硕士学位，1998 年获北京化工大学博士学位。北京化工大学材料科学与工程学院系主任，中国石化北京燕山分公司 – 北京化工大学合成橡胶联合实验室主任。中国化工学会会士，兼任中国化学会高分子学科委员会委员、首都女教授协会副会长、中国化工学会女科技工作者委员会副主任委员、中国合成橡胶工业协会理事等职务。

吴一弦主要从事高分子化工与材料的科学研究与技术开发，形成了烯烃可控聚合与大分子工程特色研究方向，取得了一系列创新性成果并已实现产业转化和工业应用。曾荣获国家技术发明奖二等奖 2 项，以及全国新世纪巾帼发明家新秀奖、中国青年科技奖、中国青年女科学家奖、侯德榜化工科技成就奖等奖励。

一、异烯烃可控阳离子聚合与高性能丁基橡胶制备

丁基橡胶是制造飞机 / 汽车轮胎不可替代的高分子材料，合成技术受国外垄断，1999 年之前我国丁基橡胶全部依赖进口。吴一弦提出活性中心微环境调控聚合反应新思路，发明异丁烯可控阳离子聚合方法，开发了丁基橡胶聚合新工艺。2002 年，中国石化股份公司采用其研究成果与技术方案，解决了我国首套 3 万吨 / 年丁基橡胶工业生产中的重大技术难题，使我国成为世界上少数掌握丁基橡胶关键技术的国家之一，引领了我国该领域产业技术发展。“异丁烯可控阳离子聚合与丁基橡胶聚合新工艺”荣获 2006 年国家技术发明奖二等奖。在此基础上，她带领团队研究开发出新引发体系核心技术，并于 2011 年实现在 4.5 万吨 / 年丁基橡胶装置上工业化应用，促进了产业升级和高质量发展。

二、烯烃可控配位聚合与高性能烯烃基弹性体制备

通过先进催化剂构筑、烯烃配位聚合及高性能烯烃基聚合物弹性体设计合成三个方

面开展基础研究与技术开发，调控聚合物分子链微观结构、共聚组成、序列结构及拓扑结构，实现了烯烃高效配位聚合与烯烃聚合物的结构与性能调控，形成了一系列自主知识产权技术，创制了具有高无规序列结构含量的乙丙橡胶、高反应活性的长链支化乙丙橡胶及新结构的聚烯烃弹性体。在此基础上完成了具有高催化活性和优异共聚性能的先进催化剂工程化，并实现催化剂在乙烯、丙烯及环状烯烃高效连续聚合的工程放大试验（规模：1000 吨 / 年），试生产高性能新型链结构乙烯 / 丙烯共聚弹性体系列产品，填补了国内空白。

研发高活性高定向性的先进催化剂和丁二烯可控配位聚合方法，发展了调控微观结构（顺 -1,4≥98.3%）与大分子链结构的核心技术，创建了配位聚合反应与聚合物分子量在线调控技术。中国石化股份公司采用该成果建设了国内首套 3 万吨 / 年高性能稀土顺丁橡胶工业生产装置，实现了规模化连续稳定生产，为生产绿色轮胎提供了高性能合成橡胶基础材料，打破了该关键基础材料长期依赖进口的局面。“烯烃可控配位聚合与高性能弹性体制备技术”荣获 2020 年度国家技术发明奖二等奖。

三、超高分子量聚烯烃特种橡胶及其制备

超高分子量聚烯烃特种橡胶是武器装备用关键基础材料，仅德国和俄罗斯掌握生产技术，2018 年之前我国全部依赖进口。吴一弦带领研究团队发明了通过稳定与保护活性中心调控活性链增长的方法，解决了高活性引发中心及快速链增长过程中的关键科学问题，发明了具有自主知识产权的可控聚合方法与成套制备技术，解决了聚合反应放大过程中的工程化难题，创制了超高分子量聚烯烃特种橡胶，攻克了超高分子量聚合物工程技术难题，并建成了世界上首条超高分子量聚烯烃特种橡胶全流程中试生产线。通过调节引发体系及聚合反应工艺条件，设计合成了分子量在 100 万～500 万的高分子量和超高分子量聚烯烃特种橡胶系列产品，填补了国内相关技术与产品空白；通过可控阳离子聚合方法在国际上率先实现了设计合成分子量高达 800 万甚至 1200 万以上的超高分子量聚烯烃特种橡胶产品，引领了该领域技术发展。研究成果应用于首套 4.5 万吨 / 年工业化，实现了特种橡胶材料国产化及其实际装备应用。

Awardee of Industrial Innovation Prize, Wu Yixian

Wu Yixian, female, was born in Putian City of Fujian Province in February 1967. She received the degrees of BSc (1986), MSc (1991) and PhD (1998) from Beijing University of Chemical Technology. Her scientific research interests focus on: Controlled/living polymerization of C_2～C_5 olefins, styrene and its derivatives; Macromolecular engineering *via* controlled/living polymerization; Advanced synthetic rubber for tire manufacture; and Advanced thermoplastic elastomer for biomedical and energy applications. The fundamental research and innovation technology from her laboratory had been successfully applied in industry for the synthetic rubber production. Two projects have been awarded the second grade prize of National Technology Innovation by national level bodies. She was awarded the title of National Women Inventor, Distinguished Young Scholars in China, and Distinguished Young Woman Scientist in China. She was also elected as a Fellow of Chemical Industry and Engineering Society of China.

Wu Yixian proposed a novel research idea for the controlled cationic polymerization of isobutylene by adjusting the environment surrounding the active centers and the propagating chain ends. She and her research group invented the polymerization method for the controlled cationic polymerization and developed the novel polymerization process for synthesis of butyl rubber. The scientific research results and the corresponding techniques were successfully applied in the first industry set of (scale: 30000 t/a) butyl rubber production in China in 2002. Furthermore, the advanced initiating system was successfully developed for industrial production (scale: 45000 t/a) of butyl rubber in 2011, leading to the industrial upgrading.

The highly efficient coordination polymerization of ethylene with propylene was realized and high performance polyolefin elastomers with controlled microstructures could be achieved. The preparation of the advanced catalyst with high catalytic activity for copolymerization of ethylene with propylene was scaled up and the high performance and special microstructure terpolymer of ethylene-propylene-nonconjugated diene were produced in a complete set with a scale of 1000 t/a for the first time in China.

Prof. Wu and her research group developed the advanced rare earth metal catalysts with both high catalytic activity and high 1,4-addition selectivity for the controlled coordination polymerization of butadiene. The high performance polybutadiene with cis-1,4 microstructure contents of more than 98.3% could be successfully synthesized with coordination polymerization process of butadiene. The first industrial plant (scale: 30000 t/a) was successfully constructed for production of high performance polybutadiene with high cis-1,4 microstructure in large scale on the basis of the above advanced rare earth catalyst system and the controlled coordination polymerization process.

Wu Yixian and her research group focused on the controlled polymerization process to achieve the ultra-high molecular weights of more than 1000000 or more than 8000000 or even more than 12000000 for the resulting polymers. The first production line (scale: 100 t/a) was successfully built for the production of a series of the polyolefin specialty rubber with ultra-high molecular weights from 1000000 to 14000000. The above advanced technology has been also used in industry for production of a series of the polyolefin specialty rubber with ultra-high molecular weights (scale: 45000 t/a). The polyolefin specialty rubbers with ultra-high molecular weights have been confirmed for application in manufacturing the special equipment in China.

产业创新奖获得者

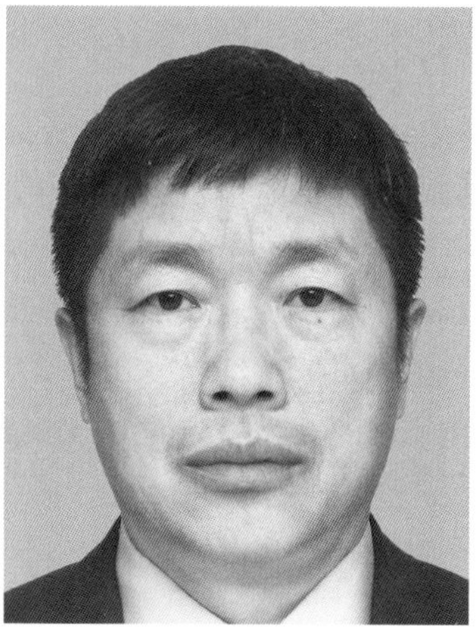

张 海 军

张海军，1968 年 3 月出生于山东省聊城市。1992 年毕业于上海医科大学（现复旦大学医学院），后入职北京积水潭医院。1994—1999 年先后在德国拜耳、德国费森尤斯担任主管和经理职务，并进入美国加利福尼亚大学尔湾分校参加 HCEMBA 学习。2003 年回国创办山东百多安医疗器械有限公司，担任董事长兼首席科学家；其间获得中欧国际工商管理学院 MBA，在奥尔堡大学攻读医学博士学位。2016 年组建生物医用材料改性技术国家地方联合工程实验室，任实验室主任。2018 年以来，在同济大学、山东大学、山东理工大学担任讲座教授、特聘教授，兼任中国医工交叉与转化协同创新平台理事长、中国塑料加工工业协会医用塑料专委会主委、中国医学装备协会心血管专委会秘书长等职。

张海军从事生物医用材料改性技术研究，针对心血管、神经外科、肿瘤等重大疾病和关键科学问题，在植入和介入医疗器械领域开拓创新，在中心血管通路定位、药物球囊超声控释、锌合金血管支架降解、人工颅骨仿生结构等领域作出了一系列开创性工作。曾荣获国家科技进步奖二等奖、中国产学研创新成果奖一等奖、国家发明专利优秀奖等国家和省部级奖励 18 项。

一、创建血管通路数字诊疗技术体系，研制首台中心血管通路心电超声多普勒设备

带领团队攻克了生物特征识别用回波信号相位信息缺失、超声视野盲区和显影暗区、有机硅材料不导电和力学强度低等科学难题，在靶血管智能筛选、平面穿刺复合显像、体内生物电精准导航三方面取得系列技术创新，建立起全新的中心血管通路技术体系，完成系列医疗器械自主研制和产业化。

创建靶血管分析与筛选技术：发明基于超声信号的生物特征识别技术，大幅提升图像质量；提出基于彩色超声多普勒血流测定穿刺靶区多参数选择方法，实现对靶血管直径、向心血流速度等生物特性的精准分析和筛选，为提高穿刺成功率提供重要保证。

创建平面穿刺复合增强显像技术：发明新型超声换能器和图像空间复合增强显示技术，采用平面进针操作，实现穿刺过程从体表到靶血管的全程实时监控，提高了穿刺成功率，降低了刺穿风险和并发症发生率。

创建血管内生物电精准导航技术：发明新型血管通路导管，实现生物电信号感知和传输，创建中心血管通路心电精准导航技术替代X线定位，降低了导管尖端定位系统误差。

二、创新阻塞性血管疾病干预策略并进行临床转化

发明非对称药物涂层技术：冠脉支架药物非对称分布于支架表面，管壁方向采用多层药物涂覆，药物靶向平稳释放防止平滑肌增生和支架内再狭窄，管腔方向药物含量少，减少对血管内皮修复抑制，快速内皮化可降低血栓事件发生率；与同期进口支架对照，显示了产品的远期安全性。

开发可吸收锌合金冠脉支架系统：在国际上首先揭示了锌铜合金在血管内的降解规律，血管内膜修复良好，显影清晰，血流通畅；发明第一个超塑性锌铜合金冠脉内支架，技术达到国际领先水平，并在中国、美国、欧盟获得专利保护；建立第一条锌合金材料熔炼、毛细管制备、激光雕刻、双向电化学抛光、非对称药物涂层、表面磷酸缓冲层改性、球囊制备、组装灭菌的全产业链规模化生产线，率先完成临床前研究并启动临床试验，顺利通过国家创新医疗器械特别审查。

研发超声控释球囊药物释放技术：针对药物球囊生物利用度低的难题，将载药微囊均匀涂层在球囊表面，输送抗增生药物，可有效防止药物在导管输送过程中的损失；当球囊进入靶病变部位，利用微囊对超声响应性，通过超声促使药物在血管靶病变部位定向释放。临床试验证实产品药物生物利用率较进口产品提高3.5倍，并通过国家创新医疗器械特别审查，同时完成2项注册临床研究。

三、创建医用和仿生材料改性技术体系

带领团队开发等离子处理、化学枝接、梯度微纳多孔氧化膜、导电控制剂调控、POSS结构交联等技术，构建植介入器械材料功能改性技术体系，使其具有抗凝、抗菌、超滑、导电和抗撕裂性能，产品性能高于国外同类产品。

表面改性技术：①抗凝改性：利用等离子溅射在特定环境中改变高分子材料表面拓扑结构形成氨基官能基团，与肝素化学交联键接枝，共聚于高分子材料表面止血小板吸附和凝集，防止凝血和血栓生成；②抗菌改性：利用介入医用材料的渗透性，形成抗菌成分储存池，药物可长期释放，降低感染发生率；③超滑改性：通过等离子处理和化学枝接，实现超滑性能，提高临床操作成功率，降低患者黏膜损伤；④导电改性：材料功能控制剂促使局部电子跃迁形成隧道电流，降低电阻，可收集体内生物电信号，根据心电P波变化实现精准导航。

抗撕裂改性技术：通过结构控制剂在高分子材料的三维网格中形成稳定交联，使医用导管力学性能提高近 1 倍，体内断管严重并发症发生率从 6.7‰降低到 0.3‰以下。

仿生功能材料改性：模拟人体自然颅骨结构，设计三层结构仿生人工颅骨，上、下表层为与皮质骨相似的致密层，以保证力学强度；中间为三维仿骨小梁结构松质骨层；表面修饰骨诱导成分，促进修复材料与组织的融合。通过无模具成型技术，实现仿生颅骨快速精准个性化定制，可完美修复缺损、缩短患者等待和手术时间、降低手术感染的发生率，突破生长期儿童颅骨修复禁区。

Awardee of Industrial Innovation Prize, Zhang Haijun

Zhang Haijun was born in Liaocheng City of Shandong Province in March 1968. He graduated from Shanghai Medical University with a master's degree in 1992. In 1992—2003, he worked in Beijing Jishuitan Hospital, Bayer AG and Fresenius AG, and studied in HCEMBA at the University of California, Irvine. In 2003—2016, he set up Shandong Branden Medical Devices Co., Ltd, obtained his MBA degree from CEIBS and study for MD degree in Aalborg University. In 2016, he established the National United Engineering Laboratory for Biomedical Material Modification and served as the director of the laboratory. Since 2018, he has served as professor at Tongji University.

He developed the first international ECG color Doppler system and catheter to solve the three international problems of target vessel intelligent screening, non-blind area puncture and bioelectrical navigation; invent asymmetric drug coating technology to reduce the incidence of long-term adverse cardiac events of coronary stents. He also created ultrasound controlled drug release balloon to achieve targeted release of anti proliferative drugs. Additionally, he revealed the degradation law of zinc alloy stent in vivo for the first time, established the whole industry chain of zinc alloy stent, and started the first clinical study of zinc stent registration in the world. So far, he has won the second Prize of National Science and Technology Progress, the first prize of China's Industry-University-Research Innovation Achievement Award, and the National Invention Patent Excellence Award , etc.

区域创新奖获得者

阿吉艾克拜尔·艾萨

阿吉艾克拜尔·艾萨，1965年9月出生于新疆维吾尔自治区阿图什市。1999年获中国科学院上海药物研究所理学博士学位。1999—2022年在中国科学院新疆理化技术研究所工作，2006年4月—2021年2月任中国科学院新疆理化技术研究所副所长，2022年9月起任新疆医科大学校长。先后担任中国科学院干旱区植物资源化学重点实验室主任、中国科学院中亚药物研发中心主任、民族药关键技术与工艺国家地方联合工程研究中心主任、中国－乌兹别克斯坦新药“一带一路”联合实验室主任。兼任国家药典委员会第十二届民族医药专业委员会副主任、全国天然样品技术委员会天然产物样品标准工作组专家委员。

阿吉艾克拜尔·艾萨从事中药民族药学研究，系统性、创造性地构建了民族药产学研创新体系。经过20余年努力，探索出我国与中亚五国医药科技创新及成果转化的国际合作新模式，成为国家“一带一路”倡议在医药领域的重要典范。曾荣获新疆科技进步奖一等奖3项、专利奖一等奖1项，以及科技进步奖突出贡献奖和中乌友谊突出贡献奖。

一、解析特色药材活性成分，发现先导化合物，为新药研究奠定基础

在新疆和中亚药用植物化学成分与功能研究中，分离鉴定了3251个化合物，包括26种新骨架类型和1018个新化合物，其化学结构和生物活性的多样性为创新药物研究提供了更多新先导或线索。发现对叶大戟中的2个新大环二萜能逆转肿瘤多药耐药，经结构修饰得到1个衍生物，其活性是维拉帕米的4.5倍，已成为候选药物；伊犁绢蒿和驱虫斑鸠菊中的15个倍半萜具有抗白癜风活性，其中1个独特的5/5/4三环新骨架倍半萜被选为国际热点化合物，绢蒿甲酯A和斑鸠菊大苦素活性优于8-甲氧沙林，首次将倍半萜用于抗白癜风新药开发；瘤果黑种草籽中的4个新骨架生物碱具有降糖作用，被选为国际热点化合物，为降糖药物开发提供了新选择；新疆鼠尾草中的2个高度变异螺环新骨架

二萜对 3 种肿瘤细胞具有细胞毒作且效果优于顺铂，为抗肿瘤药物研究提供了天然药源分子。

二、构建“一带一路”中亚国家国际科技合作创新体系，研发创新药物，主导在中亚国家转化上市

建成我国首个在乌兹别克斯坦的药品 GMP 生产技术平台，与周边国家共建 5 个联合实验室，形成了我国在中亚唯一的新药研发转化实体，推动多中心临床研究在中亚开展，主导了创新药物研发、注册和生产，实现药品海外上市。发现中亚特色天然药物汝坦具有治疗新冠肺炎的新用途，鉴定出其中 21 个高活性成分的化学结构，阐释了其药效物质基础。临床研究结果表明，汝坦安全性良好，可显著降低中度新冠肺炎患者炎症反应，2020 年在乌兹别克斯坦生产并上市；合作发现了具有抗新冠病毒作用的核苷类化合物 VV116，并开发为口服有效的候选药物，临床试验结果表明 VV116 可将患者进展为危重型及死亡的风险降低 92% 且安全性良好，2021 年在乌兹别克斯坦生产并上市。

基于上述工作，在乌兹别克斯坦首次建立中药研发、中试和生产平台，得到乌兹别克斯坦有关部门认可，促进了中药法规、标准与乌兹别克斯坦卫生体系的衔接融合，推动了中药民族药的海外转化。其中，乃孜来颗粒 2021 年获得乌兹别克斯坦临床批件，成为首个通过乌兹别克斯坦新药临床审批的中药复方新药；艾拉片、莎毕娅片和安娜凝胶等品种完成研发和中试，已申请乌兹别克斯坦临床批件。

三、研制民族药国家标准样品，形成地产中药民族药自主研发体系，开发民族药原创新药

针对民族药物质基础不清、作用机制不明、质控水平较低、产业创新滞后等难题，从国家标准样品入手，突破系列关键技术，构建规模化制备平台，率先研制出 19 件民族药国家标准样品，在民族药有效成分定量、生产过程质控、药效评价等方面发挥了示范引领作用，显著提升了民族药新药的自主研发能力。发现棉花花的黄酮类成分具有改善学习记忆的功效，揭示其拮抗 Aβ 所致的氧化应激损伤、直接或间接抑制炎症的作用机制，阐明了金丝桃苷、异槲皮素和槲皮黄苷是主要药效成分，利用高速逆流色谱技术研制出上述成分的国家标准样品，并应用于新药工艺研究和质控体系，研发出维药首个有效部位新药棉花花总黄酮片，已转让新疆药企并进入Ⅱ期临床；发现一枝蒿酮酸是道地药材一枝蒿的质量标志物，利用反复重结晶技术研制出国家标准样品，提升了新药乃孜来颗粒的质控水平，推动其进入Ⅱ期临床。建立上市药复方一枝蒿颗粒的质控体系，保障了药材、饮片、中间体和制剂的全过程质量可控，推动药品海外上市并完成大龄儿童的临床试验；发现石榴皮中安石榴苷是治疗妇科炎症的主要药效成分，通过发明的异构体结构互换方法解决了高纯度异构体的纯化难题，研制出国家标准样品，保障了组分新药安娜凝胶的有效性和安全性，推动新药在乌兹别克斯坦临床注册。

运用国家标准样品和现代质控技术体系，开展维药经典方剂的传承创新，完成艾拉片的新药研发，获得临床批件，已转让新疆药企并进入Ⅱ期临床；开展新疆地区医院内制剂的新药开发，合作研发了苏孜阿甫片和醒脑库克亚片，进入Ⅲ期临床；提升炎消迪娜儿糖浆等 4 个上市品种的质量标准，其中 3 个纳入国家医保目录、1 个列为中药保护品种。

Awardee of Region Innovation Prize, Ajiaikebaier Aisa

Ajiaikebaier Aisa was born in Atushi City of Xinjiang Uygur Autonomous Region in September 1965. He obtained his doctor's degree at Shanghai Institute of Materia Medica of the Chinese Aacademy of Sciences (CAS) in 1999. He served as the deputy director of Xinjiang Institute of Physics and Chemistry Technology of the CAS from April 2006 to February 2021. Since September 2022, he has been working as the President of Xinjiang Medical University. He has been the Director of the Key Laboratory of Plant Resource Chemistry in Arid Zones of the CAS, the Central Asia Drug Research and Development Center, the State Joint Engineering Research Center for Key Technologies and Processes of Ethnomedicines, and the Joint Laboratory of China-Uzbekistan "One Belt, One Road" for New Drugs.

He analyzed the active ingredients of the characteristic medicinal herbs and discovered the lead compounds (Noval Medicines Research) . He also builded international scientific and technological cooperation and with Central Asian countries , researched and developed innovative medicines, and took the lead in transforming and listing them in Central Asian countries. Futhermore, he researched and developed national standard samples of ethnomedicine, completed the new drug development of Ela.Tablets, received clinical approvals, transferred those approvals to Pharmaceutical Enterprises, and started clinical trial.

区域创新奖获得者

韩 林 海

韩林海，1967 年 10 月出生于内蒙古自治区。1993 年获哈尔滨建筑工程学院（现哈尔滨工业大学）博士学位。现任广西大学校长、西部陆海新通道发展研究院院长，清华大学兼职教授。国际标准化组织混凝土、钢筋混凝土和预应力混凝土技术委员会主席顾问组委员、WG2 工作组召集人，国家技术标准创新基地（建筑工程）副理事长。

韩林海长期致力于钢管混凝土结构研究，建立了其全寿期安全性分析理论与设计技术体系，创新性发展了高性能钢管混凝土混合结构形式，实现了大型复杂土木工程主体结构体系安全适用范围的拓展。曾荣获第三届全国创新争先奖状、中国产学研合作创新奖、标准科技创新奖标准大师称号。

一、揭示钢管混凝土非线性约束效应，基于全寿期性能演化建立了混凝土本构模型与构件承载力计算体系，奠定了钢管混凝土结构设计的核心理论基础

钢管混凝土力学性能兼具优势和复杂性的根源在于钢管对混凝土的约束效应。研究揭示了该约束效应的强非线性特征及其与混凝土塑性相耦合的力学本质，进而提出综合反映钢管与混凝土几何、物理特性的约束效应系数概念，以描述钢管内混凝土的塑性应力强化与软化规律，实现了对以高离散性为特征的混凝土受力状态在应变、时间、温度多重维度上的准确定量表征，系统建立了瞬时应力、长期应力、循环应力、高温下及高温作用后钢管内混凝土的系列本构模型，从根本上纠正了基于传统定值约束理论的本构模型对其塑性应力发展规律的预测错误。

揭示压 / 拉 – 弯 – 扭 – 剪复杂受力及长期荷载作用下钢管混凝土构件的力学特性，提出其失效准则；阐明了反复荷载、撞击作用下构件的累积损伤规律、软化与卸载刚度特征；实现了荷载 – 温度 – 时间多场耦合作用下构件抗火性能的准确预测，解决了以往采用热力分离路径无法正确计算其火灾下应力重分布的难题，提出了复杂受力与长期荷载、地震、撞击及火灾作用下构件承载力计算方法。由此，系统构建了基于全寿期性能演化的钢管混凝土构件分析理论。

相关成果获2019年国家自然科学奖二等奖。

二、创新性发展了高性能钢管混凝土混合结构形式，系统构建了其全寿期分析理论与设计技术体系，拓展了大型复杂土木工程主体结构体系的安全适用范围

提出以钢管混凝土为主要构件、与其他构（部）件优化混合而成且共同工作的钢管混凝土混合结构概念，创新性发展了高性能钢管混凝土混合结构形式，包括桁式（钢管混凝土弦杆与钢腹杆混合）、加劲（钢管混凝土构件与其外包钢筋混凝土混合）、中空夹层（空心钢管混凝土构件与其内置钢管混合）等，提升了结构承载能力。发明了保障混合作用的连接节点与结构构造，突破了该类结构设计关键共性技术瓶颈。研发了钢管混凝土混合结构连接节点的三维科学测试装置，解决了钢管混凝土弦杆侧向倾斜承压测试难题，据此明晰了节点受力特性。基于试验研究，阐明了钢管混凝土混合结构受力全过程中构（部）件间混合作用效应与共同工作机制。

建立了贯通施工与服役全过程的钢管混凝土混合结构分析方法，提出其在施工期结构形式动态转换过程中的钢管初应力限值、钢管内混凝土脱空容限等关键性安全判据；明晰了其在服役期长期荷载与地震、撞击、火灾耦合作用下的工作机理，实现了其时变模拟及多工况承载力准确预测，从根本上解决了以往半经验计算方法无法实现该类结构全寿期安全性设计的难题。

混合结构形式及承载力计算方法等主要研究成果被广泛应用于我国西部多项重要工程建设，如京昆高速雅西段雅安干海子特大桥、川藏公路汶川克枯特大桥，目前正应用于在建的川藏铁路雅安至林芝段金沙江特大桥等标志性工程主体结构设计。此外，该成果还被应用于凉山金阳河特大桥、凉山州金阳县溜索改桥工程及布拖县金沙江溜索改桥工程等，为改善我国西南地区多个国家级贫困县的区域交通水平作出贡献。

主持制定我国《钢管混凝土混合结构技术标准》等6部技术标准，完善我国钢管混凝土结构领域技术标准体系；主编国际首部中空夹层钢管混凝土结构英文设计指南，主持制定国际标准ISO/DIS 16521 *Design Standard for Concrete-Filled Steel Tubular*（*CFST*）*Hybrid Structures*。相关成果荣获2022年教育部高等学校科学研究优秀成果奖自然科学一等奖、中国专利优秀奖、标准科技创新一等奖。

作为主要负责人，筹建广西西部陆海新通道发展研究院、广西大学省部共建特色金属材料与组合结构全寿命安全国家重点实验室、西部陆海新通道重大基础设施全寿命安全与耐久学科创新引智基地。

Awardee of Region Innovation Prize, Han Linhai

Han Linhai was born in Inner Mongolia Autonomous Region in October 1967. He is engaged in teaching and research in the area of structural engineering. In the past 30 years, he has focused on the concrete–filled steel tubular (CFST) structure and established its life–cycle–based analytical theory, including the discovery of new phenomenon, the revealing of characteristic mechanical trends, the invention of structural detailing, the development of novel experimental apparatus, and the accurate calculations of structural resistances. He currently serves as President of Guangxi University, and is a professor at Guangxi University and Tsinghua University.He was appointed as a committee member of the Chair Advisory Group of ISO/TC 71, and serves as the convenor of ISO/TC 71/WG 2. He currently serves as the American Society of Civil Engineers (ASCE), and the Institution of Structural Engineering (IStructE), respectively.

The research outcomes have been applied to the design of over 50 iconic constructions in sectors related to building, highway, railway, civil aviation, energy, etc. He has presided over the development of 6 technical standards on CFST structures, including the National Standard of China *Technical Standard for Concrete-Filled Steel Tubular Hybrid Structures*, GB/T 51446–2021 (Chinese Edition and English Edition) . He also is presiding over the development of an international standard ISO/DIS 16521 *Design Standard for Concrete-Filled Steel Tubular* (*CFST*) *Hybrid Structures*.

区域创新奖获得者

梅 生 伟

梅生伟，1964 年 9 月出生于新疆维吾尔自治区伊犁哈萨克自治州。1996 年获中国科学院系统科学研究所理学博士学位，1996—1998 年在清华大学电机系进行博士后研究。1998 年至今在清华大学电机系工作，先后兼任青海大学新能源光伏产业研究中心主任、青海大学副校长。作为访问教授，先后在英国布鲁内尔大学、日本上智大学、国立新加坡大学开展合作研究。美国电气和电子工程师协会、英国工程技术学会会士，中国电机工程学会、中国电工技术学会、中国自动化学会会士，国家能源局储能示范工程首席科学家，国家重点基础研究发展计划储能专项专家组成员，中国电工技术学会首届高景德科技成就奖和中国可再生能源学会优秀科技工作者奖获得者，青海最美科技工作者、中宣部最美科技工作者 100 名宣传人物。

梅生伟主要从事储能和新能源领域研究，在大规模新能源安全输送、高效消纳和清洁存储等相关领域取得了一系列开创性成果。

一、非补燃压缩空气储能技术及关键装备

2011 年，梅生伟与卢强院士提出了基于压缩热回馈的非补燃压缩空气储能技术路线，自此，他带领电—热—气—机跨学科团队历经十年攻关，突破了非稳态压缩、低㶲损换热、变工况膨胀发电、储 – 网协同控制四大关键技术。特别是针对常规压缩机电耗高、空气透平发电机惯量比低导致动态性能差两大瓶颈，原创性提出低 / 中 / 高压三段串联压缩方案，显著降低压缩电耗；进一步提出了基于轴系角速度与附加电磁转矩的空气透平气门开度控制策略，实现平滑并网，一次调频性能超越火电、抽蓄和燃气机组考核要求。主持研制高负荷 / 宽工况多级离心压缩机、大型发夹式油—气换热器、储气盐穴大尺寸交变注采井管、宽压力 – 变工况空气透平膨胀发电机四大首台套全国产化装备，形成大容量、高效率、长寿命、零排放压缩空气储能技术的完备自主知识产权体系。

主持建设的国家能源局储能示范工程“金坛60 MW/300 MWh盐穴压缩空气储能电站”是全球首座商业运行的非补燃压缩空气储能电站，储能效率达62.38%（国际最先进的美国 McIntosh 补燃式电站效率为55%）；发布标准3项，立项国家标准1项，编制18项，初步建立了非补燃压缩空气储能标准体系。主持在建11项压缩空气储能工程，总装机容量1500兆瓦，引领了大规模清洁储能技术和产业新发展。相关成果获安徽省科技进步奖一等奖和中国电工技术学会创会42年来首个技术发明奖特等奖。

二、复杂电网自组织临界理论及新能源安全输送技术

提出源荷侧设备提升抗扰能力、网侧实施主动防御的源网荷协同技术路线。针对源荷侧非线性装备，提出基于变尺度微分同胚的非线性鲁棒控制理论及设计方法，研发了发电机励磁、调速等工业控制器，避免由稳定事故引发连锁故障。在网侧建立复杂电网自组织临界理论，揭示了临界态下微小故障触发连锁故障并扩散传播的机理；提出“宏－微观协同”的整体动力学建模方法，发明了连锁故障准动态仿真技术和基于半张量积的稳定域边界机械化计算方法，实现了连锁故障传播方向、速度、范围的在线快速精准分析。主持研发了复杂交直流电力系统连锁故障预演仿真平台、风险评估预警平台、连锁故障在线主动阻断平台，构建了连锁故障主动防御系统，应用于西电东送六大交直流输电通道、24个省网公司和国务院公共安全平台，保障新能源安全输送功率1.4亿千瓦以上。相关成果获国家自然科学奖二等奖、国家科技进步奖二等奖和教育部自然科学奖一等奖。

三、工程博弈论及新能源高效消纳理论与技术

受维纳控制论反馈理念和钱学森工程控制论启发，梅生伟提出“以博弈均衡协调冲突”的新思想，针对多主体、多目标、不确定系统工程决策问题，提出非合作、合作、演化三项工程博弈建模原理与均衡分析方法，形成工程博弈新理论，系统性解决了含虚拟博弈者的多阶段动态优化决策、相互冲突的多目标优化决策和系统演化过程中不同利益主体决策相互影响三大难题。

根据非合作工程博弈原理，以电网调度和大自然（新能源出力）为博弈者，提出日前—日内—实时三阶段二人零和动态博弈调控模型及纳什－贝叶斯均衡求解算法，发明了由24小时机组组合、4小时备用整定、分钟级实时调度以及风光场站群秒级自律控制构成的新能源电力系统多时间尺度滚动优化调控技术，最大程度提升新能源消纳能力。主持研发了新能源电力系统多时间尺度鲁棒一体化调控平台，应用于青藏等地700余座风光场站，装机逾3000万千瓦，近三年支撑消纳风光电量1001亿度。全面支撑青海省域全清洁能源供电实践活动，供电区域和时长五次刷新世界纪录。相关成果获青海省科技进步奖一等奖、中国可再生能源学会科技进步奖一等奖和中电联电力科技创新大奖。国家基金委自2018年起，将工程博弈论列为控制科学与工程下的学科新方向。

Awardee of Region Innovation Prize, Mei Shengwei

Mei Shengwei was born in Ili Kazak Autonomous Prefecture of Xinjiang Uygur Autonomous Region in September 1964. He received his B.Sc. degree in mathematics from Xinjiang University in 1984, an M.Sc. degree in operations research from Tsinghua University in 1989, and a Ph.D. degree in automatic control from the Chinese Academy of Sciences in 1996. He is currently a Professor at Tsinghua University and has served as the Vice President of Qinghai University since 2020. He is an IEEE/IET fellow.

Prof. Mei engages in the research of fundamental theory and enabling technologies in energy storage and renewable energy. He has done pioneering research work in related fields, including long-distance secure transmission of large-scale renewable energy, efficient accommodation of renewable energy, and advanced technologies of clean physical storage.

He compressed air energy storage is an up-and-coming large-scale clean physical energy storage technique, broke through four key technologies: unsteady-state compressor, low-exergy-loss heat exchanger, variable-working--condition compressed-air turbine, and storage-grid coordinated control. These works created an independently owned intellectual property rights system with complete technical capabilities in this technology.

He established a fundamental theory of self-organization criticality in complex power grids, revealing the mechanism underlying the triggering and spreading of chain failures at critical states due to small failures. Based on this, he has created rapid identification techniques for vulnerable sources and high-risk fault paths in complex AC/DC power systems and online active preventing techniques for cascading failures in AC/DC systems. He also has successfully led the development of an online prevention system for blocking cascading failures in AC/DC systems and applied it to the major transmission corridors for power delivery from western to eastern China, ensuring the safe transmission of more than 140 GW of renewable energy.

Prof. Mei proposed a new idea of "coordinating conflicts in engineering decision-making through game equilibrium", addressing multi-agent, multi-objective, and uncertain system engineering decision-making problems. He developed three principles with equilibrium analysis methods for building game-theoretic models of engineering problems involving uncooperative, cooperative, and evolutionary behaviors, thereby establishing a new theoretical framework for engineering games that holistically solves three major challenges.

区域创新奖获得者

王福清

王福清，1963年4月出生于山东省滨州市。1992年获山东医科大学（现山东大学）生化药学专业硕士学位。先后担任西藏金稞集团总工程师、青藏高原特色农牧产品深加工国家地方联合工程研究中心主任、西藏天虹科技股份有限责任公司总工程师。长期兼任中国药学会理事、常务理事，中国药学会生化与生物技术药物专业委员会副主任委员，中国医药企业管理协会副会长。

王福清领导开展了大量依托西藏特色资源的科研开发工作，攻克了高原低温低氧生物加工中的多项技术难题并实现产业化，为促进西藏民族地区特色生物产业的发展作出了突出贡献。曾荣获国家和省部级科技奖励13项。

一、提升西藏特色物种牦牛深加工的高值利用

王福清带领团队开展包括青藏高原特色物种牦牛肉、奶、软骨和脏器在内的深加工高值利用技术研究，突破了牦牛乳深加工中的酶解助溶、二次护色等技术难题，实现了牦牛乳酪蛋白制造的产业化；在此基础上，进一步优化牦牛干酪素产业化工艺，发明了一种药用辅料干酪素水凝胶制备工艺技术，攻克了利用干酪素的凝胶特性制备牦牛干酪素水凝胶的技术难题，获得国家发明专利授权并完成中试规模的成果转化；利用牦牛废弃脏器——牦牛胰腺为原料，以胰腺中自身的胰蛋白酶激活羧肽酶原，凝练提取和纯化牦牛胰腺来源羧肽酶B过程中去除内源性蛋白酶的关键技术，攻克了牦牛胰腺制取高纯度羧肽酶B的技术难题；在生化提取基础上，采用原生质体融合、基因重组等微生物技术解决了重组羧肽酶原B在表达过程中易发生降解的技术瓶颈，得到大量羧肽酶原B，酶原经过酶解、激活、纯化获得活性的羧肽酶B，开发了大肠杆菌重组羧肽酶B的产业化技术，可支撑规模化生产且具有发酵单位高、成本低、无污染等优点；攻关解决了采用化学修饰法提高牦牛硫酸软骨素生物利用等技术难题，开发了以牦牛硫酸软骨素为主

要原料的保健食品。“青藏高原牦牛乳深加工技术研究与产品开发”成果获2010年国家科学技术进步奖二等奖。

二、实现高原生物制造的技术创新与产业化

通过产学研合作，实现了生物技术制造药食两用高端原料和科研试剂在西藏“零的突破”。完成西藏第一个生物制造领域国家战略性新兴产业项目的建设，建成了约28000平方米的研发、中试验证与生产车间，开发了酿酒酵母工程菌高产腺苷蛋氨酸的发酵工程与分离纯化的关键技术，攻克了在高原极端环境下采用酿酒酵母工程菌高产腺苷蛋氨酸的产业化关键技术，解决了在高原极端环境下高密度发酵过程中的发酵水平低、纯度低等技术难题，产业意义重大。

以授权发明专利“人胰岛素原C肽高产菌株的构建”关键技术为基础，通过进一步优化高效表达重组人胰岛素原C肽的基因工程菌，完善人胰岛素原C肽高密度发酵、分离纯化等规模化生产工艺，发酵液表达水平达2400mg/L以上、蛋白活性回收率高于45%、产品含量高于98%，在一定程度上解决了活性肽在发酵表达过程中易降解、表达产品难纯化和难检测三个关键技术难题，所生产的人胰岛素原C肽已经成功作为高纯科研试剂应用于科学试验，产业应用潜力巨大。

三、支撑藏中药材加工技术与质量双升级

主持建设西藏藏中药饮片加工工程研究中心，截至2022年12月，已经建成藏中药饮片检测技术研发与质量标准研究室、藏中药饮片防霉防蛀工艺开发研究室、藏中药破壁饮片加工研究室、藏中药传统饮片工程化研究与验证车间和藏中药直接口服饮片工程化验证车间，解决和优化了藏党参、藏天麻、藏玛咖、手掌参、野生灵芝孢子粉、藏贝母、大花红景天和波棱子瓜等藏中药饮片的加工关键技术，提升了上述藏中药材的质量控制技术，部分藏中药饮片的关键加工技术已完成成果转化，带动了西藏藏中药饮片行业研发的整体水平和区内藏中药饮片行业的可持续发展，成为支撑西藏藏药材产业的重要技术支撑平台。

Awardee of Region Innovation Prize, Wang Fuqing

Wang Fuqing was born in Binzhou City of Shandong Province in April 1963. He obtained his master’s degree in pharmaceutical biochemistry at Shandong Medical University now Shandong University) in 1992. From 2005 to 2023, he served as the Chief Engineer of Xizang Jinke Group Co., Ltd. Also, Director of the National and Local Joint Engineering Research Center for Deep Processing of Special Agricultural and Animal Products on the Qinghai-Tibet Plateau, and the

Chief Engineer of Xizang Tianhong Technology Co., Ltd. successively. Wang Fuqing has long been the executive director of China Pharmaceutical Association, vice chairman of the Biochemical and Biotechnology Drugs Professional Committee of China Pharmaceutical Association, vice president of the China Pharmaceutical Enterprises Association.

Wang Fuqing led a team that achieved breakthroughs in key technologies for the deep processing and high-value utilization of characteristic species from the Qinghai-Tibet Plateau, including yak meat, milk, cartilage, and organs. They constructed genetically engineered bacteria for efficient expression of recombinant human insulin precursor C-peptide, optimized high-yield adenosine amino acid brewing yeast engineered bacteria, and resolved technical challenges such as low fermentation levels and low purity during high-density fermentation processes in the extreme plateau environment. This resulted in a breakthrough in the production of dual-use high-end biological manufacturing materials and scientific research reagents in Tibet. Additionally, they made breakthroughs in the processing and quality control techniques of common Tibetan traditional Chinese medicinal herbs such as Tibetan Fritillary Bulb, supporting the double upgrading of technology and quality in the Tibetan medicinal herb industry. Based on the research achievements above, he has received 13 national and provincial-level awards.

附　　录

APPENDICES

何梁何利基金评选章程

（2020 年 5 月 27 日何梁何利基金信托委员会全体会议通过）

一、总　　则

第一条　何梁何利基金（以下称“本基金”）由何善衡慈善基金会有限公司、梁銶琚博士、何添博士、利国伟博士之伟伦基金有限公司于 1994 年 3 月 30 日捐款成立。2005 年 10 月 24 日经香港高等法院批准。基金捐款人，除了何善衡慈善基金会有限公司及利国伟博士之伟伦基金有限公司外，梁銶琚慈善基金会有限公司和何添基金有限公司各自分别为已故梁銶琚博士及已故何添博士之遗产承办人指定之慈善机构，以便根据本基金信托契约之条款行使有关权力或给予所需批准。

第二条　本基金的宗旨是：

（一）促进中国的科学与技术发展；

（二）奖励取得杰出成就和重大创新的科学技术工作者。

第三条　本基金依法登记设立何梁何利基金（香港）北京代表处，负责何梁何利基金科学技术奖评选工作，执行基金在中国内地的相关业务。

何梁何利基金（香港）北京代表处的业务主管部门为中华人民共和国科学技术部。

二、评奖条件

第四条　本基金奖励和资助致力于推进中国科学技术取得成就及进步与创新的个人。

第五条　本基金奖励和资助具备下列条件的中华人民共和国公民：

（一）对推动科学技术事业发展有杰出贡献；

（二）热爱祖国，积极为国家现代化建设服务，有高尚的社会公德和职业道德；

（三）在我国科学技术研究院（所）、大专院校、企业以及信托委员会认为适当的其他机构从事科学研究、教学或技术工作已满 5 年。

第六条　获奖候选人须由评选委员会选定的提名人以书面形式推荐。

提名人由科学技术领域具有一定资格的专家包括海外学者组成。

三、奖　　项

第七条　本基金设“何梁何利基金科学与技术成就奖”“何梁何利基金科学与技术进步奖”“何梁何利基金科学与技术创新奖”，每年评奖一次。

第八条　何梁何利基金科学与技术成就奖授予下列杰出科学技术工作者：

（一）长期致力于推进国家科学技术进步，贡献卓著，历史上取得国际高水准学术成就者；

（二）在科学技术前沿，取得重大科技突破，攀登当今科技高峰，领先世界先进水平者；

（三）推进技术创新，建立强大自主知识产权和自主品牌，其产业居于当今世界前列者。

何梁何利基金科学与技术成就奖获奖人每人颁发奖励证书和奖金 100 万港元。

第九条　何梁何利基金科学与技术进步奖授予在特定学科领域取得重大发明、发现和科技成果者，尤其是在近年内有突出贡献者。

何梁何利基金科学与技术进步奖按学科领域分设下列奖项：

（一）数学力学奖

（二）物理学奖

（三）化学奖

（四）天文学奖

（五）气象学奖

（六）地球科学奖

（七）生命科学奖

（八）农学奖

（九）医学药学奖

（十）古生物学、考古学奖

（十一）机械电力技术奖

（十二）电子信息技术奖

（十三）交通运输技术奖

（十四）冶金材料技术奖

（十五）化学工程技术奖

（十六）资源能源技术奖

（十七）生态环保技术奖

（十八）工程建设技术奖

何梁何利基金科学与技术进步奖获奖人每人颁发奖励证书和奖金 20 万港元。

第十条　何梁何利基金科学与技术创新奖授予具有高水平科技成就而通过技术创新和管理创新，创建自主知识产权产业和著名品牌，创造重大经济效益和社会效益的杰出贡献者。

何梁何利基金科学与技术创新奖分设下列奖项：

（一）青年创新奖

（二）产业创新奖

（三）区域创新奖

何梁何利基金科学与技术创新奖获奖人每人颁发奖励证书和奖金 20 万港元。

第十一条　本基金每年各奖项名额如下：

何梁何利基金科学与技术成就奖不超过5名；何梁何利基金科学与技术进步奖、何梁何利基金科学与技术创新奖总数不超过65名（原则上科学与技术进步奖和科学与技术创新奖名额的比例为3∶1至2∶1）。而奖金总额不超过该年度信托委员会审议通过的奖金总额。

具体名额根据年度资金运作情况和评选情况确定。

四、评选委员会

第十二条　本基金成立由各相关领域具有高尚道德情操、精深学术造诣、热心科技奖励事业的专家组成的评选委员会。

评选委员会委员经过信托委员会批准、颁发聘任书后，独立行使职能，负责评选工作。

第十三条　评选委员会委员最多不超过24人，其中主任一人、副主任二人、秘书长一人，由内地学者和海外学者出任。

评选委员会委员内地学者和海外学者的比例，原则上每四名委员中，内地学者为三人，海外学者为一人。

评选委员会主任、副主任由基金信托契约补充条款规定的信托委员兼任。其中主任由补充契约所指明的与科技部有关的信托委员兼任，副主任二人分别由补充契约所指明的与教育部有关的信托委员和补充契约所指明的国际学者信托委员兼任。评选委员会秘书长由信托委员会任命并征得捐款人同意的人选担任。

评选委员会委员实行任期制，一任三年，可以连聘连任。

评选委员会委员原则上每三年更换四分之一（不包括主任、副主任及秘书长）。

此外，评选委员会委员的聘任，贯彻相对稳定和适度更新的原则。其办法由评选委员会制定。

评选委员会办公室设在北京，挂靠科学技术部。

第十四条　评选委员会根据评选工作需要，可组织若干专业评审组、奖项评审组，根据提名人的提名推荐材料对被提名人进行初评，产生获奖候选人，提交评选委员会终评。

专业评审组、奖项评审组的评委由评选委员会任命。

第十五条　本基金各奖项获奖人由评选委员会会议评定。

何梁何利基金科学与技术进步奖、何梁何利基金科学与技术创新奖的获奖人，由评选委员会根据专业评审组、奖项评审组的评选结果，评选审定。

何梁何利基金科学与技术成就奖获奖人，由评选委员会全体会议根据评选委员提名评选产生。评选委员会设立预审小组，必要时对候选人进行考察和听证。

第十六条　评选委员会会议贯彻“公平、公正、公开”原则，实行一人一票制，以无记名形式表决确定获奖人。何梁何利基金科学与技术进步奖、何梁何利基金科学与技术创新奖的候选人，获半数赞成票为获奖人。何梁何利基金科学与技术成就奖的候选人，获三分之二多数赞成票为获奖人。

第十七条　评选委员会在评定获奖人名额时，应适当考虑奖种、学科和区域之间的平衡。

五、授　　奖

第十八条　评选委员会评选结果揭晓前须征求获奖人本人意愿，并通知捐款人及信托委员会。遵照捐款人意愿，获奖人应承诺于获奖后，继续在国内从事科学研究和技术工作不少于三年。

第十九条　本基金每年适当时候举行颁奖仪式，由评选委员会安排向何梁何利基金各奖项获得者颁发证书和奖金，并通过新闻媒体公布获奖人员名单及其主要贡献。

六、出版物和学术会议

第二十条　本基金每年出版介绍获奖人及其主要科学技术成就的出版物。

出版物的编辑、出版工作由评选委员会负责。

第二十一条　本基金每年举办学术报告会、研讨会，由评选委员会委员、获奖人代表介绍其学术成就及相关学科领域的进展。

根据基金财政状况，本基金各专业领域专题学术讨论会可在海外举办。

本基金学术论坛由评选委员会负责组织。

七、附　　则

第二十二条　本基金评选委员会每年例会一次，总结当年工作，部署下一年度工作，研究和决定重大事宜。

第二十三条　本章程由本基金评选委员会解释。

第二十四条　本章程自 2020 年 5 月 27 日施行。

REGULATIONS OF HO LEUNG HO LEE FOUNDATION ON THE EVALUATION AND EXAMINATION OF ITS PRIZES AND AWARDS

(Adopted at the Plenary Meeting of the Trust Board on May 27, 2020)

I General Provisions

Article 1 Ho Leung Ho Lee Foundation (hereinafter referred to as " the Foundation") was established on March 30, 1994 in Hong Kong with funds donated by the S H Ho Foundation Limited, Dr. Leung Kau-Kui, Dr. Ho Tim and Dr. Lee Quo-Wei's Wei Lun Foundation Limited. With the approval of the High Court of Hong Kong, apart from S H Ho Foundation Limited and Wei Lun Foundation Limited (donors of the Foundation), Leung Kau-Kui Foundation Limited and Ho Tim Foundation Limited have respectively been nominated by the estates of the late Dr. Leung Kau-Kui and Dr. Ho Tim to and they can as from October 24, 2005 exercise the powers or give the necessary approvals under the terms of the Foundation's trust deed.

Article 2 Purposes of the Foundation are:

(1) To promote the development of science and technology in China.

(2) To reward the scientific and technical personnel with outstanding achievements and great innovations.

Article 3 The Beijing Representative Office of the Ho Leung Ho Lee Foundation (Hong Kong) is established through registration in accordance with the law. It is responsible for selecting the winners of science and technology prizes and awards granted by the Ho Leung Ho Lee Foundation, and carries out the works related to the Foundation on the mainland of China.

The Ministry of Science and Technology of the People's Republic of China acts as the competent authority responsible for the work of the Beijing Representative Office of the Ho Leung Ho Lee Foundation (Hong Kong).

II Criteria for Awards

Article 4 The Foundation shall grant awards and prizes to individuals who are devoted to the achievements, progress and innovations of China's science and technology.

Article 5 The Foundation shall grant awards and prizes to the citizens of the People's Republic of China who meet the following criteria:

(1) Having made outstanding contributions in promoting the development of science and technology.

(2) Being patriotic, vigorously working for the modernization drive of the country, and preserving lofty social morality and professional ethics.

(3) Being with at least five years of scientific researches, teaching or technical working experience in China's science and technology research institutes, institutions for higher learning and universities, enterprises and other organizations which the Board of Trustees regards as appropriate.

Article 6 Candidates for the awards and prizes of the Foundation shall be recommended in writing by nominators identified by the Selection Board.

Nominators should be qualified experts (including those overseas) in various fields of sciences and technology.

Ⅲ Awards and Prizes

Article 7 The Foundation sets three annual prizes. They are the Prize for Scientific and Technological Achievements of Ho Leung Ho Lee Foundation, the Prize for Scientific and Technological Progress of Ho Leung Ho Lee Foundation, and the Prize for Scientific and Technological Innovation of Ho Leung Ho Lee Foundation.

Article 8 The Prize for Scientific and Technological Achievements of Ho Leung Ho Lee Foundation shall be awarded to the outstanding science and technology personnel as follows:

(1) Those who have devoted to scientific and technological progress in China for a long time, having made significant contributions and world-class academic achievements.

(2) Those who have made great breakthroughs in the frontline of science and technology, attaining high levels in science and technology and leading the trend in specific areas in the world.

(3) Those who have made great efforts in pushing forward the technology innovation and have built up powerful self intellectual property and brand of its own so that its industry ranks the top of today's world.

Each winner of the Prize for Scientific and Technological Achievements of Ho Leung Ho Lee Foundation will receive a certificate and the amount of the prize of HK $ 1000000.

Article 9 The Prize for Scientific and Technological Progress of Ho Leung Ho Lee Foundation is for those who have made important inventions, discoveries and achievements in specific subject areas, especially having remarkable contributions in recent years.

The following prizes of the Prize for Scientific and Technological Progress of Ho Leung Ho Lee Foundation are set up by subjects:

(1) Award for Mathematics and Mechanics

(2) Award for Physics

(3) Award for Chemistry

(4) Award for Astronomy

(5) Award for Meteorology

(6) Award for Earth Sciences

(7) Award for Life Sciences

(8) Award for Agronomy

(9) Award for Medical Sciences and Materia Medica

(10) Award for Paleontology and Archaeology

(11) Award for Machinery and Electric Technology

(12) Award for Electronics and Information Technology

(13) Award for Communication and Transportation Technology

(14) Award for Metallurgy and Materials Technology

(15) Award for Chemical Engineering Technology

(16) Award for Resources and Energies Technology

(17) Award for Ecology and Environmental Protection Technology

(18) Award for Engineering and Construction Technology

Each winner of the Prize for Science and Technological Progress of Ho Leung Ho Lee Foundation will be awarded a certificate and the amount of the prize of HK $ 200000.

Article 10 The Prize for Scientific and Technological Innovation of Ho Leung Ho Lee Foundation is for the outstanding contributors who have made high level achievements in science and technology, created industry with self intellectual property and famous brands through technology and management innovation, and thus have created great economic and social benefits for the society.

The following prizes of the Prize for Scientific and Technological Innovation of Ho Leung Ho Lee Foundation are set up:

(1) Award for Youth Innovation

(2) Award for Industrial Innovation

(3) Award for Region Innovation

Each winner of the Prize for Scientific and Technological Innovation of Ho Leung Ho Lee Foundation will be awarded a certificate and the amount of the prize of HK $ 200000.

Article 11 Annual quotas of awardees of each prize of Ho Leung Ho Lee Foundation are as follows:

There should be no more than 5 awardees each year for the Prize for Scientific and Technological Achievements of Ho Leung Ho Lee Foundation; and the total number of the winners of the Prize for Scientific and Technological Progress of Ho Leung Ho Lee Foundation and the Prize for Scientific and Technological Innovation of Ho Leung Ho Lee Foundation should be no more than 65 (The proportion of the awardees of the Prize for Scientific and Technological Progress of Ho

Leung Ho Lee Foundation and the Prize for Scientific and Technological Innovation of Ho Leung Ho Lee Foundation is in principle from 3 : 1 to 2 : 1) . And the total amount of all the Prizes awarded should not exceed the total amount of prize moneys of the year as approved by the Board of Trustees for that year.

The number of winners of each prize should be decided according to the situation each year of the operation of the Foundation's funds and the results of evaluation and selection for the year.

Ⅳ Selection Board

Article 12 A Selection Board shall be constituted under the Foundation, consisting of scholars who are highly respected in ethics, with accomplishments in academic researches and devotion to the work of award of science and technology prizes.

Members of the Selection Board shall independently exercise the powers and are responsible for the evaluation work after they have been appointed with the approval of the Board of Trustees and received the letters of appointment.

Article 13 The total number of the members of the Selection Board should be no more than 24. Among them, there will be one Chair, two Vice Chairs and one Secretary-General. Both local and overseas scholars could be members of the Selection Board.

For every four members of the Selection Board, the ratio between local and overseas scholars should in principle be 3 : 1.

The Chair and the two Vice Chairs of the Selection Board should also be members of the Board of Trustees as stated in the Foundation's Supplemental trust deed. Among them, the Chair should be the member of the Board of Trustees who is related, as stated in the Foundation's Supplemental trust deed, to the Ministry of Science and Technology. And the two Vice Chairs should respectively be the member of the Board of Trustees who is related, as stated in the Foundation's Supplemental trust deed, to the Ministry of Education and the international scholar member of the Board of Trustees as mentioned in the Foundation's Supplemental trust deed.

Secretary General of the Selection Board should be appointed by the Board of Trustees with the agreement of the donors as well.

A system of the set term of office is instituted for members of the Selection Board. Each term of office of the members of the Selection Board is 3 years. A member of the Selection Board may serve consecutive terms.

In principle, the members of the Selection Board shall be altered a quarter every 3 years (except Chair, Vice Chair and Secretary General.)

Besides, the appointment of the members of the Selection Board should be in line with the principles of comparative stability and proper renewal. The Selection Board will be responsible for formulation of the ways of selection.

The office of the Selection Board is located in Beijing and affiliated to the Ministry of Science and Technology of China.

Article 14 Several specific professional evaluation panels or prize evaluation panels may be set up under the Selection Board when it is necessary. The first round of evaluation is done according to recommendation materials submitted by the nominators with a candidate list as the results. This list will be submitted to the Selection Board for a final evaluation.

Members of the professional evaluation panels and prize evaluation panels shall be appointed by the Selection Board.

Article 15 Winners of the prizes of the Foundation are evaluated and decided by the Selection Board.

The Selection Board shall evaluate and determine the winners of the Prize for Scientific and Technological Progress of Ho Leung Ho Lee Foundation and the Prize for Scientific and Technological Innovation of Ho Leung Ho Lee Foundation on the basis of results of the work of the professional evaluation panels or the prize evaluation panels.

The Prize for Scientific and Technological Achievements of Ho Leung Ho Lee Foundation should be decided on a plenary meeting of the Selection Board and on the basis of the nomination of the Selection Board. The Selection Board may set up preliminary evaluation panel to exercise the right of examination and hearing of the candidates when necessary.

Article 16 The Selection Board shall work with the principles of "Fairness, Justness and Openness" and "One Member One Vote" . Decisions on winners of prizes of the Foundation are made in a way of anonymous ballot by the members of the Selection Board. The endorsement of at least half of the members of the Selection Board is a must for a candidate to win the Prize for Scientific and Technological Progress of Ho Leung Ho Lee Foundation and the Prize for Scientific and Technological Innovation of Ho Leung Ho Lee Foundation; while at least two-third of favorable votes of the total number is a must for candidates to win the Prize for Scientific and Technological Achievements of Ho Leung Ho Lee Foundation.

Article 17 The Selection Board should take the balance between types of prize, between subjects and between regions into consideration in the process of evaluation.

V Awarding

Article 18 The Selection Board must ask for the winners' willingness prior to any public announcement of the results of evaluation and selection, and notify both the donors and the Board of Trustees. According to the wishes of the donors, the winners are required to stay in China and continue to carry on scientific researches or technological work for no less than 3 years after receiving the prizes.

Article 19 An award granting ceremony will be held each year at a proper time, in which the winners shall be granted with certificates and prizes as arranged by the Selection Board. The list of awardees and their major contributions will be publicized through media.

Ⅵ Publications and Academic Seminars

Article 20 The Foundation shall make a publication yearly to introduce the awardees and their major scientific and technological achievements.

The Selection Board is responsible for editing and publication of the publications.

Article 21 The Foundation shall organize academic seminars every year, in which members of the Selection Board and representatives of the awardees introduce their academic achievements and updated progress in the related areas and make relevant reports where appropriate.

Should the financial situation of the Foundation permits, the academic seminars of specific subjects of the Foundation may be held abroad.

The Selection Board is responsible for the organizing academic forums of the Foundation.

Ⅶ Supplementary Provisions

Article 22 The Selection Board of the Foundation holds a meeting annually to summarize the work of the year, to plan the work of the following year and to study and decide on the relevant important issues.

Article 23 The Selection Board of the Foundation shall have the right of explanation of the Articles of this regulation.

Article 24 This regulation becomes effective on May 27, 2020.

关于何梁何利基金获奖科学家异议处理若干规定

（2009年5月20日何梁何利基金信托委员会会议通过）

一、总　　则

为了正确处理对何梁何利基金获奖人提出异议的投诉事件，弘扬科学精神，崇尚科学道德，抵御社会不正之风和科研不端行为，提升何梁何利基金科学与技术奖的权威性和公信力，制定本规定。

二、基本原则

处理对获奖人投诉事件，贯彻以事实为依据，以法律为准绳的原则，遵循科学共同体认同的道德准则，区别情况，妥善处置。

三、受　　理

涉及对获奖科学家主要科技成果评价、知识产权权属以及与奖项有关事项提出异议的署名投诉信件，由评选委员会受理，并调查处理。

匿名投诉信件，原则上不予受理。但涉及获奖人因科研不端行为受到处分、学术资格被取消或与其学术著作、奖项评选相关重要情况的，应由评选委员会跟进调查核实处理。

四、调　　查

评选委员会受理投诉后，由评选委员会秘书长指定评选委员会办公室专人按以下工作程序办理：

1．将投诉信函复印件送交该获奖人的专业评审组负责人，征求意见。

2．专业评审组负责人有足够理由认为投诉异议不成立，没有必要调查的，评选委员会秘书长可决定终止处理。

专业评审组负责人认为投诉异议有一定依据，有必要进一步调查的，由评选委员会办公室向获奖人所在部门或单位发函听证。

3．获奖人所在部门或单位经调查，认为投诉异议不成立或基本不能成立的，应请该单位出具书面意见。评选委员会秘书长可据此决定终止处理。

获奖人所在部门或单位根据投诉认为获奖人涉嫌科研不端行为的，评选委员会应建议该部门或单位根据国家有关规定调查处理，并反馈查处信息。

4．调查结果应向信托委员会报告。

五、处理决定

获奖人所在部门或单位经调查认定获奖人确属科研不端行为，并作出相应处理的，评选委员会秘书长应当参照《中华人民共和国科学技术进步法》第七十一条规定，提出撤销其奖励决定（草案），经评选委员会主任批准后，提交信托委员会审议。

六、公　　告

因获奖人科研不端行为，撤销其奖励的决定经信托委员会审议通过后，由评选委员会在何梁何利基金年报上公告，并通知本人，返回奖励证书、奖金。

信托委员会对获奖人撤销奖励的决定是终局决定。

七、附　　则

本规定自 2009 年 6 月 1 日起试行。

附:《中华人民共和国科学技术进步法》第七十一条:

"违反本法规定，骗取国家科学技术奖励的，由主管部门依法撤销奖励，追回奖金，并依法给予处分。

违反本法规定，推荐的单位或者个人提供虚假数据、材料，协助他人骗取国家科学技术奖励的，由主管部门给予通报批评；情节严重的，暂停或者取消其推荐资格，并依法给予处分。"

REGULATIONS ON HANDLING THE COMPLAINT LODGED AGAINST THE PRIZE-WINNER WITH HO LEUNG HO LEE FOUNDATION

(Adopted at the Meeting of the Board of Trustees on May 20, 2009)

Ⅰ General Principle

For the purpose of handling properly the objection lodged against the prize-winner with Ho Leung Ho Lee Foundation, promoting scientific spirits and upholding scientific ethics, preventing social malpractice or misconduct in scientific research, and improving the public credibility and authority of Ho Leung Ho Lee Foundation with respect to awards for science and technology, the Selection Board hereby formulates the regulations as stipulated below.

Ⅱ Basic Principle

The Selection Board shall handle the complaint lodged against any prize-winner in accordance with the principle of taking the facts as the basis and taking the law as the criterion, and deal with each case properly by following the moral standard recognized by the scientific community.

Ⅲ Acceptance

For any duly signed letter of objection against a prize-wining scientist with respect to the appraisal of his major scientific and technological achievement, the ownership of intellectual property right and other prize-related matter, the Selection Board shall be responsible for acceptance of the letter of objection and for further investigation and handling thereof.

The Selection Board shall, in principle, not accept a letter of objection written or sent in an anonymous manner. However, if it is mentioned in the letter of objection that, due to misconduct of the prize-winner in the scientific research, the discipline measure is imposed against him, or his academic qualification is cancelled, or there is any other important matter concerning his academic publication and prize selection, such a letter of objection must be accepted by the Selection Board, followed by further investigation, verification and handling.

Ⅳ Investigation

Upon acceptance of a letter of objection, the Secretary General of the Selection Board shall designate a special person in the Office of Selection Board to handle the letter of objection according to the procedures as follows:

1. A copy of the letter of complaint shall be sent to the person-in-charge of the specialized evaluation team determining to grant the award to the prize-winner for soliciting his comment.

2. When the person-in-charge of the specialized evaluation team concludes with sufficient reason that the objection cannot be established and it is not necessary to make further investigation, the Secretary General of the Selection Board can make a decision as to terminate the handling of the letter of objection.

When the person-in-charge of the specialized evaluation team deems that the objection can be established on basis of facts but should be proved by further investigation, the office of the Selection Board shall issue a notification to the working unit of the prize-winner to request his presence at a hearing to be held.

3. If the working unit of the prize-winner deems that the objection cannot be established or basically cannot be established after investigation, the working unit is obligated to produce a formal document in writing to state its opinion. Then the Secretary General of the Selection Board has the right to make a decision as to the termination of the handling of the letter of objection.

In case the working unit of the prize-winner deems that the prize-winner commits malpractice or misconduct in proof of the letter of objection, the Selection Board is obligated to propose that the working unit carry out investigation in accordance with government regulations before making a response by sending a feedback to the Selection Board.

4. The investigation results should be reported to Ho Leung Ho Lee Foundation's Board of Trustees.

V Decision

Once the working unit of the prize-winner proves with further investigation that the prize-winner commits malpractice or misconduct, and takes discipline measure against the prize-winner, the Secretary General of the Selection Board should draft a proposal, in accordance with Article 71 of the *Law of the PRC on, Science and Technology Progres*s, on withdrawal of the prize awarded to the prize-winner. The proposal needs to be further approved by the Director of the Selection Board before being submitted to Ho Leung Ho Lee Foundation's Board of Trustees for deliberation.

Ⅵ Announcement

The Selection Board shall announce its decision with respect to withdrawal of the prize from the prize-winner, due to his malpractice or misconduct, in its annual report with approval of the Ho Leung Ho Lee Foundation's Board of Trustees, and shall notify the prize-winner that the prize and prize-winning certificate are to be cancelled. The decision to withdraw the prize from the prize-winner made by Ho Leung Ho Lee Foundation's Board of Trustees shall be final.

Ⅶ Appendix

These regulations shall enter into trial implementation on June 1, 2009.

Appendix: Article 71 of the *Law of the People's Republic of China on Science and Technology Progress* stipulates as follows:

The competent authority shall, in accordance with law, withdraw a prize and a bonus and take disciplinary action against anyone who is engaged in fraudulent practice for winning the National Science and Technology Prize.

For anyone or any working unit, which offers false data, false material, or conspire with others in fraudulent practice for winning the National Science and Technology Prize, the competent authority shall circulate a notice of criticism of such malpractice or misconduct; if the circumstances are serious, the competent authority shall suspend or cancel the working unit's eligibility for recommendation of any prize-winning candidate, and shall punish it in accordance with law.

关于何梁何利基金评选工作若干问题的说明

何梁何利基金是由香港爱国金融实业家何善衡、梁銶琚先生、何添先生、利国伟先生于1994年3月30日在香港创立的，以奖励中华人民共和国杰出科学技术工作者为宗旨的科技奖励基金。截至2010年，已有901位获奖科学家获得此项殊荣。经过16年的成功实践，何梁何利基金科技奖已经成为我国规模大、层次高、影响广、在国内外享有巨大权威性和公信力的科学技术大奖。为便于科技界、教育界和社会各界进一步了解基金宗旨、基本原则、评选标准和运行机制，在2010年10月颁奖大会期间，何梁何利基金评选委员会秘书长段瑞春就基金评选章程、评选工作以及社会各界所关心的有关问题，做了如下说明。

一、什么是何梁何利基金评选章程?

何梁何利基金评选章程是评选工作的基本准则。评选章程以基金《信托契约》为依据，由何梁何利基金信托委员会全体会议审议通过和发布。第一部评选章程诞生于1994年3月30日基金成立之时，保障了评选工作从一开始就步入科学、规范、健康的轨道运行。1998年5月11日适应香港九七回归和国内形势发展，对评选章程做过一次修订。2007年5月15日基金信托委员会会议决定再次修改评选章程，其主要目的，一是根据2005年10月12日香港高等法院批准生效的《补充契约条款》，对评选章程有关条款做相应修改，使之与基金《信托契约》及其《补充契约条款》保持一致。二是将评选委员会适应我国创新国策、改革评选工作的成功经验上升为章程，使之条文化、规范化、制度化，进一步提升各奖项的科学性、权威性。

二、根据《补充契约条款》，评选章程做了哪些重要修改?

何梁何利基金是依据香港法律创立的慈善基金。当初，根据香港普通法原则，实行信任委托制度，由捐款人与信托人签订《信托契约》，经香港终审法院批准成立。信托委员会是基金的最高权力机构，决定基金投资、评选和管理等重大事项。自1994年3月基金成立以来，当年四位创立者中，梁銶琚先生、何善衡先生、何添先生都在九旬高寿与世长辞。我们永远缅怀他们的崇高精神。由于他们的离去，《信托契约》有关捐款人的权利与义务主体出现缺位，从法律意义上影响到基金决策程序的进行。2005年10月，经香港高等法院批准《信托契约补充条款》将基金“捐款人”统一修订为原捐款人或者其遗产承办人指定的慈善基金，从而实现了捐款人从老一辈爱国金融家向其下一代的平稳过渡。依据此项修订，现基金捐款人为4个法人，即何善衡慈善基金有限公司、梁銶琚慈善基金有限公司、何添基金有限公司、利国伟先生和其夫人的伟伦基金有限公司。为此，评选章程也做了相应修改。

三、何梁何利基金奖励对象应当具备什么条件？

何梁何利基金奖励对象为中华人民共和国公民，获奖人应具备下列三个条件：一是对推动科学技术事业发展有杰出贡献；二是热爱祖国，有高尚的社会公德和职业道德；三是在国内从事科研、教学或技术工作已满5年。

1994年3月30日，何梁何利基金成立时，香港、澳门尚未回归祖国。鉴于当时历史状况，评选章程关于奖励对象为中华人民共和国公民的规定，仅适用祖国内地科技工作者，不包括在香港、澳门地区工作的科技人员。在“一国两制”的原则下，香港和澳门先后于1997年7月1日和1999年12月20日回归祖国。祖国内地与港澳特区科技合作与交流出现崭新局面。而今，香港、澳门特别行政区科技人员，是中华人民共和国公民中的“港人”“澳人”，符合章程的要求。为此，自2007年起，何梁何利基金奖励对象扩大到符合上述条件的香港特别行政区、澳门特别行政区科学技术人员。

四、现行评选章程对基金奖项结构是如何规定的？

在中央人民政府和香港特区政府的关怀和指导下，16年来，何梁何利基金已经形成了科学合理的奖项结构和严谨、高效、便捷的评选程序。始终保持客观、公正、权威和具有公信力的评选纪录。现行评选章程规定基金设“科学与技术成就奖”“科学与技术进步奖”“科学与技术创新奖”。

每年，“科学与技术成就奖”不超过5名，授予奖牌、奖金100万港元；“科学与技术进步奖”和“科学与技术创新奖”总数不超过65名，分别授予相应的奖牌、奖金20万港元，其中，“科学与技术进步奖”和“科学与技术创新奖”的数量按3∶1至2∶1的比例，由评选委员会具体掌握。

五、“科学与技术成就奖”的评选标准是什么？

根据评选章程，符合下列三类条件的杰出科技工作者，均可获得“科学与技术成就奖”。一是长期致力于推进国家科学技术进步，贡献卓著，历史上取得国际高水平学术成就者；二是在科学技术前沿，取得重大科技突破，攀登当今科技高峰，领先世界先进水平者；三是推进技术创新，建立强大自主知识产权和自主品牌，其产业居于当今世界前列者。符合上述标准的获奖人选，既包括毕生奉献我国科技事业、其卓越成就曾达到世界一流水平的资深科学家，也包括以科学研究或技术创新领域的重大突破或突出业绩，使我国取得世界领先地位的中青年杰出人才。在征求意见过程中，我国科技界对此普遍赞同，认为这样修订丝毫没有降低标准，而是使基金的科技大奖进一步向国际规范靠拢，为在研究开发和创新第一线拔尖人才的脱颖而出注入强大精神动力，也使基金科技奖励更加贴近建设创新型国家的主旋律。

六、“科学与技术进步奖”的评选标准是怎样规定的？

评选章程规定，“科学与技术进步奖”授予在特定学科领域取得重大发明、发现和科技成果者，尤其是在近年内有突出贡献者。需要说明的，一是这里所说的“特定学科”包括：数学力学、物理学、化学、天文学、气象学、地球科学、生命科学、农学、医学和药学、古生物学和考古学、机械电力技术、电子信息技术、交通运输技术、冶金材料技术、化学工程技术、资源环保技术、工程建设技术等17个领域，每一领域设一个奖项。原评选章程用“技术科学奖”涵盖了机电、信息、冶金、材料、工程、环保等技术领域，修订后的章程从学科领域之间平衡考虑，将其分别设立奖项。二是“科学与技术进步奖”评选政策，重在考察被提名人“近年内”的突出贡献。所谓“近年内”是指近10年内。三是随着科学技术飞速发展，新兴学科、交叉学科、边缘学科层出不穷。这些学科的被提名人宜按其最主要成就、最接近学科领域归类。关注新兴、交叉、边缘学科优秀人才，是评选委员会的一项政策。有些确实需要跨学科评议的特殊情况，将作为个案协调处理，但不专门设立新兴学科、交叉学科、边缘学科等奖项。

七、“科学与技术创新奖”的评选标准是怎样规定的？

设立“科学与技术创新奖”是基金评选工作的重要改革。评选章程规定：“科学与技术创新奖”授予具有高水平科技成就而通过技术创新和管理创新，创建自主知识产权产业和著名品牌，创造重大经济效益和社会效益的杰出贡献者。这里需要说明的是，创新，是一个经济学的范畴，指的是有明确经济、社会目标的行为。有人解释为“科学思想在市场的首次出现”。何梁何利基金为适应我国提高自主创新能力，建设创新型国家的重大决策设立这个奖项，评选章程所称的“科学与技术创新”，第一，要以高水平的科学技术成就为起点，实现科技成果转化为现实生产力，完成科技产业化的过程。第二，就创新活动而言，是指在高水平科技成就基础上的技术创新和管理创新，包括原始创新、集成创新和在他人先进技术之上的再创新，但应有自主知识产权产业和著名品牌，创造出重大经济效益和社会效益，对于创新成果在教育、节能环保、生态平衡、国家安全、社会公益事业等领域产生的巨大社会效益，将和可计量的经济效益一样，获得评选委员会的认可。第三，任何一项重大创新都是团队作战的成果，“科学与技术创新奖”的得主，可以是发挥核心作用的领军人物，也可以是实现技术突破的关键人物。当然，这里所说的领军人物本身要有科技成就，而不只是行政管理和组织协调工作。

八、怎样理解“科学技术创新奖”所分设的奖项?

根据评选章程,“科学技术创新奖”分设青年创新奖、产业创新奖和区域创新奖等三个奖项。青年创新奖授予在技术创新和管理创新方面业绩突出、年龄不超过45周岁的优秀科技人才;区域创新奖授予通过技术创新、管理创新和区域创新,对区域经济发展和技术进步,尤其是对祖国内地、边远、艰苦地区和少数民族地区发展作出突出贡献的人物;产业创新是指通过创新、创业,大幅度推进技术进步和产业升级,包括对传统产业技术改造和新兴产业的腾飞跨越作出贡献的优秀人才。分设上述三个奖项,是评选政策的安排,其本身并不是相互独立的创新门类。因此,“科学技术创新奖”仍然按照创新奖的基本要求统一评选,适当注意三类奖项的结构平衡,不按区域创新奖、产业创新奖、青年创新奖分组切块进行评审。

九、“科学与技术进步奖”和“科学与技术创新奖”评选标准有何差别?

从原则上讲,“科学与技术进步奖”按照学科领域设置,“科学与技术创新奖”基于创新业绩设置,二者有交叉和关联之处,又有重要区别,评选标准的政策取向和侧重有所不同。《评选章程》要求“科学与技术进步奖”获奖人必须是重大发明、发现和科技成果的完成人或主要完成人。而“科学与技术创新奖”的获奖人是在高水平科技成就基础上的创新实践者。前者,重在考察其发明、发现和其他科技成就的水平及其在国内国际的学术地位;而后者,重点考察其产业高端技术创新和管理创新的业绩,包括经济社会效益、自主知识产权和著名品牌建设。当然,“科学与技术创新奖”得主的领军人物本身要有高水平的科技成就,而不只是战略决策、行政管理和组织协调工作。

十、“科学与技术进步奖”“科学与技术创新奖”获奖人能否获得“科学与技术成就奖”?

何梁何利基金的宗旨是鼓励我国优秀科学技术工作者,无所畏惧地追求科学真理,勇攀当代科学技术高峰。已经获得“科学与技术进步奖”“科学与技术创新奖”的科技工作者,在获奖后,再接再厉,开拓进取,在科学技术前沿取得新的重大科技突破,领先世界先进水平者;或者在产业高端作出新的重大技术创新,建立强大自主知识产权和自主品牌,使我国产业跃居当今世界前列者;如果在前次获奖后取得的新的杰出成就达到“科学与技术成就奖”标准,可以推荐为“科学与技术成就奖”被提名人的人选,按照《评选章程》规定程序参评,也有望摘取“科学与技术成就奖”的桂冠。

十一、评选委员会按照怎样的程序进行各奖项评选工作?

每年,基金评选委员会按照下列程序开展评选工作:

（一）提名

每年年初，评选委员会向国内外2000多位提名人发去提名表，由其提名推荐获奖人选，并于3月31日前将提名表返回评选委员会。评选办公室将对提名材料进行形式审查、整理、分组、印刷成册。

（二）初评

每年7月中旬，评选委员会召开当年专业评审会，进行“科学与技术进步奖”“科学与技术创新奖”的初评。其中，“科学与技术进步奖”初评，按照学科设立若干专业评审组进行；“科学与技术创新奖”成立一个由不同行业和领域专家组成的评审组进行初评。经过初评，以无记名投票方式，产生一定差额比例的候选人，提交评选委员会会议终评。

（三）预审

根据《评选章程》，“科学与技术成就奖”候选人由评选委员会委员在初评结束后提名。每年8月，评选委员会成立预审小组进行协调、评议，必要时进行考察和听证，产生“科学与技术成就奖”候选人，并形成预审报告，提交评选委员会会议终评。

（四）终评

每年9月中旬评选委员会召开全体会议进行终评。对候选人逐一评议，最后，根据基金信托委员会确定的当年获奖名额，进行无记名投票表决。“科学与技术进步奖”“科学与技术创新奖”的候选人，获半数以上赞成票为获奖人。“科学与技术成就奖”的候选人，获三分之二多数赞成票为获奖人。

（五）授奖

每年10月的适当时候，何梁何利基金举行颁奖大会，向获奖人颁发奖牌、奖金。

十二、何梁何利基金获奖人有哪些权利和义务？

《世界人权宣言》宣布：“人人对他所创造的任何科学、文学或艺术成果所产生的精神的和物质的权利，享有受保护的权利。”知识产权是精神权利和经济权利的总和，其本原和第一要义，是给人的智慧、才能和创造性劳动注入强大精神动力。科技奖励是确认和保护精神权利的重要制度，何梁何利基金“科学与技术成就奖”“科学与技术进步奖”“科学与技术创新奖”获奖人的权利是，享有何梁何利基金获奖科学家的身份权、荣誉权；享有接受何梁何利基金颁发的奖金的权利，该奖金个人所有；有从第二年起成为基金提名人，向基金提名推荐被提名人的权利。根据基金《信托契约》和评选章程，获奖人有义务在获得基金奖励后继续在中华人民共和国从事科学与技术工作不少于三年，为我国科技进步与创新作出更多贡献。

十三、评选委员会委员和专业评委是怎样产生的?

评选委员会是何梁何利基金评选工作的执行机构，通过全体会议审议、决定各奖项获奖人，行使最终评选决定权。根据评选章程，评选委员会由最多不超过20名委员组成。评选委员会主任由科技系统的信托委员担任，副主任委员两人，分别由教育部系统的信托委员和补充契约所指明的国际学者信托委员担任。评选委员会秘书长由信托委员会任命并征得捐款人代表同意的人选担任。

评选委员会委员由信托委员会任命，委员名单通过何梁何利基金出版物、网站公布。

按《评选章程》规定，评选委员会委员的聘任条件是：第一，要具备高尚道德情操，能够公正履行评选委员的职责；第二，要具备精深学术造诣，能够对其所属领域科技成就作出科学性和权威性评价；第三，要热心祖国科技奖励事业，愿意为之作出无私奉献；第四，评选委员会委员的结构配置，原则上每一领域有一名委员，国内评委和海外评委按照三比一的比例安排；第五，评选章程还规定了评选委员会委员的更新和替换制度，以保障评选委员会的生机和活力。

每年7月何梁何利基金召开专业评审会议，进行初评。初评是评选工作的第一道关口。其十多个“科学与技术进步奖”评审组和“科学与技术创新奖”的专业评委，由评选委员会根据工作需要，从250人左右的评审专家库或历年获奖科学家中，按《评选章程》规定的上述条件遴选。

十四、怎样理解基金公平、公正、公开的评选原则?

科学精神的精髓是求实、求是、求真。科技奖励评选工作必须坚持以诚信为本，践行实事求是的方针。何梁何利基金从一开始就贯彻“公平、公正、公开”的评选原则，保持良好的评选记录，得到社会各界的高度评价和充分肯定。所谓公平，体现在所有被提名者，不论职务、职位、学衔、资历，也不论年龄、民族、性别，在评选章程确定的评选标准面前一律平等。所谓公正，是指评选工作严格按照章程确定的评选标准和评选程序进行，无论初评的专业评委，还是终评的评选委员会委员，有权作出独立判断，按一人一票的制度行使表决权，最终依据评委共同体的意志决定获奖人，不受任何单位或个人的干扰。所谓公开，是指何梁何利基金评选章程、评选标准及其解释、评选委员会委员、逐年获奖人材料等，通过年报、网站等向社会公开，接受社会公众的监督和指导。自2006年起，评选委员会在部分省市和部门建立联络员，加强同社会各界的联系。何梁何利基金评选实践经验凝练到一点，就是贯彻“公平、公正、公开”的评选原则，是何梁何利基金的指导方针，是评选委员会的工作纪律，是基金的立业之本、权威之根、公信力之源泉，是一个具有国内和国际影响力的科技大奖的生命线。今后，基金将一如既往恪守“三公”原则，本着对科学负责、对基金负责、对科技共同体负责的精神，做好评选工作，使何梁何利基金科学与技术奖经得起历史的检验。

十五、何梁何利基金有无异议处理程序？

为了弘扬科学精神，崇尚科学道德，抵御社会不正之风和科研不端行为，提升何梁何利基金科学与技术奖的权威性和公信力，基金于 2009 年 5 月 20 日制定并发布了《关于何梁何利基金获奖科学家异议处理若干规定》，自发布之日起试行。

根据该项决定，凡涉及对获奖科学家主要科技成果评价、知识产权权属以及与奖项有关事项提出异议的署名投诉信件，由评选委员会受理，并调查处理。匿名投诉信件，原则上不予受理。但涉及获奖人因科研不端行为受到处分、学术资格被取消或与奖项评选相关重要情况的，应跟进调查核实，酌情处理。

评选委员会的处理原则是，以事实为依据，以法律为准绳，遵循科学共同体认同的道德准则，区别情况，正确处置。经调查，认定获奖人确属科研不端行为，将参照《中华人民共和国科学技术进步法》第七十一条规定，报基金信托委员会审议并作出相应的处分决定，直至公告撤销其奖励的决定，并通知本人，返回奖励证书、奖金。

十六、何梁何利基金未来发展目标是什么？

在中央人民政府和香港特别行政区政府的指导下，在我国科技界、教育界和社会各界的共同努力下，何梁何利基金已经成为我国规模大、权威性高、公信力强的社会力量奖励，成为推进我国科技进步与创新的强大杠杆，在国内外影响和声誉与日俱增。在历年颁奖大会上，党和国家领导人亲临颁奖，发表重要讲话，给予基金同仁极大鼓舞和力量。何梁何利基金同人将不负众望，不辱使命，承前启后，继往开来，在新的起点上总结经验，开拓创新，突出特色，丰富内涵，朝着办成国际一流的科技奖励的方向迈进，为祖国的科技进步和创新，为建设富强民主、文明和谐的社会主义现代化国家而不懈努力！

EXPLANATIONS ON SEVERAL ISSUES ON THE SELECTION WORK OF HO LEUNG HO LEE FOUNDATION

Ho Leung Ho Lee Foundation ("the Foundation") is a scientific and technological award foundation established on March 30, 1994 in Hong Kong by patriotic Hong Kong financial industrialists Ho Sin Hang, Leung Kau-Kui, Ho Tim, Lee Quo-Wei for the purpose of awarding prominent scientific and technological workers of the People's Republic of China. Up to 2010, there were 901 scientists who received this special honor. Within the 16 years of successful practice, HLHL Foundation Scientific and Technological Awards have become major scientific and technological awards of large scale, high standard and extensive influence in China that enjoy enormous prestige and public trust both domestically and abroad. In order for the circle of science and technology, the circle of education, and other various social circles to further understand the Foundation's purpose, basic principles, award selection criteria and operation mechanisms, Mr. Duan Ruichun, secretary general of the Selection Board of HLHL Foundation, made the following explanations during the awards ceremony in October 2010 with respect to the Foundation's selection regulation, selection work and other issues that various social circles are concerned about.

I. What is the Regulation of Ho Leung Ho Lee Foundation on the Selection of the Award Winners of its Prizes?

The Regulation of Ho Leung Ho Lee Foundation on the Selection of the Award Winners of its Prizes ("Selection Regulation") is the fundamental guideline of the award selection work. The Selection Regulation is based on the Foundation's Trust Agreement and deliberated, adopted and published by the plenary meeting of HLHL Foundation Broad of Trustees. The birth of the first selection regulation on March 30, 1994, the very day when the Foundation was established, guaranteed the operation of the selection work in a scientific, regulated and healthy track from the very beginning. On May 11, 1998, a revision was made to the Selection Regulation to adapt to the return of Hong Kong to China and the development of domestic situation. On May 15, 2007, it was resolved at the meeting of the Foundation's Broad of Trustees that another revision would be made to the Selection Regulation. The main purpose of the revision was that, on the one hand, relevant modifications would be made to certain terms and conditions in the Selection Regulation in accordance with the Supplementary Terms to the Trust Agreement which took effect upon approval by the Hong Kong SAR High Court on October 12, 2005 so that the Foundation's Trust Agreement became consistent with its Supplementary Terms to the Trust Agreement while, on the other hand, the successful experience of the Selection Board in adapting to China's national innovation policy and reforming its selection work was elevated to become part of the selection regulation so that the experience was embodied in agreement terms, standards and systems to further improve the scientific and authoritative features of different award categories.

Ⅱ. What are the Important Modifications to the Selection Regulation Made in Accordance with the Supplementary Terms of the Trust Agreement?

HLHL Foundation is a charity foundation established in accordance with the laws of the Hong Kong SAR. In its early days, the trust system was established in accordance with the principles in Hong Kong's common law and the foundation was established upon the approval of the Hong Kong Supreme Court after the donors and the trustees signed the Trust Agreement. The Board of Trustees is the supreme body of power of the Foundation that decides on major matters of the foundation in investment, award selection and management. After the foundation was established in March 1994, Mr. Ho Sin Hang, Mr. Leung Kau-Kui and Mr. Ho Tim of the four founders, whose sublime and noble spirits we will all cherish forever, passed away in their nineties. Due to their decease, the main parties to the rights and obligations of donors in the Trust Agreement became absent, which affected the operation of the Foundation's decision-making procedures in terms of law. In October 2005, it was uniformly revised in the Supplementary Terms of the Trust Agreement, upon the approval of the Hong Kong SAR High Court, that the "donors" of the Foundation became the charity foundations designated by the original donors or their estate administrator. Thus a peaceful and smooth transition was achieved with respect to donors from the old generation patriotic financers to the charity foundations run by their next generation. According to the revision, the current donors of the Foundation are four legal persons, namely the S. H. Ho Foundation Limited, the Leung Kau-Kui Foundation Limited, the Ho Tim Foundation Limited, and the Wei Lun Foundation Limited of Mr. Lee Quo-Wei and his wife. And the relevant modifications were made to the Selection Regulation accordingly.

Ⅲ. What Conditions Need the Winners of the Awards of HLHL Foundation Have?

The winners of the awards of HLHL Foundation shall be the citizens of the People's Republic of China. And they also need to meet the following three conditions: First, they shall have made prominent contributions in the development of the undertakings in science and technology. Second, they shall love the motherland and exhibit noble social ethics and good professional ethics. Third, they shall have engaged in scientific and technological research work, teaching work or technical work for no less than five years in China.

When HLHL Foundation was established on March 30, 1994, Hong Kong and Macao were not returned to the motherland yet. In view of the historical situation then, the provision in the Selection Regulation that the winners of the awards shall be citizens of the People's Republic of China only applied to scientific and technological workers in China's mainland and scientific and technological workers in Hong Kong and Macao were excluded. Then Hong Kong and Macao were returned to the motherland under the principle of "one country, two systems" respectively on July 1st, 1997 and December 20, 1999. And a brand new situation emerged in the cooperation and exchange between the mainland of China and the Hong Kong and Macao SARs. Now, the scientific and technological workers in the Hong Kong and Macao SARs are " Hong Kong people" and " Macao people" among the citizens of the People's Republic of China and thus meet the conditions in the Selection Regulation. Therefore, the scope of the scientists eligible to the awards of HLHL Foundation was expanded from 2007 to include scientific and technological personnel in the Hong Kong and Macao SARs who meet the above conditions.

Ⅳ. What are the Provisions on the Structure of the Award Categories in the Prevailing Selection Regulation?

Under the care and guidance of the Central People's Government and the government of the Hong Kong SAR, HLHL Foundation has formed during 16 years a scientific and rational structure of the award categories and a selection regulation of meticulousness, high efficiency, convenience and swiftness. It has always retained its objective, fair, authoritative selection performance and won good public trust. As provided in the prevailing Selection Regulation, the Foundation sets up the Prize for Scientific and Technological Achievements, the Prize for Scientific and Technological Progress, and the Prize for Scientific and Technological Innovation.

Each year there will be no more than five winners of the Prize for Scientific and Technological Achievements. Each of them will be given a medal and a prize of HKMYM one million. The total number of the winners of the Prize for Scientific and Technological Progress and the Prize for Scientific and Technological Innovation will not exceed 65. Each winner will be given a corresponding medal and a prize of HKMYM 200000. Among these, the proportion of the winners of the Prize for Scientific and Technological Progress to those of the Prize for Scientific and Technological Innovation will range from 3 : 1 to 2 : 1. The proportion will be determined by the Selection Board on the basis of specific situation.

Ⅴ. What are the Selection Criteria on the Prize for Scientific and Technological Achievements?

According to the Selection Regulation, all outstanding scientific and technological workers who meet the following three conditions are eligible to be honored with the Prize for Scientific and Technological Achievements. The first condition is that the scientist has been committed for a long time to promoting the scientific and technological achievements of the state in China and he or she has made eminent contribution and obtained high-level international academic achievements in his career. The second condition is that the scientist has obtained major scientific and technological breakthroughs in the frontiers of science and technology, mounted the peak of the science and technology of the present age, and obtained achievements of a world-leading standard. Third, the scientist has promoted technological innovation and established powerful independently-owned intellectual property and brand. And the industry in which the scientist works is one of the leading industries in the world. The candidates who meet the above standards include both senior scientists who have devoted their whole life to Chinese scientific and technological undertakings and obtained eminent achievements that were once first-rate in the world and youth and middle-aged outstanding talents who have made major breakthroughs or prominent achievements in the area of scientific and technological research and technical innovation so that China got a world-leading position in the area. During the process of opinion solicitation, the Chinese scientific and technological circle expressed general approval of the revision and indicated that such revision lowered the standard by not a slight bit while pushing the Foundation's awards one step further and closer to international standards. It injected powerful spiritual impetus for top-level talents to excel in the frontline of research and development and innovation. The revision also drew the Foundation's scientific and technological awards more closer to the mainstream ideology of building an innovative country.

VI. What are the Provisions on the Selection Criteria of the Prize for Scientific and Technological Progress?

It is provided in the Selection Regulation that the Prize for Scientific and Technological Progress will be honored to scientists who have made major inventions, discoveries and scientific and technological results in particular disciplinary areas, particularly those who have made prominent contributions in recent years. First, it needs to be noted that the "particular disciplines" stated here include 17 disciplines, namely mathematics and mechanics, physics, chemistry, astronomy, meteorology, earth sciences, life sciences, agronomy, medical sciences and materia medica, paleontology and archeology, technology of machinery and electronics, information technology, communication and transportation technology, metallurgical materials technology, chemical engineering technology, resources and environment protection technology, and engineering and construction technology. One award category is established for each of these areas. In the original selection regulation, the Award of Technical Sciences is set up to cover various technical areas including machinery, electronics, information, metallurgy, material science, engineering and environment protection. The revised procedure sets up different award categories for these areas out of the consideration on the balance between various disciplinary areas. Second, the selection policy on the Prize for Scientific and Technological Progress focuses on examining and reviewing the prominent contribution of the nominees "within recent years" . And "within recent years" refers to within the recent ten years. Third, as emerging disciplines, interdisciplines, and fringe disciplines come up one after another with the rapid development of science and technology, the nominees from these disciplines should desirably be classified according to their most important achievements and the closest disciplines to which these belong. To pay more attention to the excellent talents from emerging disciplines, interdisciplines and fringe disciplines is one policy of the Selection Board. The special cases that truly need cross-disciplinary review and deliberation will be processed through coordination as separate cases. But no prize category will be established particularly for emerging disciplines, interdisciplines and fringe disciplines.

VII. What are the Provisions on the Selection Criteria of the Prize for Scientific and Technological Innovation?

Setting up the Prize for Scientific and Technological Innovation is an important reform of the Foundation's selection work. It is provided in the Selection Regulation that " the Prize for Scientific and Technological Innovation will be awarded to scientists who have high-level scientific and technological accomplishments and who have established an industry with independently-owned intellectual property and famous brand, created significant economic and social benefits, and made prominent contribution" . It needs to be noted here that, as a term in economics, innovation refers to acts with specific economic and social goals. Some people defines it as the "first presence of an idea in science on the market" . HLHL Foundation set up the innovation award to adapt to China's important decision to improve the ability to independent innovation and build an innovative country. For the purpose of the Selection Regulation, to make "scientific and technological innovation" first needs to make high-level scientific and technological achievements as its starting point to realize the transformation of scientific and technological achievements into real productive force and complete the process of scientific and technological industrialization. Second, innovation activities refer to technological and managerial innovations on the basis of high-level scientific and technological achievements. These include original innovation, integration innovation and re-innovation on the basis of other people's advanced technology. And such innovations should create independently-owned intellectual properties and famous brands and create significant economic and social benefits. Besides, the Selection Board also accepts and approves, in the same way as measurable economic benefits, the enormous social benefits created by innovation results in the areas of education, energy preservation and environment protection, ecological balance, national security, and social public interest undertakings. Third, as any major innovation is the result of teamwork, the winner of the Prize for Scientific and Technological Innovation may be either a leading person that plays the key role or a key person who has achieved technical breakthroughs. Naturally, the leading person here needs to have his or her own scientific and technological accomplishments in addition to conducting administrative management, organization and coordination work.

Ⅷ. How should the Award Categories Set Up in the Prize for Scientific and Technological Innovation be Understood?

In accordance with the Selection Regulation, the Prize for Scientific and Technological Innovation includes three award categories of the Award for Youth Innovation, the Award for Region Innovation and the Award for Industrial Innovation. The Award for Youth Innovation will be given to excellent scientific and technological talents not older than 45 years old who have achieved prominent performance in technical and managerial innovation. The Award for Region Innovation will be given to people who have made prominent contributions to regional economic development and technological progress through technical, managerial and regional innovations, particularly those who have made contributions to China's inland, remote regions, regions of harsh conditions, and regions of ethic minorities. The Prize for Industrial Innovation will be given to excellent talents who have made contributions through innovation and entrepreneurship to greatly promote technical progress and industrial upgrading, which include both the technical transformation of traditional industries and the leap-forwards of emerging industries. The above three award categories are set up according to the arrangement in selection policy. These do not define mutually-independent types of innovation. Therefore, the selection of the winners of the Prize for Scientific and Technological Innovation will be conducted as a whole part in accordance with the basic requirements on the Prize while proper attention will be paid to retain the structural balance between these three award categories. Selection and evaluation will not be conducted in a manner that the Award for Region Innovation, the Award for Industrial Innovation and the Award for Youth Innovation are separated and form different groups.

Ⅸ. What are the Differences in the Selection Criteria of the Prize for Scientific and Technological Progress and the Prize for Scientific and Technological Innovation?

In principle, the Prize for Scientific and Technological Progress has award categories set up in accordance with different disciplines while the Prize for Scientific and Technological Innovation has award categories based on innovation results. The two prizes have overlaps and connections while there are important differences between them. And the policy orientations and stresses in their selection criteria are also different. The Selection Regulation requires that the winners of the Prize for Scientific and Technological Achievements must be completers or major completers of major inventions, discoveries and scientific and technological research results while the winners of the Prize for Scientific and Technological Innovation are scientists in innovative practices on the basis of high-level scientific and technological achievements. The former focuses on examining the standard and value of a scientist's invention, discovery or other scientific and technological achievement and its domestic and international academic status. The latter focuses on examining a person's performance in high-end industrial technical and managerial innovations, including economic and social benefits, independently-owned intellectual properties and building of famous brands. Naturally, the winners of the Prize for Scientific and Technological Innovations need to have high-level scientific and technological achievements as leading persons in addition to just conducting strategic decision making, administrative management, organization and coordination work.

X. Can the Winners of the Prize for Scientific and Technological Progress and the Prize for Scientific and Technological Innovation Be Honored with the Prize for Scientific and Technological Achievements?

The purpose of HLHL Foundation is to encourage excellent Chinese scientific and technological workers to dauntlessly pursue the truth of science and courageously mount the peaks in modern science and technology. The scientific and technological workers who have won the Prize for Scientific and Technological Progress and the Prize for Scientific and Technological Innovation may continue to forge ahead and break new grounds. And they may achieve new important breakthroughs in the frontiers of science and technology and lead in the cutting edge area of the world. Or they may make new important technical innovations in the high-end areas of an industry and create powerful independent intellectual properties and independent brands so that China's relevant industries become industrial leaders in the world. If such scientists' new outstanding achievements obtained after the previous prize winning meet the criteria for the Prize for Scientific and Technological Achievement, these scientists may be recommended as candidates to be nominated to the Prize for Scientific and Technological Achievements. They will participate in the evaluation in accordance with the procedures as provided in the Selection Regulation. And it is hopeful that they may become the laureates of the Prize for Scientific and Technological Achievements.

XI. In Accordance with What Procedures Will the Selection Board Conduct the Selection Work for Various Award Categories?

Each year, the Foundation's Selection Board will carry out selection work in accordance with the following procedure:

A. Nomination. In the beginning of each year, the Selection Board will send nomination forms to over 2000 domestic and foreign nominators. The nominators will recommend candidates for award winners and return the nomination form to the Selection Board by March 31st. The Selection Office will conduct the formal examination, arranging, assorting, and printing of the nomination materials and bind them into booklets.

B. Preliminary Evaluation. In the middle of July each year, the Selection Board will hold the year's specialized evaluation meeting and conduct the preliminary evaluation for the Prize of Scientific and Technological Progress and the Prize for Scientific and Technological Innovation. In the preliminary evaluation, that of the Prize for Scientific and Technological Progress will be conducted with a number of specialized evaluation groups formed according to different disciplines. The preliminary evaluation of the Prize for Scientific and Technological Innovation will be conducted by an evaluation group consisting of experts from different industries and areas. After the preliminary evaluation, candidates will be determined with a proportion of competitive selection by means of secret ballot and submitted to the meeting of the Selection Board for final evaluation.

C. Preliminary Review. In accordance with the Selection Regulation, the candidates of the Prize for Scientific and Technological Achievements will be nominated by the members of the Selection Board upon the conclusion of the preliminary evaluation. Each August, the Selection Board will form a preliminary evaluation group to conduct coordination and evaluation. Inspection tours and hearings will be made when necessary. Then the candidates for the Prize for Scientific and Technological Achievements will be determined and a preliminary review report will be prepared and submitted to the meeting of the Selection Board for final evaluation.

D. Final Evaluation. In the middle of September each year, the Selection Board will hold a plenary meeting to conduct final evaluation. Candidates will be evaluated one by one. And finally a secret ballot will be made on the selection in accordance with the numbers of prize winners of the year determined by the Trust Board of the Foundation. The candidates for the Prize for Scientific and Technological Progress and the Prize for Scientific and Technological Innovation will become prize winners with over half of the votes in favor. The candidates for the Prize for Scientific and Technological Achievements will become prize winners with over two thirds of the votes in favor.

E. Award Ceremony. At a proper time in October each year, HLHL Foundation will hold an award ceremony to present medals and prizes to the winners.

XII. What Are the Rights and Obligations of the Winners of the Awards of HLHL Foundation?

The *Universal Declaration of Human Rights* states that "Everyone has the right to the protection of the moral and material interests resulting from any scientific, literary or artistic production of which he is the author." Intellectual property rights are the sum of both spiritual and economic rights. Its origin and primary significance is to inject powerful spiritual drive to people's wisdom, talent and creative labor. Scientific and technological awards are important systems to recognize and protect spiritual rights. The rights of the winners of the Prize of Scientific and Technological Achievements, the Prize for Scientific and Technological Progress, and the Prize for Scientific and Technological Innovation of HLHL Foundation are the enjoyment of the right of status and the right of honor of the prize-winning scientists of HLHL Foundation, the enjoyment of the right to accept the prize money granted by HLHL Foundation which shall be owned personally by the prize winners, and the right to become a nominator of the Foundation from the year next to the prize winning to recommend nominees to the Foundation. In accordance with the Foundation's Trust Agreement and Selection Regulation, the prize winner is obligated to continue to engage in scientific and technological work in the People's Republic of China for three years after prize winning so as to make more contribution to China's scientific and technological advancement and innovation.

XIII. How are the Members of the Selection Board and the Specialized Evaluators Selected?

The Selection Board is the implementing body of the selection work of HLHL Foundation. It conducts deliberation through plenary meeting, decides on the winners of the award categories, and exercises the right of decision in final evaluation. In accordance with the Selection Regulation, the Selection Board consists of no more than twenty members at the most. The chairman of the Selection Board shall be a member of the Board of Trustees for the circle of science and technology. The two vice chairmen of the board shall be a member of the Board of Trustees from the bodies under the Ministry of Education and a member of the Board of Trustees who is an international scholar as specified in the Supplementary Terms to the Trust Agreement. The secretary general of the Selection Boards shall be appointed by the Board of Trustees upon the consent of the representatives of the donors.

The members of the Selection Board are appointed by the Board of Trustees. And the list of such members will be published through the publications and website of HLHL Foundation.

As provided in the Selection Regulation, the conditions for the appointment of a member of the Selection Board are: First, the person needs to have noble ethics and the ability to fairly perform the duties of the member of the Selection Board. Second, the person needs to have sophisticated academic accomplishment and the ability to make scientific and authoritative evaluation on the scientific and technological achievements in his or her own specialized field. Third, the person needs to have enthusiasm on the motherland's undertakings in scientific and technological awards and the willingness to make selfless contributions to these undertakings. Fourth, with respect to the structural distribution of the members of the Selection Board, there shall be one member from each area in principle and the proportion between domestic and overseas members shall be 3 : 1. Fifth, the Selection Regulation provides for the renewal and replacement system of the members of the Selection Board so as to ensure the liveliness and vigor of the board.

Each July, HLHL Foundation holds a specialized evaluation meeting to conduct the preliminary evaluation. The preliminary evaluation is the very first step in the selection work. About a dozen of evaluation groups for the Prize for Scientific and Technological Progress and the specialized evaluators of the Prize for Scientific and Technological Innovation will be selected by the Selection Board on the basis of working needs and in accordance with the above conditions as provided in the Selection Regulation from an evaluation expert pool containing about 250 persons or the prize winners in previous years.

XIV. How should People Understand the Foundation's Selection Principles of Fairness, Justice and Openness?

The essence of the scientific spirit is to be practical, honest and truth–seeking. The selection work for the scientific and technological awards must adhere to the principle of sincerity and follow the guideline of doing things with a realistic and pragmatic approach. HLHL Foundation persistently carries out the selection principle of fairness, justice and openness from the very beginning. It retains good selection records and wins high praises and full recognition from various social circles. The principle of fairness is embodied in the provision that all the nominees, regardless of their jobs, positions, academic titles or work experiences and also their age, ethnic group or gender, are equal with respect to the selection criteria determined in the Selection Regulation. The principle of justice refers to the provision that the selection work is carried out strictly in accordance with the selection criteria and procedures determined in accordance with the Selection Regulation. Any person as either a specialized evaluator in the preliminary evaluation or a member of the Selection Board in final evaluation has the right to make independent judgment and exercise the right to vote under the system of one vote for one person. The prize winners are eventually determined according to the common will of all the evaluators free from the intervention of any entity or individual. The principle of openness refers to the practice that HLHL Foundation's Selection Regulation, Selection Criteria, and their explanations and the information about the members of the Selection Board and the prize winners of different years are published to the society through annual report and website to receive supervision and guidance from the public in the society. From 2006, the Selection Board has appointed liaison persons in some governmental departments, provinces and cities to strengthen its contact with various social circles. One viewpoint that can summarize the practical experience of the award selection of HLHL Foundation is to carry out the selection principle of "fairness, justice and openness." It is the guideline of HLHL Foundation, the working discipline of the Selection Board, and the cornerstone of the Foundation, the root of its authoritativeness and the source of its public trust. It is the lifeline of this major scientific and technological award with both domestic and international influence. From now on, the Foundation will adhere to this three–word principle as always. It will carry out the selection work well with the spirit of being responsible to science, to the Foundation, and to the scientific and technological community so that the scientific and technological awards of HLHL Foundation can stand the test of the history.

XV. Does HLHL Foundation Have Dispute Handling Procedures?

With a view to carrying forward the spirit of the science, advocating the ethics of the science, guarding against the unhealthy tendencies in the society and the improper conducts in scientific and technological research, and enhancing the authoritativeness and public trust of HLHL Foundation's scientific and technological awards, the Foundation formulated and published on May 20th, 2009 *Several Provisions on Handling the Disputes on the Prize-Winning Scientists of Ho Leung Ho Lee Foundation*. It took effect from the date of publication.

In accordance with the resolution on the document, the Selection Board will accept, investigate and handle all the signed complaint letters on the disputes with respect to the evaluation of the main scientific and technological research results, the ownership of relevant intellectual properties, and the matters about award categories related to a prize-winning scientist. In principle, anonymous complaint letters will not be accepted and handled. However, where such anonymous complaint letters involve the information that a prize winner has been punished due to improper conducts in scientific and technological research, that his academic title or qualification was cancelled, or other information related to the award evaluation, follow-up action shall be taken to investigate and verify. Such disputes shall then be handled according to actual situation.

The complaint handling principle of the Selection Board is to take facts as the basis and the law as the criterion, follow the ethical principles commonly accepted by the science community, distinguish different situations, and handle correctly. Where it is determined upon investigation that a prize winner really involves in improper conducts in scientific and technological research, the case will be referred to the Board of Trustees of the Foundation for deliberation with reference to the provisions in Article 71 of the *Law of the People's Republic of China on, Science and Technology Progress*. The board will make resolutions on corresponding punishment up to that of a public announcement to cancel its reward. The person involved will be notified of the decision and required to return his certificate and prize money.

XVI. What are the Goals of HLHL Foundation on Its Future Development?

Under the guidance of the Central People's Government and the government of the Hong Kong SAR and with the joint efforts of China's scientific and technological circle, education circle and various social circles, HLHL Foundation has already become an awarding organization founded with social resources that is of large scale, high authoritativeness, and strong public trust in China. It becomes a powerful lever to push forward China's scientific and technological advancement and innovation. Its domestic and foreign influence and reputation also grow constantly. China's state and CPC leaders attended in person the award ceremonies in the previous years. They presented the awards and delivered important speeches to give great encouragement and power to our colleagues working with the Foundation. The people of HLHL Foundation will live up to the expectations of the people and their own commitment. They will build on the past and usher in the future. They will summarize their experiences and move on from a new starting point. They will explore and innovate, highlight the Foundation's features, enrich its connotations, and advance in the direction of making it an internationally first-rate scientific and technological award. They will work hard and relentlessly for the motherland's scientific and technological advancement and innovation and for building China into a wealthy, democratic, civilized and harmonious socialist modern country!

关于何梁何利基金（香港）北京代表处公告

（2019 年 11 月 20 日北京市公安局批准）

何梁何利基金是香港爱国金融家何善衡、梁銶琚、何添、利国伟先生基于崇尚科学、振兴中华的热忱，各捐资 1 亿港元于 1994 年 3 月 30 日在香港注册成立的社会公益性慈善基金。其宗旨是奖励中华人民共和国杰出科学技术工作者，服务祖国科技进步与创新伟业。

根据《中华人民共和国境外非政府组织管理法》，经申请，并经北京市公安局批准，何梁何利基金（香港）代表处自 2019 年 11 月 20 日在北京宣告成立。

何梁何利基金（香港）代表处负责基金在中国境内开展活动，执行评选委员会指定提名、初评、终评和颁奖大会等日常事务。举办基金学术论坛、图片展。出版《何梁何利奖》等刊物。

特此公告。

何梁何利基金（香港）北京代表处

2020 年 1 月 1 日

PUBLIC ANNOUNCEMENT OF THE BEIJING REPRESENTATIVE OFFICE OF THE HO LEUNG HO LEE FOUNDATION (HONG KONG)

(Approved by Beijing Municipal Public Security Bureau on November 20, 2019)

With their fervor for advocating science and rejuvenating the Chinese nation, four patriotic financial industrialists in Hong Kong—Mr. Ho Sin-Hang, Mr. Leung Kau-kui, Mr. Ho Tim and Mr. Lee Quo-Wei—each donated 100 million HK dollars to register the establishment of the Ho Leung Ho Lee Foundation in Hong Kong on March 30, 1994. The Ho Leung Ho Lee Foundation is aimed to reward the outstanding science and technology workers of the People's Republic of China and to serve the great undertaking of advancing scientific and technological progress and innovation in the motherland.

The Ho Leung Ho Lee Foundation submitted an application in accordance with *The Law of the People's Republic of China on Administration of Activities of Overseas Nongovernmental Organizations in the Mainland of China*. With the approval of the application by the Beijing Municipal Public Security Bureau, the Beijing Representative Office of the Ho Leung Ho Lee Foundation (Hong Kong) was announced to be established on November 20, 2019 in Beijing.

The Beijing Representative Office of the Ho Leung Ho Lee Foundation (Hong Kong) is responsible for conducting activities of the Ho Leung Ho Lee Foundation in the mainland of China, and handling day-to-day affairs of the Selection Board of Ho Leung Ho Lee Foundation such as designating nominees, holding preliminary and final evaluations, and holding the awarding ceremony of the Ho Leung Ho Lee Foundation. It is also responsible for organizing academic forum and photo exhibition of the Ho Leung Ho Lee Foundation, and publishing periodicals including the *Ho Leung Ho Lee Prize*.

The public announcement is hereby given.

Beijing Representative Office of the
Ho Leung Ho Lee Foundation (Hong Kong)
January 1, 2020

何梁何利基金捐款人简历

捐款者何善衡慈善基金会有限公司之创办人

何 善 衡

何善衡博士，1900年出生，广东省番禺市人。

何博士于1933年创办香港恒生银号，其后又创办恒昌企业及大昌贸易行。1952年恒生银号改为有限公司，1959年改称恒生银行，何氏一直担任董事长一职。1983年，于恒生银行成立50周年时，何氏因年事关系，改任恒生银行名誉董事长至病逝。

何博士经营之业务包括银行、贸易、信托、财务、酒店、保险、地产、船务、投资等。

何博士热心慈善公益不遗余力。1970年设立何善衡慈善基金会，资助国内外慈善事业，包括地方建设、教育、医疗、科学等，帮助社会造就人才，尤其对广州市及其家乡一带贡献很多。1978年创办恒生商学书院，免费提供教学，并曾任多所学校校董。1971年获香港中文大学荣誉社会科学博士衔，1983年获香港大学荣誉法律博士衔，1990年及1995年分别获中山大学荣誉顾问衔及名誉博士学位，1993年获广州市荣誉市民及番禺市荣誉市民称谓。

何善衡博士于1997年12月4日在香港病逝，享年97岁。

梁 銶 琚

梁銶琚博士，1903年出生，广东顺德人。

梁博士为恒昌企业之创办人，曾任恒生银行董事、大昌贸易行副董事长，亦为美丽华酒店企业有限公司、富丽华酒店有限公司、Milford国际投资有限公司等董事以及恒生商学书院校董等。

梁博士早年在穗、港、澳等地经营银号和贸易，为大昌贸易行创办人之一，为工作经常往返国内各大商埠及海外大城市，或开设分行，或推进业务，并与合伙股东制定运作规章，积极培育人才；梁博士领导华商参与国际贸易，并于20世纪60年代协助香港政府重新厘定米业政策，对香港的安定繁荣有卓越贡献。

梁博士宅心仁厚，精于事业，淡泊声名，热心公益。数十年来对社会福利、教育、医疗事业捐助良多，堪称楷模。较为显著者包括捐款建成纪念其先父之圣高隆庞女修会梁式芝书院，纪念其先母之保良局梁周顺琴学校，香港大学梁銶琚楼，香港中文大学梁銶琚楼，香港浸会学院"梁銶琚汉语中心"，岭南学院梁銶琚楼，广州中山大学捐建两千两百座位的梁銶琚堂与梁李秀娱图书馆，赞助杨振宁博士倡议之中山大学高级学术研究中心基金会及中国教育交流协会留学名额，为清华大学设立"梁銶琚博士图书基金"，中国人民解放军第四军医大学"梁銶琚脑研究中心"，清华大学建筑馆——梁銶琚楼。

在香港的其他教育捐助包括：顺德联谊总会梁銶琚中学，顺德联谊总会梁李秀娱幼稚园（屯门），顺德联谊总会梁李秀娱幼稚园（沙田），香港励志会梁李秀娱小学，恒生商学书院，劳工子弟学校新校，九龙乐善堂陈祖泽学校礼堂，乐善堂梁銶琚学校，乐善堂梁銶琚书院，香港大学黄丽松学术基金，香港女童军总会沙田扬坑营地及梁李秀娱花园；在医疗卫生方面包括：医务卫生署土瓜湾顺德联谊总会梁銶琚诊所，香港防癌会，香港放射诊断科医生协会，玛丽医院"梁銶琚糖尿病中心"，玛丽医院放射学图书博物馆教学资料和医院员工的福利，香港大学医院在山东省为胃癌研究工作经费，支持张力正医生在葛量洪医院的心脏病手术和医疗的发展经费及捐助圣保禄医院设立心脏中心并以"梁銶琚心脏中心"命名；在社会福利捐献包括：九龙乐善堂梁銶琚敬老之家，东区妇女福利会梁李秀娱晚晴中心，香港明爱，西区少年警讯活动及跑马地鹅颈桥区街坊福利会等；向宗教团体的捐助包括：资助基督教"突破机构"开设青年村——信息站，赞助"志莲净苑"重建基金及大屿山"宝莲禅寺"筹募兴建天坛大佛基金等。

多年来，梁博士对家乡顺德的地方建设、科技教育、医疗事业亦大量资助，其中包括捐资成立国家级重点中学梁銶琚中学，中学的科学楼并增置教学仪器，北头学校，梁銶琚图书馆及图书，增设杏坛医院230张病床、独立手术室及分科设备仪器等，杏坛康乐活动中心，北头大会堂及北头老人康乐中心，北头乡每户开建水井一口，修葺北头主路及河道两岸，北头乡蚕房四座，梁銶琚夫人保健中心（即妇产幼儿医院），梁銶琚夫人幼儿园及梁銶琚福利基金会。

1987年梁博士荣获香港中文大学颁授荣誉社会科学博士学位，1990年被广州中山大学聘为名誉顾问，1992年获顺德市（今顺德区）颁授为首位荣誉市民，1994年国务院学位委员会批准清华大学授予梁博士名誉博士学位；同年4月，国务院总理李鹏为梁博士题词"热心公益，发展教育"，以赞扬其贡献。1995年6月21日，香港大学向已故梁銶琚博士追授名誉法学博士文凭。

在海外方面，梁博士亦曾捐助英国牛津大学、苏格兰Aberdeen大学医学院与加拿大多伦多颐康护理中心。

梁銶琚博士于1994年11月10日在香港病逝，享年91岁。

何　　添

何添博士于1933年加入香港恒生银行有限公司（前为恒生银号），于1953年任董事兼总经理，1967—1979年任恒生银行副董事长。何添博士于2004年4月退任恒生银行董事，同时获该行委任为名誉资深顾问。何添博士曾任多个上市公司董事职位，包括美丽华酒店企业有限公司（董事长）、新世界发展有限公司、新鸿基地产有限公司、熊谷组（香港）有限公司及景福集团有限公司。

何添博士积极参与公职服务，他为香港中文大学联合书院永久校董、香港中文大学校董会校董、恒生商学书院校董、邓肇坚何添慈善基金创办人之一、香港何氏宗亲总会永久会长、旅港番禺会所永久名誉会长及金银业贸易场永远名誉会长。

何添博士于1982年获香港中文大学颁授荣誉社会科学博士学位；1997年获香港城市大学颁授名誉工商管理学博士学位；1999年获香港大学颁授荣誉法律博士学位；于1988年、1993年、1995年及2004年分别获广州市、番禺市、顺德市及佛山市授予荣誉市民的称号；又于1996年11月出任中华人民共和国香港特别行政区第一届政府推选委员会委员。

何添博士于2004年11月6日在香港病逝，享年95岁。

捐款者伟伦基金有限公司之创办人

利　国　伟

利国伟博士于1946年加入香港恒生银行有限公司（前为恒生银号），1959年12月任该行董事，1976年1月任副董事长，1983—1996年2月做执行董事长，1996年3月至1997年12月任非执行董事长，1998年1月至2004年4月任名誉董事长，退任后续任名誉资深顾问。

在公职方面，利国伟博士1963—1982年为香港中文大学司库，1982—1997年为该大学校董会主席，并于1994年11月30日起被该校委为终身校董。利博士亦曾先后任香港李宝椿联合世界书院创校主席及名誉主席。此外，亦曾任江门市五邑大学名誉校长。

利国伟博士曾先后任香港行政局议员7年，立法局议员10年，银行业务咨询委员会委员 14 年，教育委员会主席 7 年，教育统筹委员会主席 5 年。

利国伟博士历年获香港及海外多所大学颁授荣誉博士学位，这些学校分别为香港中文大学（1972）、英国赫尔大学（University of Hull）（1985）、英国伯明翰大学（University of Birmingham）（1989）、香港大学及香港城市理工学院（即现时之香港城市大学）（1990）、香港理工学院（即现时之香港理工大学）及香港浸会学院（即现时之香港浸会大学）（1992）、英国伦敦市政厅大学（London Guildhall University）（1993）、清华大学及香港公开进修学院（即现时之香港公开大学）（1995）。利博士于 1971 年及 1995 年分别获选为英国银行学会及美国塔夫斯大学（Tufts University）院士，并于 1991 年、1993 年、1995 年、1996 年及 2003 年分别获选为英国牛津大学圣休学院（St Hugh's College，Oxford University）、爱丁堡皇家医学院（Royal College of Physicians of Edinburgh）、香港心脏专科学院、香港内科医学院以及英国剑桥李约瑟研究所荣誉院士，并于 1993 年获广州市政府、开平市政府及江门市政府颁授荣誉市民名衔。此外，利博士在南华早报及敦豪国际（香港）有限公司主办之 1994 年香港商业奖中获商业成就奖。利博士于 1995—2003 年受聘为中国老教授协会名誉会长，并于 1997 年荣获香港特别行政区政府颁授“大紫荆勋章”，2006 年获香港证券专业学院授予荣誉会员衔。

多年来，利国伟博士对其原籍之开平地方建设、教育及医疗事务多所资助，对江门市亦捐赠不少。此外，对清华大学、上海市和广州市之其他机构亦分别作出捐献。

利国伟博士于 2013 年 8 月 10 日在香港病逝，享年 95 岁。

BRIEF INTRODUCTION TO THE DONORS TO HO LEUNG HO LEE FOUNDATION

Brief Biography of Dr. S. H. Ho

Dr. S. H. Ho, the founder of the S. H. Ho Foundation Ltd. which donated to Ho Leung Ho Lee Foundation, born in 1900, was a native of Panyu, Guangdong Province. He cofounded Hang Seng Ngan Ho in Hong Kong in 1933 and later, the Hang Chong Investment Co Ltd. and the Dah Chong Hong Ltd. In 1952, Hang Seng Ngan Ho was incorporated and in 1959, was renamed Hang Seng Bank Ltd. From 1960 until 1983, Dr. Ho served as Chairman of the Bank. In 1983, on the 50th anniversary of the Bank, he became its Honorary Chairman until he passed away.

Dr. Ho was involved in a wide range of businesses, including banking, trade, trusteeship, financing, hotels, insurance, property, shipping and investment.

Dr. Ho was a philanthropist who was committed to promoting charitable causes. In 1970, he founded the S. H. Ho Foundation Ltd to support charitable causes in China and overseas, including regional construction, education, medical services, scientific research and the training of new talent. His contributions to Guangzhou and his homeland were particularly notable. In 1978, he founded the Hang Seng School of Commerce to provide free education to aspiring youths. He also sat as director on many school boards. In 1971, he was conferred the Honorary Degree of Doctor of Social Science by The Chinese University of Hong Kong and in 1983, an Honorary Degree of Doctor of Laws by The University of Hong Kong. In 1990, he became an Honorary Adviser to the Zhongshan University in Guangzhou and was conferred the Honorary Doctorate's degree by that University in 1995. He was made an Honorary Citizen of Guangzhou and of Panyu in 1993.

Dr. S. H. Ho passed away peacefully in Hong Kong on December 4, 1997 at the age of 97.

Brief Biography of Dr. Leung Kau-Kui

The late Dr. Leung Kau-Kui was born in 1903, a native of the City of Shunde in Guangdong Province. Dr. Leung made his mark in the businesses of foreign exchange and trading in Guangzhou, Hong Kong and Macau early in his career. He was a pioneer in leading Chinese businessmen to participate in international trades.

Throughout his career, Dr. Leung held directorships in various companies. He was a director of the Hang Seng Bank, founder of Hang Chong Investment Co. Ltd., and one of the founders and Vice-Chairman of the Dah Chong Hong Ltd. —a leading Chinese-owned trading firm in Hong Kong during the colonial days. He was also a director of Miramar Hotel and Investment Co. Ltd. Furama Hotel Co. Ltd., Milford (International) Investment Co. Ltd., and a director of the Hang Seng School of Commerce.

Dr. Leung travelled regularly and extensively to cities in China and overseas to set up branches for Dah Chong Hong Ltd. as well as to promote and develop businesses for his partners. During the 60's, he helped to restructure the import procedures of rice to Hong Kong from Thailand contributing significantly to the stability and prosperity of Hong Kong.

Benevolent, enterprising and self-effacing, Dr. Leung was a committed contributor to charitable causes. He gave generously to education, medical social services and religious organisations. Among the charitable causes which he had supported were: the Missionary Sisters St. Columban Leung Shek Chee College in memory of his late father, the Po Leung Kuk Leung Chou Shun Kam Primary School in memory of his late mother, The University of Hong Kong's KK Leung Building, The Chinese University of Hong Kong's Leung Kau-Kui Building, Lingnan College's Leung Kau-Kui Building, the Hong Kong Baptist College's (now the Hong Kong Baptist University) School of Continuing Education Leung Kau-Kui Hanyu Institute, K. K. Leung Architectural Building of Beijing's Tsinghua University, Guangzhou's Zhongshan University's Leung Kau-Kui Hall and Leung Lee Sau Yu Library, and The K. K. Leung Brain Research Centre of the Fourth Military Medical University in Xian, China. He also sponsored the Foundation of Zhongshan University Advanced Research Centre and the China Educational Exchange Association's Scholarships for Overseas Studies, both of which were promoted by Professor Yang Chen Ning. He also set up the Book Foundation of Dr. Leung Kau-Kui for Tsinghua University.

In Hong Kong, his other contributions were supports given to: Shun Tak Fraternal Association Leung Kau-Kui College, Shun Tak Fraternal Association Leung Lee Sau Yu Kindergarten (Tuen Mun), Shun Tak Fraternal Association Leung Lee Sau Yu Kindergarten (Shatin), The Endeavourers Leung Lee Sau Yu Memorial Primary School, Hang Seng School of Commerce, the assembly hall of Lok Sin Tong Chan Cho Chak Primary School, Lok Sin Tong Leung Kau-Kui Primary School, Lok Sin Tong Leung Kau-Kui College, Dr. Raymond Huang Foundation of the University of Hong Kong, S. T. F. A. Leung Kau-Kui Clinic of the Medical and Health Department, The Hong Kong Anti-Cancer Society, Queen Mary Hospital's Leung Kau-Kui Diabetes Centre and donations to upgrade the Radiology Library/Museum as well as teaching materials and staff welfare of the Hospital. He also contributed to the Department of Medicine of the University of Hong Kong to do research work on gastric cancer in Shandong Province, China. Dr. Leung also made generous contributions to the religions bodies, which included assisting the Christian Break-through Organization in establishing and donating to the Youth Village-Information Centre, redevelopment foundation of the Buddhist Chi Lin Nunnery, as well as the construction fund of the Buddha Statue at Po Lin Monastery on Lantau Island.

Dr. Leung was generous and zealous in promoting education in science and technology and medical services in his hometown, Shunde. In particular, he was the first donor working to improve the public amenities of his native Beitou Village. Notable projects which he supported in Shunde included multipurpose halls, hospitals, child care and nursery centres, schools, kindergartens, libraries, sports and recreational centres as well as welfare institutions.

Dr. Leung received an Honorary Degree of Doctor of Social Sciences from The Chinese University of Hong Kong in 1987 and became an Honorary Adviser to Guangzhou's Zhongshan University in 1990. In 1992, the government of Shunde named him an Honorary Citizen. He was conferred an Honorary Doctorate by Tsinghua University in 1994. In April 1994, Premier Li Peng praised him for his enthusiastic support of charitable causes and development of education in China.

Dr. Leung had also donated to overseas institutions such as the Oxford University of United Kingdom, the medical school of Aberdeen University in Scotland, and the Yee Hong Geriatric Centre in Toronto, Canada.

Dr. Leung passed away peacefully in Hong Kong on November 10, 1994 at the age of 91.

Brief Biography of Dr. Ho Tim

Dr. Ho Tim joined Hang Seng Bank Ltd (formerly Hang Seng Ngan Ho) in Hong Kong in 1933, was appointed its Director and General Manager in 1953 and Vice-Chairman from 1967 to 1979. In April 2004, he retired from the Board of Hang Seng Bank Limited and was named one of the Bank's Honorary Senior Advisers. Dr. Ho held directorships in a number of listed companies. He was the Chairman of Miramar Hotel and Investment Co. Ltd.; a Director of New World Development Co. Ltd., Sun Hung Kai Properties Ltd., Kumagai Gumi (Hong Kong) Ltd. and King Fook Holdings Ltd.

Dr. Ho was active in public service. He was a Permanent Member of the Board of Trustees of the United College of The Chinese University of Hong Kong, a Council Member of The Chinese University of Hong Kong, a Board Member of the Hang Seng School of Commerce, one of the founders of the Tang Shiu Kin and Ho Tim Charitable Fund, Permanent President of the Ho's Clansmen Association Ltd., Honorary President of the Panyu District Association of Hong Kong and Honorary Permanent President of the Chinese Gold & Silver Exchange Society.

In 1982, The Chinese University of Hong Kong conferred on Dr. Ho the Honorary Degree of Doctor of Social Science; in 1997, an Honorary Doctorate Degree of Business Administration by The City University of Hong Kong; and in 1999, an Honorary Degree of Doctor of Laws by The University of Hong Kong. He was made an Honorary Citizen of Guangzhou, Panyu, Shunde and Foshan in 1988, 1993, 1995 and 2004 respectively by the respective municipal governments. He was appointed a member of the Selection Committee of the First Government of the Hong Kong

Special Administrative Region of the People's Republic of China in November 1996.

Dr. Ho Tim passed away peacefully in Hong Kong on November 6, 2004 at the age of 95.

Brief Biography of Dr. Lee Quo-Wei

Dr. Lee Quo-Wei, the founder of Wei Lun Foundation Limited which donated to Ho Leung Ho Lee Foundation, joined Hang Seng Bank (formerly Hang Seng Ngan Ho) in Hong Kong in 1946. He was appointed a Director of the Bank in December 1959 and elected Vice-Chairman in January 1976. He became Executive Chairman of the Bank from 1983 until February 1996; non-executive Chairman from March 1996 to December 1997. He was appointed Honorary Senior Advisor of the Bank after his appointment as Honorary Chairman from January 1998 to April 2004.

Dr. Lee was well-known for his active involvement in public services. He had been Treasurer of the Chinese University of Hong Kong from 1963 to 1982, the Chairman of the Council of the University from 1982 to 1997 and a Life Member of the Council of the University since 30 November 1994. He was the Founding Chairman and later the Honorary Chairman of the Li Po Chun United World College of Hong Kong as well as the Honorary President of Jiangmen's Wuyi University.

He was a member of the Executive Council in Hong Kong for 7 years and a member of the Legislative Council for 10 years. He was also a member of the Banking Advisory Committee for 14 years, Chairman of the Board of Education for 7 years and Chairman of the Education Commission for 5 years.

Several universities in Hong Kong and overseas had conferred Honorary Doctorate Degrees on Dr Lee, including The Chinese University of Hong Kong in 1972, University of Hull (United Kingdom) in 1985, University of Birmingham (United Kingdom) in 1989, University of Hong Kong in 1990, City Polytechnic of Hong Kong (presently known as the City University of Hong Kong) in 1990, Hong Kong Polytechnic (now the Hong Kong Polytechnic University) and Hong Kong Baptist College (now the Hong Kong Baptist University) in 1972, London Guildhall University (United Kingdom) in 1993, Tsinghua University (Beijing of China) and the Open Learning Institute (now the Open University of Hong Kong) in 1995. Dr Lee was also elected to a fellowship of the Chartered Institute of Bankers, London in 1971 and Tufts University (USA) in 1995 as well as honorary fellowships of St Hugh's College, Oxford University; Royal College of Physicians of Edinburgh; Hong Kong College of Cardiology; and Hong Kong College of Physicians; and Needham Research Institute, Cambridge in 1991, 1993, 1995, 1996 and 2003 respectively. In 1993, he was made an Honorary Citizen of Guangzhou, Kaiping and Jiangmen by the three municipal governments. In the 1994 South China Morning Post/DHL Hong Kong Business Awards, he was awarded Businessman of the year. Dr Lee had been engaged Honorary President of

China Senior Professors Association from 1995 to 2003. In July 1997, he was awarded the Grand Bauhinia Medal by the Hong Kong Special Administrative Region Government. In 2006, he was elected Honorary Fellow for the year by the Hong Kong Securities Institute.

Over the years, Dr Lee had donated generously to his homeland Kaiping, helping to improve infrastructure, education and medical services. He had also made significant contributions to Jiangmen. In addition, he had made donations to Tsinghua University in Beijing and other institutions in the cities of Shanghai and Guangzhou.

Dr Lee Quo-Wei passed away peacefully in Hong Kong on August 10, 2013 at the age of 95.

何梁何利基金信托人简历

朱 丽 兰

朱丽兰，女，1935 年 8 月出生于上海。教授，原科学技术部部长，现任全国人大常委会委员、全国人大教科文卫委员会主任委员。曾就读于上海中西小学，毕业于第三女中。1956 年在苏联敖德萨大学高分子物理化学专业学习，1961 年获优秀毕业生文凭。回国后在中国科学院化学研究所工作到 1986 年。长期从事高分子反应动力学、高分子材料剖析及结构表征研究。所承担的高分子材料剖析、性能结构形态关系的研究项目曾分别获国家级重大科研成果奖及应用成果奖，多次在国内外发表学术论文。曾任中国科学院化学研究所研究室主任和所长职务。

1979—1980 年，在德国费拉堡大学高分子化学研究所做访问学者。在科研工作中，发展了一种新的染色技术用于制备样品，被称为一种突破，在国内外同行中享有较高声誉。

1986—2001 年，曾任国家科委副主任、常务副主任、科学技术部部长。任国家科委、科技部领导期间，组织制订并实施了国家高技术研究发展计划（“863”计划）、国家发展基础研究的攀登计划以及高技术产业化的火炬计划等。倡导和推行新的专家管理机制，提出了一系列适应当代高技术发展规律并结合中国国情的管理理论与政策、方法，出版了专著《当代高技术与发展战略》《发展与挑战》等，并获中国材料研究学会成就奖。由于在推动国际科技合作以及促进中国国家高技术研究发展与产业化方面成绩卓著，1993 年获美洲中国工程师协会颁发的杰出服务奖；1998 年获德国联邦总统星级大十字勋章。

朱丽兰曾任中国工程院主席团顾问，中国科学院学部主席团顾问，国家科技领导小组成员，中央农村工作领导小组成员，国家信息化领导小组成员，国家奖励委员会主任委员等职。现任中国化学会常务理事会理事，中国对外友好协会常务理事，中国自然辩证法研究会理事，中国材料研究学会理事，并被聘为北京理工大学、国家行政学院、清华大学、中国科学院化学研究所兼职教授。

朱丽兰是国际欧亚科学院院士、亚太材料科学院院士。

孙　　煜

孙煜自2020年12月起任中银香港（控股）有限公司及中国银行（香港）有限公司副董事长兼总裁。彼时为战略及预算委员会和可持续发展委员会委员。调任前，于2020年3月—2020年12月出任集团非执行董事和风险委员会委员。

孙煜于1998年加入中国银行，2012年7月—2014年12月任中银香港全球市场总经理，2015年3月—2018年11月任中国银行伦敦分行行长、中国银行（英国）有限公司行长，2015年12月—2018年11月兼任中国银行伦敦交易中心总经理。此前，先后担任中国银行全球金融市场部总监、金融市场总部总监（代客）、金融市场总部总监（证券投资）和上海市分行副行长。2018年9月—2019年2月任中国银行海外业务总监，2019年2月—2020年12月任中国银行副行长，并于2019年2月—2020年12月兼任中银航空租赁有限公司（于香港上市）董事长，于2019年11月—2020年12月兼任中国银行上海人民币交易业务总部总裁，于2019年12月—2020年12月兼任中国银行北京市分行行长。

孙煜目前亦兼任多项职务，包括中国银行（英国）有限公司董事长、中银保险（国际）控股有限公司董事长、中银集团人寿保险有限公司董事长以及中银香港慈善基金董事局主席。孙煜现任多项公职，包括香港中资银行业协会会长、外汇基金咨询委员会委员、银行业务咨询委员会委员、财资市场公会议会委员、香港总商会理事会理事、香港贸易发展局“一带一路”及大湾区委员会委员、香港交易所风险管理委员会成员、香港印钞有限公司董事、香港银行学会副会长等。

孙煜于1998年毕业于南开大学，获经济学硕士学位。

钟　登　华

钟登华，1963年11月出生。天津大学工学博士。曾任教育部党组成员、副部长，现任中国农业大学党委书记。2009年当选中国工程院院士。

长期从事水利工程领域的人才培养和科学研究工作。提出了水利工程智能仿真与实时控制理论方法与技术、水利工程地质精细建模与分析理论方法与技术、水利工程建设智能控制数字大坝理论方法与技术。

先后承担并完成10余项国家重大工程的科技攻关或技术开发任务，研究成果在我国80多项水利水电工程中得到推广应用，在提高工程设计水平与效率、保证工程质量和节省工程投资方面发挥了重要作用。作为第一完成人获国家科技进步奖二等奖2项。

施 颖 茵

汇丰集团董事总经理

恒生银行执行董事兼行政总裁

施颖茵是汇丰集团董事总经理。她亦是恒生银行有限公司执行董事兼行政总裁、恒生银行（中国）有限公司董事长兼非执行董事、恒生保险有限公司董事长及恒生指数有限公司的恒生指数顾问委员会主席。

在加入恒生银行前，施女士曾担任香港汇丰的行政总裁。她通过客户管理及建立伙伴合作关系，并与政府及监管机构协调，推动汇丰的业务发展以达致其策略目标，同时改善雇员福祉。她亦曾为香港上海汇丰银行有限公司执行委员会成员。

施女士于汇丰集团内拥有丰富经验，曾在市场推广、信用卡、消费贷款和按揭等业务部门出任要职，并曾担任香港零售银行及财富管理业务主管和亚太区分销策略及客户提案主管。此前，施女士曾被借调至中国台湾地区，出任信用卡部门主管，期内成功将该项业务转亏为盈。

加入汇丰前，施女士为数码通电讯客户关系总经理，并曾于香港及加拿大多家环球金融机构工作，包括花旗集团及美国运通。

施女士现时服务多个公共机构及业界团体，包括：

- 鹰君集团有限公司独立非执行董事
- 恒生商学书院校董会主席
- 香港金融管理局金融基建及市场发展委员会委员
- 香港公益金董事、第二副会长兼筹募委员会联席主席及执行委员会委员
- 香港恒生大学校董会主席
- 何梁何利基金信托委员会委员
- 香港银行学会副会长、荣誉银行专业会士
- 财资市场公会议会成员

• 妇女事务委员会非官方成员

施女士为香港银行公会前主席。

霍 泰 辉

霍泰辉毕业于香港大学医学院，后于香港中文大学取得医学博士学位，专研新生儿科。曾在香港大学及玛丽医院担任儿科学系讲师，后于英国牛津大学约翰·拉德克利夫医院及加拿大麦克马斯特大学医疗中心的初生儿科部门工作多年。于 1984 年加入香港中文大学，曾任多项重要职务，包括 1995—2004 年出任儿科学系系主任，2004—2012 年出任医学院院长，2013—2021 年出任大学副校长，负责对外事务及大学拓展筹募。现为香港中文大学儿科学系荣休教授。

致力推动医学教育，培养新一代的医疗专业人才。其研究范畴是新生儿科，包括小儿呼吸系统疾病、传染性疾病、生长发育及医学教育。曾于国际医学期刊发表多篇研究论文，并为国内外多份学术期刊的编委会成员。英国皇家内科医学院（伦敦及爱丁堡）及英国皇家儿科医学院荣授院士，香港医学专科学院院士（儿科）及香港儿科医学院院士，香港儿科医学会终身荣誉会员。

积极参与社会服务，曾出任政府及专业团体多个委员会顾问，建树良多。曾任香港儿科医学院主席（2003—2006 年）、香港医院管理局医疗服务发展委员会主席（2005—2012 年）、香港医学专科学院副主席（一般事务）（2012—2016 年）。现为香港医务委员会初步侦讯委员会主席、香港中文大学医院董事局成员及香港儿童医院管治委员会成员。

曾获多项奖誉，包括亚洲杰出儿科医生奖、中大校长模范教学奖、中大医学院杰出教学奖以及五次荣获医学院最杰出教师奖。此外，亦获香港特别行政区政府委任为太平绅士及颁授银紫荆星章，表扬其对公共医疗服务的杰出贡献。

BRIEF INTRODUCTION TO THE TRUSTEES OF HO LEUNG HO LEE FOUNDATION

Brief Biography of Professor Zhu Lilan

Professor Zhu Lilan, female, born in Shanghai in August 1935, is the member of the Standing Committee of the National People's Congress, the director of the Science, Education, Culture and Health Commission of the National People's Congress, former minister of the Ministry of Science and Technology of China. From 1956 to 1961, Professor Zhu studied in the Aodesa University of former Soviet Union majoring in macromolecule physical chemistry. After graduated from the university as an excellent student, Professor Zhu worked in the Institute of Chemistry, Chinese Academy of Sciences till 1986. For a long time, Professor Zhu had been conducted the research of macromolecule reactivity dynamics, macromolecule material analysis and structure token. The research project had got the national award of Grand Research Achievements and Award of Application Achievements. During this period, Professor Zhu served as the director of the research department and the director of the Institute of Chemistry, Chinese Academy of Sciences.

From 1979 to 1980, Professor Zhu was a visiting scholar in macromolecule institute in Fleberg University in Germany. In her research, she developed a kind of new dyeing technique for the sample producing, which was considered a break through at that time and won high reputation in the research circle.

From 1986 to 2001, Professor Zhu was appointed vice-minister of the State Science and Technology Commission and minister of the Ministry of Science and Technology of China. During this period, Professor Zhu organized the formulating and implementation of the National High-Tech Development Plan (863 Plan), National Climbing Plan for the Basic Research, and Torch Program for the High-Tech Industrialization. Professor Zhu advocated and implemented the new expertise management mechanism, put forward a series of management theories and policies which suit to the development of high-tech and the situation of China, published her monograph *High-tech, Development Strategy in the Contemporary Era, Development and Challenge.* Owing to her outstanding contribution to promoting international science and technology cooperation and the development of China's high-tech research and industrialization, Professor Zhu was awarded the Outstanding Service Prize in 1993 by the American Association of Chinese Engineers, and the Germany Federal President Star Great Cross Medal in 1998.

Professor Zhu has been the counselor of Chinese Academy of Engineering Presidium, the counselor of Chinese Academy of Science Presidium, the member of State Science and Education Steering Group, member of Central Rural Work Steering Group, member of State Informationalization Steering Group, director-commissioner of State Award Commission. Professor Zhu is now the member of China Chemistry Society Administrative Council, the administrative member of the board of the Association of China Foreign Friendship Relations, the member of board of China Natural Dialectic Seminar, the director of China Material Seminar. Professor Zhu is also the concurrent Professors of Beijing University of Science and Technology, National Administration College, Tsinghua University, Chemistry Institute of Chinese Academy of Sciences. Professor Zhu is the academician of International Europe and Asia Academy of Science, and the academician of Asian and Pacific Material Academy of Science.

Brief Biography of Mr. Sun Yu

Mr. Sun has been appointed as Vice Chairman and Chief Executive of BOC Hong Kong (Holdings) Limited and Bank of China (Hong Kong) Limited since December 2020. He is a member of each of the Strategy and Budget Committee and the Sustainability Committee. Prior to the re-designation, Mr.Sun was a Non-executive Director and a member of the Risk Committee of the Group from March 2020 to December 2020.

Mr. Sun joined BOC in 1998. He served as the Executive Vice President of BOC from February 2019 to December 2020, and as Chief Overseas Business Officer of BOC from September 2018 to February 2019. From March 2015 to November 2018, Mr.Sun served as General Manager of London Branch of BOC, CEO of Bank of China (UK) Limited, and also served as General Manager of London Trading Center of BOC from December 2015 to November 2018. Mr.Sun previously served as Director of Global Financial Markets Department, Director of Financial Markets Unit (Client Business), Director of Financial Markets Unit (Securities Investments) and Deputy General Manager of the Shanghai Branch of BOC. He served as General Manager of Global Markets of BOCHK from July 2012 to December 2014. He was also Chairman of the Board of Directors of BOC Aviation Limited (listed in Hong Kong) from February 2019 to December 2020, President of Shanghai RMB Trading Unit of BOC from November 2019 to December 2020 and General Manager of Beijing Branch of BOC from December 2019 to December 2020.

Mr. Sun holds other roles with the group, including Chairman of the Board of Directors of Bank of China (UK) Limited, Chairman of BOC Insurance (International) Holdings Company Limited, Chairman of BOC Group Life Assurance Company Limited and Chairman of BOCHK Charitable Foundation. Mr.Sun also holds a number of public offices in Hong Kong. He serves as Chairman of the Chinese Banking Association of Hong Kong, and sits on the Exchange Fund Advisory Committee, the Banking Advisory Committee, the Council of Treasury Markets Association, the General Committee of the Hong Kong General Chamber of Commerce, the Belt and Road and Greater Bay Area Committee of the Hong Kong Trade Development Council, and the Risk Management Committee of the Hong Kong Exchanges and Clearing Limited. He is also Director of Hong Kong Note Printing Limited, as well as Vice President of the Hong Kong Institute of Bankers, etc.

Mr. Sun graduated from Nankai University with a Master's Degree in Economics in 1998.

Brief Biography of Mr. Zhong Denghua

Zhong Denghua was born in November 1963. He earned a doctorate in engineering from Tianjin University. Formerly served as a member of the Party Leadership Group and Vice Minister of the Ministry of Education, and currently serves as the Party Committee Secretary of China Agricultural University. He was elected a member of the Chinese Academy of Engineering in 2009.

Zhong Denghua has long been engaged in the training of talents and scientific research in the field of hydraulic engineering. He put forward theories, methodologies and developed technologies in the following areas: intelligent simulation and real–time control of hydraulic projects, precision modeling and analysis of the geological conditions of hydraulic projects, and intelligent control in the construction of hydraulic projects and digital dam.

Zhong Denghua has undertaken and completed the tasks of tackling hard–nut problems or technological development in more than 10 national major projects. The research achievements he has scored have been applied in more than 80 hydraulic and hydroelectric power projects in China, and have played important roles in improving the level and efficiency of project design, guaranteeing project quality and saving project investment. He was presented with 2 second–prizes of the State Science and Technology Advancement Award as the first complete person.

Brief Biography of Ms Diana Cesar

Managing Director, HSBC

Executive Director and Chief Executive, Hang Seng Bank

Diana Cesar is a Managing Director of the HSBC Group. She is also Executive Director and Chief Executive of Hang Seng Bank Limited, Chairman and Non–executive Director of Hang Seng Bank (China) Limited, Chairman of Hang Seng Insurance Company Limited and Chairman of the Hang Seng Index Advisory Committee of Hang Seng Indexes Company Limited.

Prior to joining Hang Seng Bank, Ms Cesar was Chief Executive of HSBC Hong Kong. She was responsible for steering the business to achieve its strategic objectives by managing client relationships and business partnerships, coordinating with the government and regulatory bodies, and improving employee well-being. She was a member of the Executive Committee for The Hongkong and Shanghai Banking Corporation Limited.

During a wide-ranging career with HSBC, Ms Cesar held leadership roles in Marketing, Credit Cards, Consumer Loans and Mortgages. She was Head of Retail Banking and Wealth Management in Hong Kong and Regional Head of Distribution Strategy and Consumer Propositions for Asia Pacific. Earlier in her career at HSBC, she was seconded to Taiwan, Province of China as Head of Credit Cards and successfully turned the business around.

Prior to joining HSBC, Ms Cesar was General Manager for Customer Relations for SmarTone Telecom. She has also worked in Canada and Hong Kong for other global financial institutions, including Citibank and American Express.

Ms Cesar also holds various industry and civic appointments, including:

- Great Eagle Holdings Limited–Independent Non-executive Director
- Hang Seng School of Commerce–Chairman of the Board of Directors
- Hong Kong Monetary Authority–Member of the Financial Infrastructure and Market Development Subcommittee
- Justice of the Peace appointed by the Government of the Hong Kong SAR
- The Community Chest of Hong Kong–Director, Second Vice President and Campaign Committee Chairman, and Member of Executive Committee
- The Hang Seng University of Hong Kong–Chairman of the Board of Governors
- The Ho Leung Ho Lee Foundation–Member of the Board of Trustees
- The Hong Kong Institute of Bankers–Vice President and Honorary Certified Banker
- Treasury Markets Association–Council Member
- Women's Commission–Non-official Member

Ms Cesar is also a former Chairperson of the Hong Kong Association of Banks.

Brief Biography of Mr. Fok Tai-Fai

Fok Tai-Fai graduated in Medicine from The University of Hong Kong (HKU) and received his Doctor of Medicine (MD) from The Chinese University of Hong Kong (CUHK). A paediatrician by training, he served in HKU and Queen Mary Hospital as a Lecturer in Paediatrics, and spent a number of years working in the Neonatal Units at the John Radcliffe Hospital in the University of Oxford, UK and the McMaster University Medical Centre, Canada. Professor Fok joined CUHK in 1984 and had served in various key positions including Chairman of the Department of Paediatrics (1995—2004), Dean of the Faculty of Medicine (2004—2012), and Pro-Vice-Chancellor/Vice-President (External Affairs and Institutional Advancement) from 2013 to 2021. Professor Fok is the Emeritus Professor in the Department of Paediatrics of CUHK.

Professor Fok is dedicated to nurturing the next generation of medical professionals. His research interest is in newborn care, especially the prevention and management of respiratory conditions, newborn infection, newborn growth, and medical education. Professor Fok has published extensively in international journals, and served on the editorial boards of international and national medical journals. He is a Fellow of the Royal College of Physicians of Edinburgh, Royal College of Physicians of London, Royal College of Paediatrics and Child Health, Hong Kong Academy of Medicine (Paediatrics) and Hong Kong College of Paediatricians. He has also been elected as Honorary Life Member of the Hong Kong Paediatric Society.

Professor Fok has served on many government committees and advisory bodies and has contributed significantly to the community. He was the President of the Hong Kong College of Paediatricians (2003—2006), Chairman of the Medical Services Development Committee of Hong Kong Hospital Authority (2005—2012), and Vice-President (General Affairs) of the Hong Kong Academy of Medicine (2012—2016). He is the Chairman of the deemed Preliminary Investigation Committee of the Medical Council of Hong Kong, and a member of the Board of Directors of CUHK Medical Centre and the Hospital Governing Committee of the Hong Kong Children's Hospital.

Professor Fok has received many honours and awards throughout his career, including the Outstanding Asian Paediatrician Award, the Vice-Chancellor's Exemplary Teaching Award of CUHK, and Master Teaching Award of the Faculty of Medicine. He received the Outstanding Teacher Award of the Faculty of Medicine five times. He was also awarded the honours of Justice of Peace and Silver Bauhinia Star by the HKSAR Government for his distinguished contribution to the public healthcare sector.

何梁何利基金评选委员会成员简历

评选委员会主任
朱丽兰

朱丽兰，女，1935 年 8 月出生，浙江湖州人，教授。现任中国发明协会理事长，澳门特别行政区科技奖励委员会主任。曾任国家科委副主任（1986 年）、国家科学技术部部长（1998 年），全国人大常委会教科文卫委员会主任委员（2001 年），中国工程院主席团顾问，中国科学院学部主席团顾问，国家科教领导小组成员，国家科技奖励委员会主任委员，澳门特别行政区科学技术委员会顾问等职。

在中国科学院化学所从事高分子材料剖析及结构形态表征、反应动力学研究期间，承担了多项国家、国防重点科研攻关项目，曾获国家级、省部级重大科研成果奖及应用成果奖。担任全国人大常委会教科文卫委员会主任委员期间，负责组织完成《科技进步法》《义务教育法》的修订和实施；组织实施一批关系到社会、民生、科技、文化、卫生等重要法律的立法调研与修法任务，为法制建设奠定重要基础。

发表了多篇有关高技术发展现状及对策和管理方面的文章，出版了《当代高技术与发展战略》《发展与挑战》等专著。曾获中国材料研究学会成就奖。由于在推动中国高技术发展及国际科技合作方面成绩显著，获美洲中国工程师协会颁发的杰出服务奖、德国总统颁发的德意志联邦共和国大十字勋章、乌克兰总统二级勋章。

评选委员会副主任
钟登华

钟登华，1963 年 11 月出生。天津大学工学博士。曾任教育部党组成员、副部长，现任中国农业大学党委书记。2009 年当选中国工程院院士。

长期从事水利工程领域的人才培养和科学研究工作。提出了水利工程智能仿真与实时控制理论方法与技术、水利工程地质精细建模与分析理论方法与技术、水利工程建设智能控制数字大坝理论方法与技术。

先后承担并完成 10 余项国家重大工程的科技攻关或技术开发任务，研究成果在我国 80 多项水利水电工程中得到推广应用，在提高工程设计水平与效率、保证工程质量和节省工程投资方面发挥了重要作用。作为第一完成人获国家科技进步奖二等奖 2 项。

评选委员会副主任
霍泰辉

霍泰辉毕业于香港大学医学院，后于香港中文大学取得医学博士学位，专研新生儿科。曾在香港大学及玛丽医院担任儿科学系讲师，后于英国牛津大学约翰·拉德克利夫医院及加拿大麦克马斯特大学医疗中心的初生儿科部门工作多年。于 1984 年加入香港中文大学，曾任多项重要职务，包括 1995—2004 年出任儿科学系系主任，2004—2012 年出任医学院院长，2013—2021 年出任大学副校长，负责对外事务及大学拓展筹募。现为香港中文大学儿科学系荣休教授。

致力推动医学教育，培养新一代的医疗专业人才。其研究范畴是新生儿科，包括小儿呼吸系统疾病、传染性疾病、生长发育及医学教育。曾于国际医学期刊发表多篇研究论文，并为国内外多份学术期刊的编委会成员。英国皇家内科医学院（伦敦及爱丁堡）及英国皇家儿科医学院荣授院士，香港医学专科学院院士（儿科）及香港儿科医学院院士，香港儿科医学会终身荣誉会员。

积极参与社会服务，曾出任政府及专业团体多个委员会顾问，建树良多。曾任香港儿科医学院主席（2003—2006 年）、香港医院管理局医疗服务发展委员会主席（2005—2012 年）、香港医学专科学院副主席（一般事务）（2012—2016 年）。现为香港医务委员会初步侦讯委员会主席、香港中文大学医院董事局成员及香港儿童医院管治委员会成员。

曾获多项奖誉，包括亚洲杰出儿科医生奖、中大校长模范教学奖、中大医学院杰出教学奖以及五次荣获医学院最杰出教师奖。此外，亦获香港特别行政区政府委任为太平绅士及颁授银紫荆星章，表扬其对公共医疗服务的杰出贡献。

评选委员会秘书长
段 瑞 春

段瑞春，1943 年 2 月出生。上海交通大学工学学士，中国科学院研究生院理学硕士，北京大学法学硕士。20 世纪 90 年代，任国家科委政策法规与体制改革司司长、国务院知识产权办公会议办公室主任，2000—2007 年任国务院国有重点大型企业监事会主席。现任中国科学技术法学会名誉会长，曾任中国民营科技促进会会长、中国产学研合作促进会常务副会长。

我国知识产权、科技政策和企业创新领域著名专家，具有自然科学、经济管理和法律科学复合型知识结构。曾主持起草我国《技术合同法》《科学技术进步法》《促进科技成果转化法》《国家科技奖励条例》等法律法规；参加多项知识产权法律的制定和修改工作；担任中美、中欧、中俄科技合作知识产权谈判首席代表、中国“入世”知识产权谈判主要代表；《国家知识产权战略》总报告评审组组长；何梁何利基金《信托契约》《评选章程》主要制定者之一。

其研究成果于 1992 年获得国家科委科技进步奖一等奖、1993 年获得国家科技进步奖二等奖，均为第一完成人。2004 年获我国技术市场建设功勋奖，2008 年获中国科技法学会杰出贡献奖，2017 年获中国科技法学会终身成就奖。撰写出版《国际合作与知识产权》《技术合同原理与实践》《技术创新读本》《科技政策多维思考》等多部著作。主编《光荣、责任与梦想》《情系科学春天》等何梁何利基金文献。

评选委员会委员
马 永 生

马永生，1961 年 10 月出生于内蒙古自治区呼和浩特市。石油地质学家、沉积学家。1980 年至 1990 年先后就读于中国地质大学（原武汉地质学院）和中国地质科学院，获博士学位。现任中国石化集团公司副总经理、总地质师。2009 年当选中国工程院院士。

长期从事中国油气资源勘探理论研究和生产实践，

在中国海相碳酸盐岩油气勘探理论和技术方面取得了多项创新性成果，成功指导发现了普光、元坝等多个大型、特大型天然气田，为国家重大工程“川气东送”提供了扎实的资源基础。他在非常规天然气领域的前瞻性研究，为中国第一个页岩气田——涪陵页岩气田的发现作出了重要贡献。他的科研成果对缓解我国天然气供需矛盾、发展地区经济与环境保护起到了重要的促进作用。

获国家科技进步奖一等奖 2 项；2007 年获何梁何利科学与技术成就奖，同年获第十次李四光地质科学奖；2013 年被评为国家首批“万人计划”杰出人才。由于他在石油工业界的杰出成果，2017 年国际小行星中心将国际编号为 210292 号小行星命名为“马永生星”。

评选委员会委员
王 小 凡

王小凡，著名癌症生物学家。1955 年出生于乌鲁木齐市，1982 年毕业于武汉大学生物化学专业，同年考入中国科学院遗传研究所，并在当年举办的首届“中美生物化学联合招生项目”（CUSBEA）中取得第一名的成绩赴美留学。1986 年获加州大学洛杉矶分校博士学位，之后在麻省理工学院师从癌症生物学家 Robert A. Weinberg 从事博士后研究。1992 年被聘为杜克大学药理学和肿瘤生物学系助理教授，成为最早在杜克大学执教的华人教授之一。1998 年成为终身教授，2003 年晋升为正教授。现任杜克大学医学中心药理学和肿瘤生物学 Donald and Elizabeth Cooke 终身讲席教授。

王小凡在细胞信号转导、DNA 损伤与修复、癌症转移分子机制、肿瘤微环境等多个领域均有重要学术贡献，尤其在 TGF-β 相关研究领域取得了令人瞩目的成绩。先后发表了 100 多篇学术论文，其中在 *Cell*、*Nature*、*Science*、*Cancer Cell*、*Nature Cell Biology* 等高水平杂志上发表论文 20 余篇。王小凡长期坚持通过多种渠道为中国的教育科技事业建言献策，推动、促成了一系列改善中国教育科研环境的政策制度，目前担任中国国务院侨办海外专家咨询委员会委员。

评选委员会委员
杨 祖 佑

杨祖佑，1940 年出生。获美国康奈尔大学博士学位。先后任普渡大学航空宇宙工程系主任，工学院院长；曾兼任美国国家科学基金会智能制造工程中心共同主任，同时任阿姆斯特朗（首位登陆月球者）杰出宇航讲座教授。现任美国圣塔芭芭拉加州大学校长（1994 年始任），美国国家工程院院士，美国航天、机械学会 Fellow，中国工程院海外院士。兼任美、中、印、日、加“三十米望远镜”计划（简称 TMT 计划）主席，太平洋滨 42 所大学联盟主席（包括北大、清华、复旦、科大、浙大、南京），美国总统科学奖章评委，科维理科学基金会理事，曾任美国大学联盟（AAU，包括 62 所顶尖研究型大学）主席，芬兰千禧科技奖评委。共获 7 所大学荣誉博士。

长期致力于教学及科研。从事宇航结构、颤振、控制转型至地震、制造、材料（LED）及生物工程等方面的研究，亲任博士论文主席指导 60 篇，发表期刊论文 200 余篇，学术会议论文 200 余篇，有限元教科书 1 本（被 40 余所美国大学采用，有中文、日文版）。

曾获 2008 年美国航天学会结构、振动、材料奖（SDM Award），美国工程教育学会最高李梅金质奖章以及十余次最佳教学奖。

评选委员会委员
杨 纲 凯

杨纲凯，1948 年 7 月出生于上海市。自 1973 年起任职香港中文大学，曾任物理系主任、理学院院长、研究院院长、副校长。现任香港中文大学敬文书院院长、物理系教授，香港特别行政区教育统筹委员会委员、课程发展议会主席。曾任香港特别行政区大学教育资助委员会委员及香港研究资助局主席，亚太物理联会秘书长、副会长。1965—1972 年就读于美国加州理工学院，主修物理，1969 年获学士学位，1972 年获博士学位。1972—1973 年在美国普林斯顿大学从事教学及研究。

长期从事理论物理学研究，包括基本粒子、场论、高能唯象、耗散系统及其本征态展开，对光学、引力波等开放系统的应用作出贡献，其主要研究成果载于有关国际杂志，包括 Microscopic derivation of the Helmholtz force density，Phys Rev Lett 47，77；Late time tail of wave propagation on curved spacetime，Phys Rev Lett 74，2414；Quasinormal mode expansion for linearized waves in gravitational systems，Phys Rev Lett 74，4588；Quasinormal modes of dirty black holes，Phys Rev Lett 78，289 等。1999 年被选为美国物理学会院士，2004 年被选为国际欧亚科学院院士。

评选委员会委员
吴 伟 仁

吴伟仁，1953 年出生，中国探月工程总设计师，航天测控通信和深空探测工程总体技术专家。中国工程院院士，国际宇航科学院院士，全国政协常委。我国深空探测领域主要开拓者之一和航天战略科学家。

先后获国家科技进步奖特等奖 3 项，一等奖 2 项；获首届全国创新争先奖章，何梁何利科学与技术成就奖，钱学森最高成就奖等。2020 年获国际宇航联合会最高奖——世界航天奖。鉴于他在航天领域的杰出贡献，国际天文学联合会将国际永久编号 281880 小行星命名为“吴伟仁星”。

评选委员会委员
张 立 同

张立同，女，1938 年 4 月出生于重庆，著名航空航天材料专家。1961 年毕业于西北工业大学。1989—1991 年在美国 NASA 空间结构材料商业发展中心做高级访问学者。现任西北工业大学教授、博士生导师、超高温结构复合材料技术国家重点实验室学术委员会副主任。1995 年当选中国工程院院士。

致力于航空航天材料及其制造技术研究，在薄壁复杂高温合金和铝合金铸件的无余量熔模精密铸造技术及其理论基础研究中取得丰硕成果。揭示了叶片变形规律、粗糙度形成规律和陶瓷型壳中温和高温软化变形机理。创新发展了高温合金无余量熔模铸造技术、铝合金石膏型熔模铸造技术、高温合金熔模铸造用中温和高温抗蠕变陶瓷型壳材料、高温合金泡沫陶瓷过滤净化材料技术等。相关成果成功用于航空发动机和飞机构件生产中。

突破大型空间站用陶瓷基复合材料技术，建立了具有自主知识产权的制造工艺、制造设备与材料环境性能考核三个技术平台，打破了国际技术封锁。

获国家技术发明奖一等奖 1 项，国家科技进步奖一、二、三等奖 4 项，国家级教学成果奖二等奖 1 项，获授权国家发明专利 64 项。

评选委员会委员
张 恭 庆

张恭庆，1936 年 5 月 29 日出生于上海。1959 年毕业于北京大学数学系，毕业后留校工作至今。1978 年作为我国改革开放后第一批赴美访问学者赴美进修。现为北京大学教授、中国科学院院士、发展中国家（第三世界）科学院院士、高校数学研究与人才培养中心主任，还担任多个国际核心刊物的编委。

著名数学家。发展无穷维 Morse 理论为临界点理论的统一框架，并首次将其应用于偏微分方程的多解问题，其著作成为该领域的基本文献。发展了集值映射的拓扑度理论以及不可微泛函的临界点理论，使之成为研究数学物理方程以及非光滑力学中的一类自由边界问题的有效方法。

曾荣获全国科技大会奖（1978）、国家自然科学奖三等奖（1982）、国家自然科学奖二等奖（1987）、陈省身数学奖（1986）、有突出贡献的中青年科学家（1984）、第三世界科学院数学奖（1993）、华罗庚数学奖（2009）、北京大学国华奖、方正教学特等奖（2011）等。

评选委员会委员
陈 佳 洱

陈佳洱，1934 年 10 月 1 日出生于上海市。中国科学院院士、第三世界科学院院士。现任北京大学物理学教授，国家重点基础研究计划（“973”计划）专家顾问组副组长，国际科联中国协调委员会副主席等职。

曾任北京大学校长和研究生院院长、国家自然科学基金委员会主任、中国科学院数理学部主任和中科院主席团成员以及中科院研究生院物理科学学院院长等职。

长期致力于低能粒子加速器及其应用的教学与科研工作，善于把握学科前沿发展与国家需求的结合，前瞻性地部署物理研究与人才培养，开拓发展我国的射频超导加速器、超灵敏加速器质谱计、射频四极场加速器、高压静电加速器等，是我国低能粒子加速器的奠基者和领头人之一。

陈佳洱长期在北京大学和国家自然科学基金委等单位担任领导工作，并曾担任国家中长期科技规划领导小组成员等职，为我国科学技术中长期规划的制订与相关的科教事业的发展作出了重要贡献。

评选委员会委员
郝 吉 明

郝吉明，1946 年 8 月出生于山东省，著名环境工程专家。1970 年毕业于清华大学，1981 年获清华大学硕士学位，1984 年获美国辛辛那提大学博士学位。现任清华大学教授、博士生导师、教学委员会副主任、环境科学与工程研究院院长，兼任国家环境咨询委员会委员、中国环境与发展国际合作委员会委员。2005 年当选中国工程院院士，2018 年当选美国国家工程院外籍院士。

致力于中国空气污染控制研究 40 余年，主要研究领域为能源与环境、大气污染控制工程。主持全国酸沉降控制规划与对策研究，划定酸雨和二氧化硫控制区，被国务院采纳实施，为确定我国酸雨防治对策起到主导作用。建立了城市机动车污染控制规划方法，推动了我国机动车污染控制进程。深入开展大气复合污染特征、成因及控制策略研究，发展了特大城市空气质量改善的理论与技术方法，推动我国区域性大气复合污染的联防联控。长期开展大气污染控制关键技术研究，在燃煤烟气除尘脱硫脱硝、机动车污染控制等领域作出贡献。

获国家科技进步奖一等奖 1 项、二等奖 2 项，国家自然科学奖二等奖和国家技术发明奖二等奖各 1 项，国家教学成果奖一等奖 2 项。2006 年获国家教学名师称号，获 2015 年度哈根－斯密特清洁空气奖及 2016 年 IBM 全球杰出学者奖。

评选委员会委员
赵 宇 亮

1985 年获四川大学放射化学学士学位，从事核燃料研究。1989 年赴日本原子力研究所进修，在东京都立大学获硕士、博士学位，从事原子核裂变碎片质量测量的研究，与日本同事一起发现了 113 号新元素（Nh），是元素周期表中亚洲国家发现的唯一元素。

2001 年回国，率先提出纳米生物安全性问题并创建第一个实验室。率先揭示了无机和碳纳米材料的生物安全性规律与肿瘤纳米药物的化学生物学机制。部分研究成果被 ISO 颁布为国际标准。曾获国家自然科学奖二等奖（2012 年，2018 年）、中国科学院杰出科技成就奖（2019 年）、何梁何利基金科学与技术进步奖（2020 年）、中国侨界贡献奖（2020 年）、TWAS 化学奖、中国毒理学杰出贡献奖、全国优秀科技工作者等。2015 年创建中国药学会纳米药物专业委员会，2011 年创建中国毒理学会纳米毒理学专业委员会，大力推动了纳米生物学这个学科交叉前沿在我国的起步和发展。

中国科学院院士，发展中国家科学院院士，中国医学科学院学部委员，国家纳米科学中心主任。目前担任中国生物材料学会候任理事长，中国化学会副理事长，中国药学会副理事长，爱思唯尔学术期刊 *Nano Today* 主编等。

评选委员会委员
钱 绍 钧

钱绍钧，1934 年出生于浙江省平湖市。1951 年考入清华大学物理系，后在北京俄语专科学校和北京大学物理系、物理研究室（现技术物理系）学习。现任原总装备部科技委顾问，研究员，中国工程院院士。曾任核试验基地副司令员、司令员，国防科工委科技委常任委员。

长期从事核试验放射化学诊断工作，参与了由原子弹到氢弹、由大气层到地下的一系列核试验，建立完善多项诊断方法和技术，显著提升测量精度。多次参加国防科技和武器装备发展战略研究，参与组织国家中长期科学技术发展规划专题研究。指导开展国防应用基础研究，努力促进与国家基础研究的协调链接。指导军用核技术发展，长期跟踪研究国际态势及主要国家政策演变，参与军备控制研究和“全面禁止核试验条约”谈判。

出版译著 1 部，主编专著 2 部，撰写科技论文和重要科技档案多篇，获国家科技进步奖特等奖、二等奖各 1 项，国家发明奖二等奖、三等奖各 1 项，军队科技进步奖多项。

评选委员会委员
倪 军

倪军，1961 年 11 月出生于青海省，著名制造科学专家。1982 年获上海交通大学学士学位。1984 年和 1987 年分别获得美国威斯康星大学硕士和博士学位。1987 年起在美国密歇根大学任教至今。现为美国密歇根大学吴贤铭制造科学冠名教授及机械工程系终身教授；上海交通大学校长特聘顾问、交大密西根学院荣誉院长，并同时担任美国密西根大学吴贤铭制造研究中心主任及美国国家科学基金会产学研“智能维护系统中心”共同主任。倪军教授目前担任世界经济论坛（达沃斯论坛）未来制造委员会主席。

曾担任美国国家科学基金会“可重组制造系统中心”执行主任及美国国家科学基金会产学研“制造质量测量与控制中心”主任。倪军教授主要从事先进制造科学领域中智能制造技术的研究，包括基于工业大数据分析和人工智能技术在精密质量控制、制造过程效率优化、重大装备的可靠性和健康预测管理、智能维护系统等研究。他的研究成果在众多工业领域得到成功应用。

倪军教授获得 40 多项学术成就奖。2013 年获中华人民共和国国际科技合作奖；1994 年获克林顿颁发的美国总统教授奖；2013 年获国际制造工程师协会金奖，是该奖 1955 年设立之后首位获此殊荣的华人学者；2009 年获美国机械工程学会 William T. Ennor 最高制造技术奖；2002 年当选为美国制造工程师学会 FELLOW；2004 年当选为美国机械工程学会 FELLOW；1991 年获国际制造工程师学会杰出制造工程师奖。

评选委员会委员
桑 国 卫

桑国卫，1941 年 11 月出生，浙江湖州人。临床药理学家，中国工程院院士。中国药学会理事长，“十一五”“十二五”“十三五”国家“重大新药创制”重大专项技术总师，工信部“医药工业‘十三五’发展规划”专家咨询委员会主任，中国药品生物制品检定所资深研究员，上海中医药大学名誉校长。曾任十一届全国人大常委会副委员长、农工民主党中央主席。

对长效注射与口服甾体避孕药及抗孕激素的药代动力学、种族差异及临床药理学做了系统研究，取得多项重大成果。近年来，在新药的安全性评价、质量控制和临床试验等方面进行了卓有成效的工作，为加强我国 GLP、GCP 平台建设作出了重要贡献。

获全国科技大会奖 2 项，国家科学技术进步奖二等奖 3 项，部委级科技进步奖一等奖 1 项、二等奖 4 项。1997 年获何梁何利科学与技术进步奖（医学药学奖）。2008 年获吴阶平—保罗·杨森奖特殊贡献奖。2014 年获国际药学联合会药学科学终身成就奖。

评选委员会委员
曹 雪 涛

曹雪涛，1964 年 7 月出生，山东济南人。1990 年毕业于第二军医大学。现为中国医学科学院院长、中国工程院院士、医学免疫学国家重点实验室主任，兼任中国免疫学会理事长、全球慢性疾病防控联盟主席、亚洲大洋洲免疫学会联盟主席等。担任 *Cell* 等杂志编委。

主要从事天然免疫识别及其免疫调节的基础研究、肿瘤免疫治疗应用性研究。发现了具有重要免疫调控功能的树突状细胞新型亚群；独立发现了 22 种免疫相关分子；系统研究了天然免疫识别与干扰素产生调控的新机制；探讨了表观分子在炎症与肿瘤发生发展中的作用；建立了肿瘤免疫治疗新途径并开展了临床试验。

以第一完成人获国家自然科学奖二等奖 1 项，中华医学科技奖一等奖 1 项，军队科技进步奖一等奖 1 项，上海市自然科学奖一等奖 3 项，已获得国家发明专利 16 项，获得 2 个国家Ⅱ类新药证书。研究成果入选 2011 年中国十大科技进展。获得光华工程奖、长江学者成就奖、中国青年科学家奖、中国十大杰出青年等。以通讯作者发表 SCI 收录论文 220 余篇，包括 *Cell*、*Science*、*Nature Immunology*、*Cancer Cell*、*Immunity* 等。论文被 SCI 他引 5600 多次；编写和共同主编专著 8 部。

评选委员会委员
程 序

程序，1944 年出生，江苏无锡人。1965 年毕业于北京农业大学（现中国农业大学）农学系，后入中国农业科学院作物育种栽培研究所从事研究工作。现为中国农业大学教授，博导。曾就职于北京市农科院、农业部等单位。主要研究方向为可持续农业与农村发展、农业生态与生态农业以及生物能源等。

曾主持农业现代化规律和实验基地建设（实验基地：北京市房山区窦店村）以及生态农业两个研究项目。1985 年率先引进农业可持续发展的理论，此后开始研究中国条件下农业可持续发展的途径。重点放在农牧交错生态脆弱带的生态恢复途径，以及探索可持续的集约化农业模式的研究两个方面。

作为第一完成人，先后被授予北京市科技进步奖一等奖及国家星火科技奖（等同科技进步奖）一等奖。累计获省部级科技进步奖二、三等奖 7 项，1988 年被批准为国家级有突出贡献的中青年专家。

著有《可持续农业导论》和《中国可持续发展总纲第 13 卷：中国农业与可持续发展》两部专著。

评选委员会委员
曾 庆 存

曾庆存，1935 年 5 月出生于广东省阳江市（原阳江县）。1956 年毕业于北京大学物理系。1961 年在苏联科学院应用地球物理研究所获副博士（现称博士即 Ph.D）学位。回国后先后在中国科学院地球物理研究所和大气物理研究所工作。1980 年当选中国科学院院士。现为中国科学院大气物理研究所研究员。

主要研究领域为大气科学和地球流体力学。致力于大气环流和地球流体动力学基础理论和数值模式及模拟、地球系统动力学模式、数值天气预报和气候预测理论、气候动力学和季风理论、大气边界层动力学、卫星遥感理论方法、应用数学和计算数学以及自然控制论等的研究工作。在国际上最早提出半隐式差分法和平方守恒格式，最早成功将原始方程应用于实际数值天气预告（1961）和研制成大气海洋耦合模式并用作跨季度气候预测（1990，1994），提出系统的卫星大气遥感理论（1974）以及自然控制论理论方法（1995）。

曾获国家自然科学奖二等奖 2 项和三等奖 1 项，中国科学院自然科学奖一等奖 6 项和杰出贡献奖 1 项。出版专著包括《大气红外遥测原理》《数值天气预报的数学物理基础》《短期数值气候预测原理》《千里黄云——东亚沙尘暴研究》等。发表学术文章约百篇。

评选委员会委员
蒲　慕　明

蒲慕明，1948年10月出生。1970年毕业于台湾清华大学物理系；1974年在美国约翰斯·霍普金斯大学生物物理系获博士学位；1974—1976年先后在美国Woods Hole海洋生物研究所、美国普渡大学生命科学系做博士后研究；1976年9月—1985年3月在美国加州大学尔湾分校生物物理系任助理教授、副教授、教授；1985年4月—1988年8月在美国耶鲁大学医学院分子神经生物学系任教授；1988年7月—1995年12月在美国哥伦比亚大学生物学系任教授；1996年1月—2000年10月在美国加州大学圣地亚哥分校生物学系任Stephen W. Kuffler讲座教授。1998年7月筹建神经科学研究所；2000年9月起任美国加州大学伯克利分校分子与细胞生物学系1933级讲座教授，2002年起任神经生物学部主任。中国科学院外籍院士（2011年），美国科学院院士（2009年），台湾“中央研究院”院士。现任中国科学院上海生命科学研究院神经科学研究所所长，中国科学院脑科学卓越创新中心主任。

蒲慕明教授主要从事轴突导向和突触可塑性的分子与细胞机制研究，以其卓越成就于2005年荣获中华人民共和国国际科学技术合作奖，2016年荣获Gruber神经科学奖。

蒲慕明是一位世界级科学家，曾参与清华大学生物系组建并担任首任系主任，长期担纲中国神经科学研究领军者。

蒲慕明于2017年放弃美国国籍，恢复中国国籍。

BRIEF INTRODUCTION TO THE MEMBERS OF THE SELECTION BOARD OF HO LEUNG HO LEE FOUNDATION

Zhu Lilan, Director of the Selection Board

Zhu Lilan, female, was born in August 1935 and is of the origin of Huzhou, Zhejiang Province. At present, she is the Chairman of the China Association of Inventions and the Chairman of the Committee of Science and Technology Awards of Macau Special Administrative Region. She was the vice-minister of the State Science and Technology Commission (1986), the Minister of the Ministry of Science and Technology (1998), the Director of the Education, Science, Culture and Public Health Committee of the National People's Congress (2001), the counselor of Chinese Academy of Engineering Presidium, the Advisor of the Presidential Committee of CAS Academic Board, the Member of the State Leading Group of Science, Technology and Education, the Director of the State Committee of Science and Technology Awards and the Advisor of the Macao Science and Technology Council.

When analyzing polymer materials and researching morphological structure and reaction dynamics in the Institute of Chemistry of the Chinese Academy of Sciences, Zhu Lilan undertook several national and national defense key science and technological projects and was granted the statelevel and provincelevel significant scientific and technological result awards and application result awards. When being the Director of the Education, Science, Culture and Public Health Committee of the National People's Congress, she organized the amendments to and implementation of the Science and Technology Progress Law and the Compulsory Education Law; and organized a series of investigations for making the laws and amending the important laws concerning such matters as society, people's life, science and technology, culture and health, which has provided an important basis for legal construction.

Zhu Lilan has published several articles and books on the status quo of hi-tech development and the corresponding strategies and management measures, including *Modern Hi-tech. Development Strategy in the Contemporary Era* and *Development and Challenge*. She was granted the Achievement Award by the Chinese Materials Research Society. Thanks to her significant contribution to the development of China's hi-tech development and international scientific and technological cooperation, Zhu Lilan obtained the Distinguished Service Award granted by the Chinese Institute of Engineers, USA, the Grand Cross Medal of the Federal Republic of Germany granted by German President and the Medal No. 2 of Ukraine President.

Zhong Denghua, Deputy Director of the Selection Board

Zhong Denghua was born in November 1963. He earned a doctorate in engineering from Tianjin University. Formerly served as a member of the Party Leadership Group and Vice Minister of the Ministry of Education, and currently serves as the Party Committee Secretary of China Agricultural University. He was elected a member of the Chinese Academy of Engineering in 2009.

Zhong Denghua has long been engaged in the training of talents and scientific research in the field of hydraulic engineering. He put forward theories, methodologies and developed technologies in the following areas: intelligent simulation and real–time control of hydraulic projects, precision modeling and analysis of the geological conditions of hydraulic projects, and intelligent control in the construction of hydraulic projects and digital dam.

Zhong Denghua has undertaken and completed the tasks of tackling hard–nut problems or technological development in more than 10 national major projects. The research achievements he has scored have been applied in more than 80 hydraulic and hydroelectric power projects in China, and have played important roles in improving the level and efficiency of project design, guaranteeing project quality and saving project investment. He was presented with 2 second–prizes of the State Science and Technology Advancement Award as the first complete person.

Fok Tai–Fai, Deputy Director of the Selection Board

Fok Tai–Fai graduated in Medicine from The University of Hong Kong (HKU) and received his Doctor of Medicine (MD) from The Chinese University of Hong Kong (CUHK) . A paediatrician by training, he served in HKU and Queen Mary Hospital as a Lecturer in Paediatrics, and spent a number of years working in the Neonatal Units at the John Radcliffe Hospital in the University of Oxford, UK and the McMaster University Medical Centre, Canada. Professor Fok joined CUHK in 1984 and had served in various key positions including Chairman of the Department of Paediatrics (1995—2004), Dean of the Faculty of Medicine (2004—2012), and Pro–Vice–Chancellor/Vice–President (External Affairs and Institutional Advancement) from 2013 to 2021. Professor Fok is the Emeritus Professor in the Department of Paediatrics of CUHK.

Professor Fok is dedicated to nurturing the next generation of medical professionals. His research interest is in newborn care, especially the prevention and management of respiratory conditions, newborn infection, newborn growth, and medical education. Professor Fok has published extensively in international journals, and served on the editorial boards of international and national medical journals. He is a Fellow of the Royal College of Physicians of Edinburgh, Royal College of Physicians of London, Royal College of Paediatrics and Child Health, Hong Kong

Academy of Medicine (Paediatrics) and Hong Kong College of Paediatricians. He has also been elected as Honorary Life Member of the Hong Kong Paediatric Society.

Professor Fok has served on many government committees and advisory bodies and has contributed significantly to the community. He was the President of the Hong Kong College of Paediatricians (2003—2006), Chairman of the Medical Services Development Committee of Hong Kong Hospital Authority (2005—2012), and Vice-President (General Affairs) of the Hong Kong Academy of Medicine (2012—2016). He is the Chairman of the deemed Preliminary Investigation Committee of the Medical Council of Hong Kong, and a member of the Board of Directors of CUHK Medical Centre and the Hospital Governing Committee of the Hong Kong Children's Hospital.

Professor Fok has received many honours and awards throughout his career, including the Outstanding Asian Paediatrician Award, the Vice-Chancellor's Exemplary Teaching Award of CUHK, and Master Teaching Award of the Faculty of Medicine. He received the Outstanding Teacher Award of the Faculty of Medicine five times. He was also awarded the honours of Justice of Peace and Silver Bauhinia Star by the HKSAR Government for his distinguished contribution to the public healthcare sector.

Duan Ruichun, Secretary-General of the Selection Board

Duan Ruichun, born in February 1943, is a bachelor of engineer from Shanghai Jiaotong University, a master of science from Graduate University of Chinese Academy of Science and a master of law from Peking University. In the 1990s, he was the Director of the Policy, Law and System Reform Department of the State Science and Technology Commission and the Director of the Intellectual Property Working Meeting Office of the State Council. From 2000 to 2007, he was the Chairman of the Board of Supervisors for Key Large State-Owned Enterprises of the State Council. At present, Duan Ruichun is the Chairman of the China Association for Science and Technology and the permanent vice chairman of the China Association for Promotion of Cooperation among Industries, Universities & Research Institutes.

As a famous expert in China's intellectual property rights, scientific and technological policies and enterprise innovation, Duan Ruichun possesses interdisciplinary knowledge in natural science, economic management and legal science. He has led the drafting of many Chinese laws and regulations such as the Technology Contract Law, the Scientific and Technological Progress Law and the Regulation on National Awards for Science and Technology; he has participated in drafting of and amendments to many laws on intellectual property rights; he was the chief representative of the Intellectual Property Negotiations for Scientific and Technological Cooperation between China and the United States and the main representative of intellectual property negotiations in the process of China's entry into WTO; he was the Leader of the Review Team of the general report of the National IP Strategy; and he was one of the main person formulating the Trust Deed and the Selection Articles of the Ho Leung Ho Lee Foundation.

Due to his research results, Duan Ruichun was granted the first prize of the Science and Technology Progress Award by the State Science and Technology Commission in 1992 and granted the second prize of the Science and Technology Progress Award in 1993. He was granted the recognition award of China's technology market in 2004 and the significant contribution award of the China Law Association on Science and Technology in 2008. He has written and published several books such as *International Cooperation and Intellectual Property Rights*, *Principles and Practice of Technology Contracts*, *Guidelines on Technology Innovation* and *Multi-Dimensional Thinking of Scientific and Technological Policies.*

Ma Yongsheng, Member of the Selection Board

Ma Yongsheng, a petroleum geologist and sedimentologist, was born in Hohhot City of Inner Mongolia in October 1961. He obtained his bachelor's and master's degrees from China University of Geosciences (previously known as Wuhan College of Geology) and received his Ph.D from Chinese Academy of Geological Sciences in 1990. He is now the Vice President and Chief Geologist of China Petroleum & Chemical Corporation (Sinopec Group). He has been elected as academician of Chinese Academy of Engineering in 2009.

Over the past few decades, he devoted his career to the research and application of the petroleum and natural gas exploration theory. He has made great contributions to the marine carbonates hydrocarbon exploration theory with a number of leading technological and theoretical achievements. For instance, he led the successful discovery of several giant natural gas reservoirs in China, such as the Puguang and Yuanba gas fields, establishing solid foundations for the Sichuan-to-East China Gas Transmission Project. His pioneering research in unconventional natural gas contributed significantly to the discovery of Fuling shale gas field in Chongqing, China's first large-scale shale gas field. His research accomplishments have also remarkably facilitated the mitigation of natural gas supply-demand imbalance, as well as the promotion of regional economy and environmental protection in China.

Ma has won the 1st Prize of the National Science & Technology Progress Award twice. In 2007, he won the Scientific & Technological Achievements Award granted by the Ho Leung Ho Lee Foundation. In the same year, he won Li Siguang Geoscience Prize for the 10th time. In 2013, he was selected as one of China's first six outstanding scientists supported by the National Ten-Thousand Talents Program. For his distinguished achievement in the petroleum industry, the Minor Planet Center named No. 210292 asteroid officially after him as "Ma Yongsheng Planet" in 2017.

Wang Xiaofan, Member of the Selection Board

Wang Xiaofan is a renowned cancer biologist. He was born in Urumqi in 1955.

In 1982, he graduated from Wuhan University after completing an undergraduate program in biological chemistry, and was admitted into the Institute of Genetics, the Chinese Academy of Sciences.

In the same year, he ranked the highest in the first China–United States Biochemistry Examination and Application (CUSBEA) and went to the U.S. to pursue further studies.

In 1986, he obtained the doctoral degree from the University of California, Los Angeles (UCLA) . Later he engaged in post–doctoral study by following Robert A. Weinberg, an eminent cancer biologist, at Massachusetts Institute of Technology (MIT) .

In 1992, he was engaged as an assistant professor by the Department of Pharmacology and Tumor Biology at Duke University, becoming one of the earliest Chinese professors who taught at Duke University.

He became a tenure–track professor in 1998 and was promoted to be a full professor in 2003.

He is the Donald and Elizabeth Cooke Professor of Cancer Research at the Department of Pharmacology and Cancer Biology, School of Medicine, Duke University.

Professor Wang Xiaofan has made important academic contributions in many fields including cell signal transduction, repair of DNA damage, molecular mechanism of cancer metastasis and tumor microenvironment. In particular, he has made eye–catching achievements in the field related to TGF– β . He has published more than 100 academic papers, of which more than 20 were published in high–level academic periodicals such as *Cell*, *Nature*, *Science*, *Cancer Cell* and *Nature Cell Biology*.

Over a long period of time, professor Wang Xiaofan has insisted on offering advice and putting forward suggestions on education and science and technology undertakings in China through various channels. He has promoted or brought about a series of policies and systems for improving the environment of education and scientific research in China. He currently serves as a member of the Overseas Expert Consultant Committee of Overseas Chinese Affairs Office of the State Council.

Henry T. Yang, Member of the Selection Board

Henry T. Yang was born in 1940. He obtained a Ph.D from Cornell University. He has served as Dean of the Aerospace Engineering Department and Head of the Engineering College of Purdue University. He used to be a co–director of the Smart Manufacturing Engineering center of the National Science Foundation (U. S.) and an outstanding professor of Armstrong (the first Moon lander) Astronautics Lectures. Currently, he is President of University of California Santa Barbara (since 1994), an academician of American Academy of Engineering, a fellow of both American Institute of Aeronautics and Astronautics and American Society of Mechanical Engineers, an overseas academician of Chinese Academy of Engineering and an academician of the Taiwan Academia Sinica. He is the chairman of the Thirty-metre Telescope Program (TMT Program) jointly sponsored by the United States, China, India, Japan and Canada. He is the chairman of the Association of Pacific Rim 42 Universities (including Peking University, Tsinghua University, Fudan University, University of Science and Technology of China, Zhejiang University and Nanjing University), a member of the Selection Board of the United States Presidential Medal of Science and a member of council of the Kavli Foundation. He used to be the Chairman of Association of American Universities (AAU) that consists of 62 top universities and a member of the Selection Board of Finnish Millennium Technology Grand Prize. He has been conferred seven honorary doctoral degrees.

He has been involved in teaching and research in aerospace structure, oscillation, control transition to earthquake, manufacturing, material (LED) and biological engineering. He has served as doctoral supervisor for sixty dissertations. He has published over 200 papers in journals, over 200 papers for academic conferences and one textbook on finite element (used by over forty American universities and translated into Chinese and Japanese) .

He won the SDM Award granted by the American Institute of Aeronautics and Astronautics in 2008. He won Benjamin Garver Lamme Gold Metal, the highest one granted by the American Society for Engineering Education, and over ten excellent awards for education.

Kenneth Young, Member of the Selection Board

Born in July 1948 in Shanghai, Kenneth Young has been working at The Chinese University of Hong Kong (CUHK) since 1973, and has held the position of Chairman of the Department of Physics, Dean of the Faculty of Science, Dean of the Graduate School and Pro-Vice-Chancellor/Vice-President. At present, Kenneth Young is Master of the CW Chu College and professor of physics at CUHK. He is also a member of the Education Commission (EC) and the Chairman of the Curriculum Development Council of the Hong Kong SAR. He was a member of the Hong Kong University Grants Committee and Chairman its Research Grants Council. He was the Secretary and later Vice-President of the Association of Asia Pacific Physical Societies. Kenneth Young studied at the California Institute of Technology from 1965 to 1972 and obtained the BS in physics in 1969 and the Ph.D in physics and mathematics in 1972. He was engaged in teaching and research at Princeton University from 1972 to 1973.

Kenneth Young has been engaged in physics research for a long time, on topics including elementary particles, field theory, high energy phenomenology, dissipation system and their eigenfunctions expansion, with applications to such open systems as optics and gravitational waves. Some of his publications include "Microscopic derivation of the Helmholtz force density", Phys Rev Lett 47, 77; "Late time tail of wave propagation on curved spacetime", Phys Rev Lett 74, 2414; "Quasinormal mode expansion for linearized waves in gravitational systems", Phys Rev Lett 74, 4588; "Quasinormal modes of dirty black holes", Phys Rev Lett 78, 289. Kenneth Young was elected as a Fellow of the American Physical Society in 1999 and an academician of International Eurasian Academy of Science in 2004.

Wu Weiren, Member of the Selection Board

Wu Weiren was born in 1953. He is the designer-in-chief of China's Lunar Exploration Program, expert in aerospace TT&C and communication area and overall design technology in deep space exploration program; Prof. Wu is the academician of Chinese Academy of Engineering (CAE) and the member of International Academy of Astronautics (IAA), member of the standing committee of the National Committee of the Chinese People's Political Consultative Conference (CPPCC). He is also one of the main pioneers in the Chinese deep space exploration area and aerospace strategy scientist in China.

Prof. Wu has won 3 special awards and 2 first awards of national science and technology progress award, the first national innovation award, Ho Leung Ho Lee foundation for scientific and technological achievement award and Qian Xuesen's highest achievement award, etc. Also, Prof. Wu has been given the World Space Award, the highest award of the International Astronautical Federation (IAF) in 2020. For his outstanding contributions to the field of aerospace, the International Astronomical Union (IAU) approved the official name of the asteroid numbered 281880 as "Wu Weiren star".

Zhang Litong, Member of the Selection Board

Zhang Litong, female, born in Chongqing in April of 1938, is a famous expert in aerospace materials. She graduated from Northwestern Polytechnical University in 1961. She was a senior visiting scholar in the Business Development Center of Spatial Structure Materials of NASA of the US from April 1989 to January 1991. Now, she acts as a professor and doctoral supervisor of Northwestern Polytechnical University and the deputy director of the Academic Committee of National Key Laboratory on Ultra-temperature Structure Composite Material Technology. She was elected as an academician of the Chinese Academy of Engineering in 1995.

She has been devoting himself to the research of aerospace materials and the technologies of manufacturing aerospace materials for many years and has achieved abundant research results in marginless melted module precise casting technologies and their fundamental theory research of thin–wall complex high–temperature alloy and aluminum alloy castings. She reveals the blade deformation rules, roughness generation rules and middle/high–temperature softening deformation mechanism of ceramic shells. Through independent innovation, she develops marginless melted module casting technology of high–temperature alloy, plaster–mold melted module casting technology of aluminum alloy, technology of middle/high–temperature creep–resisting ceramic shell materials for melted module casting of high–temperature alloy, and technology of foamed ceramic filtering and purifying materials for high–temperature alloy. Relevant achievements have been applied to production of aero–engines and aircraft components successfully.

After returning to China, she establishes three technology platforms with independent intellectual property rights (manufacturing process, manufacturing equipment and material and environment performance assessment), breaking international blockade on technologies.

She was awarded with one first–class prize of National Award for Technological Invention, four first–class, second–class and third–class prizes of National Award for Scientific and Technological Progress, one second–class prize of State–level Teaching Award. She is authorized with 64 national invention patents.

Zhang Gongqing, Member of the Selection Board

Zhang Gongqing was born on May 29, 1936 in Shanghai. After he graduated from the Department of Mathematics of Peking University in 1959 he worked in his university. In the year of 1978, as one of the first visiting scholars since the reform and opening–up, he made further study in the United States. Now he is a professor of Peking University, an academician of Chinese Academy of Sciences, an academician of the Academy of Sciences for the Developing World, the Director of the Research and Talent Training Center for Teaching and Learning Mathematics in Universities and Colleges, and he also serves as a member in the editorial board of many international core academic journals.

As a famous mathematician, he develops infinite dimensional Morse theory into a unified framework of the critical point theory, and is the first one to employ Morse theory as a tool to study multiple solutions to partial differential equations. His monograph is the fundamental literature of the related field. He also develops the topological degree theory of set–valued mappings and the critical point theory of non–differential functional, making them a kind of free boundary problem in the study on equations of mathematical physics and on non–smooth mechanics.

He won the Award of National Science & Technology Conference (1978), the third prize of the State Natural Sciences Award (1982), the second prize of the State Natural Sciences Award (1987), Chen Xingshen Mathematics Prize (1986), the title of the Young Scientist with Outstanding Contributions (1984), the Third World Academy of Sciences Award in Mathematics (1993), Hua Luogeng Mathematics Prize (2009), Guohua Award of Peking University, and Special Award for Teaching presented by Founder Group (2011), etc.

Chen Jiaer, Member of the Selection Board

Chen Jiaer, born on October 1, 1934 in Shanghai, is an academician of Chinese Academy of Sciences, an academician of the Academy of Sciences for the Developing World. He is currently a professor of physics at Peking University, the vice director of the Advisory Group of the National Basic Research Program of China (or 973 Program), and the vice chairman of the China Coordination Committee of the International Council of Scientific Unions.

He was the president of the Peking University and the dean of the Graduate School of Peking University, the director of the Committee of the National Natural Sciences Foundation, the director of the Division of Mathematics and Physics of the Chinese Academy of Sciences (CAS), a member of the CAS presidium, and the dean of the School of Physics of the Graduate University of CAS.

For a long time he has been devoting himself to the teaching and scientific research of the low-energy particle accelerator and its application. He is good at combining the cutting-edge development of an academic subject with national demands and planning the research in physics and talent training in a forward-looking way. He pioneered the development of RF superconducting accelerator, ultra-sensitive accelerator mass spectrometry, RF quadrupole field accelerator and electrostatic accelerator in China. He is a founder and one of the leaders in researching and developing low-energy particle accelerator in China.

Chen Jiaer was a long-time leader in Peking University and the Committee of the National Natural Science Foundation, and was also a member of the Leadership Group of Medium and Long Term Planning for Development of Science and Technology. He made important contribution to the formulation of the National Medium and Long Term Planning of Development of Science and Technology and the development of relevant science and education causes in China.

Hao Jiming, Member of the Selection Board

Hao Jiming, a well-known expert in environmental engineering, was born in Shandong

Province in August 1946. He graduated from Tsinghua University in 1970. He earned a master degree from Tsinghua University in 1981, and obtained a Ph.D from University of Cincinnati in 1984. At Tsinghua University, he is a professor, tutor for doctoral candidates, deputy director of the teaching committee, and director of the Research Institute of Environmental Science and Engineering. He is also a member on the National Environmental Consultation Committee and China Council for International Cooperation on Environment and Development. He was elected as academician of the Chinese Academy of Engineering in 2005, and was elected as foreign academician of the National Academy of Engineering in the U.S. in 2018.

Hao Jiming has dedicated himself to the research in controlling air pollution in China for more than 40 years. His main fields of research include energy and environment, and air pollution control engineering. He is in charge of national acid deposition control planning and the research in countermeasures against acid deposition. His research result on dividing the areas for controlling acid rain and carbon dioxide has been adopted by the State Council, playing a guiding role in formulating China's policies on preventing and treating acid rain pollution. He has developed the planning and methods for controlling pollution caused by motor–driven vehicles in urban areas, promoting the control of the pollution caused by motor–driven vehicles in China. He has conducted in–depth research in the characteristics, causes and control policy on air compound pollution, further developed the theoretical and technological methods on improving the air quality in mega cities, and promoted the joint efforts to prevent and control the regional air compound pollution in China. He has conducted the research in the key technologies for controlling air pollution for a long period of time, and has made contributions in the fields such as dust control, desulfurization and denitration in coal–fired flue gas, and control of the pollution caused by motor–driven vehicles.

Hao Jiming won one first–prize and two second prizes of National Award for Scientific and Technological Progress, one second prize of National Award for Natural Science and two second prizes of National Award for Technical Invention, and two first prizes of National Award in Teaching Achievement. He was granted the title of national famous teacher in 2006. He won the Haagen–Smit Clean Air Award in 2015, and the IBM Global Faculty Award in 2016.

Zhao Yuliang, Member of the Selection Board

Zhao Yuliang is a pioneer in the study of nano safety, having proposed the toxicology study of engineered nanomaterials and establishment of the first research laboratory in 2001. His work focuses on understanding the biological effects of nanomaterials, with a particular emphasis on establishing reliable and valid analytical methods for discovering their effects *in vivo*. Dr. Zhao also aims to understand the chemical mechanisms of nanosafety and ensure the safe application of nanomaterials. As a result of his research, a list of ISO standard analytical methods has been adapted by ISO/IEC 168 member countries. He has also established a nanosafety assessment framework for occupational exposure to nanomaterials, and has made significant contributions to the development of a new–concept nanomedicine for cancer therapeutics.

Dr. Zhao has received many honours and awards throughout his career, including TWAS Prize in Chemistry, CAS Outstanding Science and Technology Achievement Prize, National Prize for Natural Sciences (twice), Ho Leung Ho Lee Foundation Science and Technology Progress Prize, China Award for Outstanding Contribution on Toxicology, Beijing Award for Leading Talent in Science & Technology, etc.

Prof. Yuliang Zhao is the Director–General of National Center for Nanosciences and Technology, China. He is also Academician of Chinese Academy of Sciences, Academician of the World Academy of Sciences (TWAS), Academician of Chinese Academy of Medical Sciences, Elected President of Chinese Association for Biomaterials, Vice President of Chinese Chemical Society, Vice President of Chinese Pharmaceutical Association, Editor–in–Chief of *Nano Today*, Elsevier, Netherlands.

Qian Shaojun, Member of the Selection Board

Qian Shaojun was born in 1934 in Pinghu, Zhejiang Province. In 1951, he was admitted to the Department of Physics of Tsinghua University, and later studied Beijing Russian Language College, Department of Physics and the Research Section of Physics (now the Department of Technical Physics) of Peking University. He currently works as a consultant and research fellow of the Committee of Science and Technology of General Armament Department of the PLA, a research fellow and an academician of the Chinese Academy of Engineering. He used to be the deputy commander and the commander of the Nuclear Test Base, and was a standing member of the Committee of Science and Technology in the State Commission of Science and Technology for National Defense Industry.

He has been long engaged in the radiochemical diagnostic work of nuclear test and participated in a series of atomic bomb and hydrogen bomb nuclear tests conducted in the atmosphere or underground, in which he remarkably enhanced the measurement accuracy by establishing and improving many diagnostic approach and technology. For many times he took part in the study on the development strategy of science and technology and weaponry and equipment for national defence and participated in organizing the special research in national medium and long term scientific and technical development planning. He guided the basic study on applying research results in national defense, and worked hard to make such basic study consistent with the national basic research programs. He was put in charge of developing nuclear technology for military use, kept track of long-term changes with international situations and the policy evolvement of some leading nations, and instructed and took part in the study of arms control. He participated in the negotiation of the Comprehensive Nuclear Test Ban Treaty and guided the preparatory work for the performance of the treaty after it was signed.

His published works include a translated work, two monographs, wrote many scientific and technical papers and important scientific and technical articles for archival purpose. He won the Top Prize of the State Scientific and Technological Progress Award and the second prize of the State Scientific and Technological Progress Award once, the second prize of the State Award for Inventions and the third prize of the State Award for Inventions once, and the Military Progress Prize in Science and Technology many times.

Ni Jun, Member of the Selection Board

Ni Jun was born in Qinghai Province in November 1961. He is the Shien-Ming (Sam) Wu Collegiate Professor of Manufacturing Science and Professor of Mechanical Engineering at the University of Michigan, USA. He is the director of the Wu Manufacturing Research Center and the co-director of a National Science Foundation sponsored Industry/University Cooperative Research Center for Intelligent Maintenance Systems at the University of Michigan. Professor Ni served as the founding Dean of the University of Michigan – Shanghai Jiao Tong University Joint Institute located in Shanghai, China and is currently the Honorary Dean and Special Advisor to the President of Shanghai Jiao Tong University. Professor Ni is currently the Chairman of Global Future Council on Production at the World Economic Forum. Professor Ni served as the Deputy Director of the National Science Foundation Engineering Research Center for Reconfigurable Manufacturing Systems, and the Director of a National Science Foundation sponsored Industry/University Cooperative Research Center for Dimensional Measurement and Control in Manufacturing.

Professor Ni's research covers many topics in advanced manufacturing, including smart manufacturing technologies, and applications of industrial big data analytics and artificial intelligence in quality assurance, precision manufacturing, and intelligent maintenance systems. His research has been successfully applied by various industrial companies.

Selected honors and awards that Professor Ni received are 2013 International Science and Technology Cooperation Award from the President of People's Republic of China, 2013 Gold Medal from Society of Manufacturing Engineers, 2009 Ennor Manufacturing Technology Award from American Society of Mechanical Engineers, and 1994 Presidential Faculty Fellows Award from President Clinton. He is an elected Fellow of International Society of Engineering Asset Management, International Society for Nano-manufacturing, American Society of Mechanical Engineers, and Society of Manufacturing Engineers.

Sang Guowei, Member of the Selection Board

Sang Guowei was born in Huzhou, Zhejiang in November 1941. He is a clinical pharmacologist, an academician of the Chinese Academy of Engineering, Chairman of Chinese Pharmaceutical Association, Chief Engineer for the important specific techniques for the national "development of important new medicines" in the "11th Five-Year Plan", "12th Five-Year Plan" and "13th Five-Year Plan". He is also the director of the Expert Consultation Committee of the "Development Program of the Pharmaceuticals Industry in the 13th Five-Year Plan" of the Ministry of Industry and Information Technology, senior research fellow of National Institute for the Control of Pharmaceutical and Biological Products (NICPBP), honorary president of Shanghai University of Traditional Chinese Medicine (SHUTCM), and was the vice chairman of the 11th National People's Congress Standing Committee, and chairman of Chinese Peasants' and Workers' Democratic Party.

He has systematically studied the pharmacokinetics, race differences and clinical pharmacology of steroidal contraceptives and antiprogestogens for long-acting injection and for oral taking, and made a number of important achievements. He has done fruitful work in terms of safety evaluation, quality control and clinical trial etc. for new drugs in recent years, and has made great contributions in strengthening China's construction of the GLP and GCP platforms.

He has won two National Scientific Conference Awards (in 1978), three Second Prizes of National Science and Technology Progress Award (in 1987, 1997 and 2008), one First Prize and four Second Prizes of Science and Technology Progress Award at the ministerial and commission levels, the Science and Technology Awards of the Ho Leung Ho Lee Foundation in 1997(Medical-Pharmaceutical Award), the Special Contribution Award of the Wu Jieping-Paul Janssen Medical-Pharmaceutical Award in 2008, and the Lifetime Achievement Award in Pharmacy Science of the Federation International Pharmaceutical (FIP) in 2014.

Cao Xuetao, Member of the Selection Board

Cao Xuetao, was born in July 1964 in Jinan City, Shandong Province. In 1990, he graduated from the Second Military Medical University. He is the President of Chinese Academy of Medical Sciences (CAMS), member of the Chinese Academy of Engineering, and the Director of National Key Laboratory of Medical Immunology. Concurrently he is the President of the Chinese Society for Immunology, Chairperson of Global Alliance of Chronic Diseases (GACD), and President of the Federation of Immunological Societies of Asia-Oceania (FIMSA). He also serves as a member of the editorial board of magazines including Cell.

He is mainly engaged in fundamental research on innate immune recognition and relevant immune regulation, and applicability research on tumor immunotherapy. He has found a new dendritic cell (DC) subset with an important immune regulation function, independently identified 22 immune-related molecules, systematically studied innate immune recognition and the new mechanism for interferon production regulation, explored apparent molecular action on inflammation and cancer development and progression, established new approaches for tumor immunotherapy, and carried out relevant clinical trials.

He won the second-class prize of National Science and Technology Awards as the primary participant of a research project, a first-class prize of Chinese Medical Science and Technology Awards, a first-class prize of Military Science and Technology Progress Awards, three first-class prizes of Shanghai Science and Technology Progress Awards. He has obtained 16 national invention patents and two national category-II new medicine certificates. His research result was selected as one of the top ten results representing the scientific and technological progress in China in 2011. He was presented with Guanghua Engineering Science and Technology Award, Cheng Kong Scholar Achievement Award, China Young Scientist Award, and others. As corresponding author, he published over 220 papers in SCI-cited journals including Cell, Science, Nature Immunology, Cancer Cell, Immunity and others. His papers have been non-self-cited for over 5600 times in SCI-cited journals; he has written and served as a co-chief-editor for eight monographs. Of all the doctoral candidates under his tutorship, 11 have been presented with the awards of "national 100 excellent dissertations for doctoral degrees."

Cheng Xu, Member of the Selection Board

Cheng Xu, born in 1944, is of the origin of Wuxi, Jiangsu Province. He graduated from the Department of Agronomy of Beijing Agricultural University (Now China Agricultural University), later he worked in the Institute of Crop Breeding and Cultivation of the Chinese Academy of Agricultural Science. He is currently a professor of the China Agricultural University, and a tutor for doctoral candidates. He worked in the Beijing Academy of Agricultural Science and the Ministry of Agriculture. His major fields of research include sustainable agriculture and rural development, agricultural ecology and ecological agriculture.

He was put in charge of two research projects: one is the construction of the Agricultural Modernization and Experimental Base (location: Doudian village, Fangshan County, Beijing) and the other is Ecological Agriculture Program. In 1985, he took the lead in introducing the theory of sustainable agricultural development. From then on he started to study the way to realize sustainable agricultural development in China. He focused his research on the ecological restoration in the fragile farming-pastoral transitional zones and the exploration of the sustainable intensive agriculture.

As the main participant in completing the research project, he won the first prize of the Beijing

Science and Technology Progress Awards and the first prize of the National Sparkle Technology Award (equivalent to Science and Technology Progress Award). He was totally presented with seven second or third prizes of science and technology progress awards at provincial and ministerial level. In 1988, he was approved as a National Young & Middle-Aged Expert with Outstanding Contribution.

His works include *An Introduction to Sustainable Agriculture* and *General Program on Sustainable Development in China Volume* 13: *Agriculture in China and the Sustainable Development.*

Zeng Qingcun, Member of the Selection Board

Zeng Qingcun, born in May 1935 in Yangjiang County of Guangdong Province, graduated from the Department of Physics of Peking University in 1956. In 1961, he completed his Licentiate (namely Ph.D now) in the Institute of Applied Geophysics of the Soviet Academy of Science. After he returned to China he worked in the Institute of Geophysics and then the Institute of Atmospheric Physics of the Chinese Academy of Sciences (CAS). He was elected as an academician of the Chinese Academy of Sciences in 1980. Currently he is a research fellow of the Institute of Atmospheric physics of the CAS.

His major research field includes atmospheric sciences and geophysical fluid dynamics. He has been devoting himself to the study of the basic theory and numerical model and simulation of general atmospheric circulation and fluid dynamics, earth system dynamics model, numerical weather prediction and climatic prediction theory, climate dynamics and monsoon theory, dynamics of atmospheric boundary layer, theoretical method of satellite remote sensing, applied mathematics and numerical mathematics, and natural cybernetics. He is the first one in the world to put forward half-implicit difference scheme and square conservative scheme, applied the original equation into the actual numerical climate prediction (1961), developed the marine-atmosphere coupled mode for the extra-seasonal climate predictions (1990, 1994), and put forward the systematic theory of satellite remote sensing (1974) and the Theoretical method of natural control (1995).

He won the second prize of the State Natural Sciences Award twice and the third prize of the State Natural Sciences Awards once, the first prize of the Natural Science Award of the CAS six times and Outstanding Contribution Award once. His monographs include *Principles of the Atmospheric Remote Sensing in Infrared*, *Mathematical Physics Foundations of the Numerical Weather Prediction*, *Principles of the Short-term Numerical Climatic Prediction*, *Yellow Clouds Stretching Thousands of Miles— The research on Dust-storm in East Asia.* He has also published hundreds of academic articles.

Pu Muming, Member of the Selection Board

Pu Muming, born in October 1948, graduated from the Department of Physics, Tsing Hua University, Taiwan in 1970; He received his Ph. D. degree in biophysics from Johns Hopkins University in 1974. From 1974 to 1976, he did postdoctoral research in Woods Hole Institute of Marine Biology and Department of Life Sciences, Purdue University. From September 1976 to March 1985, he served as assistant professor, associate professor and professor in the Department of Biophysics, University of California, Irvine, USA; professor, Department of Molecular Neurobiology, Yale University School of Medicine, USA, from April 1985 to August 1988; professor, Department of Biology, Columbia University, USA, from July 1988 to December 1995; he was Stephen W.Kuffler's Chair Professor in the Department of Biology, University of California, San Diego, USA, from January 1996 to October 2000. In July 1998, he founded the Institute of Neuroscience. Since September 2000, he has been the Chair professor of the Department of Molecular and Cell Biology, University of California, Berkeley, Class 1933, and the director of the Department of Neurobiology since 2002. He is a foreign member of the Chinese Academy of Sciences (2011), a member of the American Academy of Sciences (2009), and a member of the Academia Sinica, Taiwan. He is currently the director of the Institute of Neuroscience, Shanghai Institutes for Biological Sciences, Chinese Academy of Sciences, and Director of the Center for Excellence in Brain Science Innovation, Chinese Academy of Sciences.

Professor Pu Muming, who is mainly engaged in molecular and cellular mechanisms of axon orientation and synaptic plasticity, was awarded the People's Republic of China International Science and Technology Cooperation Award in 2005 and the Gruber Neuroscience Award in 2016 for his outstanding achievements.

Professor Pu is a world-class scientist who was born in Nanjing and grew up in Taiwan. He has been engaged in scientific research in the United States for a long time. He participated in the establishment of the Department of Biology of Tsinghua University and served as the first chair of the department.

Pu renounced his US citizenship and restored his Chinese citizenship in 2017.